d holds
nclude
and Its
on and

es to
lay

of sex,
ns her
cts'

ward
while
rish

the
nes

Also by Catharine Arnold

BEDLAM: London and Its Mad

CITY OF SIN: London and Its Vices

NECROPOLIS: London and Its Dead

THE SEXUAL HISTORY OF LONDON: From Roman
Londinium to the Swinging City

UNDERWORLD LONDON

*Crime and Punishment
in the Capital City*

CATHARINE ARNOLD

**SIMON &
SCHUSTER**

London · New York · Sydney · Toronto · New Delhi

A CBS COMPANY

First published in Great Britain by Simon & Schuster UK Ltd, 2012
This paperback edition published by Simon & Schuster UK Ltd, 2013
A CBS COMPANY

1 3 5 7 9 10 8 6 4 2

Simon & Schuster UK Ltd
1st Floor
222 Gray's Inn Road
London
WC1X 8HB

www.simonandschuster.co.uk

Simon & Schuster Australia, Sydney
Simon & Schuster India, New Delhi

A CIP catalogue record for this book is available
from the British Library

Paperback ISBN: 978-1-84983-292-2
Ebook ISBN: 978-0-85720-117-1

Typeset by M Rules
Printed and bound by CPI Group (UK) Ltd, Croydon, CR0 4YY

For my husband

Till a' the seas gang dry, my dear,
And the rocks melt wi' the sun:
I will luve thee still, my dear,
While the sands o' life shall run.

Robbie Burns

Contents

Acknowledgements   ix

Introduction   1

1 CITY OF GALLOWS: Roots of the Tyburn Tree   5

2 CASTLE OF DARKNESS: Torture and Death   25
   in the Tower of London

3 FRATERNITY OF VAGABONDS: London,   46
   Den of Thieves

4 SHADES OF THE PRISON HOUSE: From   64
   Newgate Gaol to the Old Bailey

5 STAND AND DELIVER!: The Golden Age   80
   of Highway Robbery

6 THE BLACK PARADE: The Road to Tyburn   98

7 THE LONG ARM OF THE LAW: 125
   From Bow Street to Scotland Yard

8 DARKEST LONDON: The Victorian   148
   Underworld

9 THE HIDEOUS APPARATUS OF DEATH: 174
   Murder and Execution in Victorian London

10 FROM HELL!: A Murder Guide to   198
   Victorian London

11 *CRIMES PASSIONNELS, FEMMES FATALES*: 216
    Drama at the Old Bailey

12 EAST END BOYS: The Origins of 235
    London's Gangland

13 LONDON MONSTERS: Killers in the Smoke 251

14 WHO BREAKS A BUTTERFLY UPON 265
    A WHEEL?: Miscarriages of Justice and the
    Abolition of the Death Penalty

15 HARD BASTARDS AND DIAMOND GEEZERS 287
    How the Firm Ruled London

16 LONDON BABYLON: From the Old Bailey 305
    to Tyburn

    Bibliography 309
    Notes 315
    Illustration Credits 330
    Index 331

Acknowledgements

With grateful thanks to Cambridge University Library; the Hallward Library at the University of Nottingham; my agent, Charlie Viney; my editor, Kerri Sharp; Dr Simon Lee Price for his generous and helpful comments; Sue Stephens and Rory Scarfe at Simon & Schuster; Brian Catling for allowing me to share the inscription from his beautiful memorial at Tower Green; Paul Willetts; Lucille Venn; and most of all my wonderful family.

'Many cart-loads of our fellow-creatures are once in six weeks carried to slaughter.'

Henry Fielding, 1751

'The following malefactors were executed at Tyburn – John Kelly, for robbing Edward Adamson in a public street of sixpence and one farthing.'

Gentleman's Magazine, 7 March 1783

'It is frequently said by the prisoners of Newgate that the crimes of which they have been guilty are as nothing when compared with the crimes of Government towards themselves: that they have only been thieves, but that their governors have been murderers.'

Mrs Elizabeth Fry, prison reformer, 1818

Introduction

Imagine that you are standing at Marble Arch today, looking east, down the vista of eight hundred years. Picture an innumerable procession of men and women advancing from the mist, walking to their deaths from the Tower of London or Newgate Gaol to the bloody field of Tyburn. Historians can only surmise the number of those who suffered violent death here, but a modest estimate would put the figure at around 50,000. This black parade is composed of all sorts and conditions of men, from aristocrats to artisans, priests to petty thieves, and notorious murderers to young boys who have stolen a few pennies. Learned scholars and priests rub shoulders with illiterate thugs. Highwaymen swagger in their finery while fraudulent clerks twitch nervously. There are women here, too: an unrepentant murderess resplendent in black satin and an innocent maiden in her white bridal gown. Alongside them stride rebels and martyrs whose only crime was to refuse to renounce their cherished beliefs at the bidding of a tyrant.

Tyburn's dead travel along this Via Dolorosa in different ways. Some are bound with rope, tied to a horse and dragged five miles from the Tower. The majority ride in horse-drawn carts, alongside their coffins. This is, for the most part, a nameless, unrecorded crowd. Over the centuries, only the occasional figure emerges here and there from the anonymous throng. It is just for a few decades in the history of Tyburn that we will see certain characters from this procession clearly, and in detail. Mainly they pass in faceless batches of ten, fifteen, twenty: laughing boys; women with babies at the breast; men and women drunk, cursing, crying, praying. Some of the women will be burnt alive. Of the men, all will hang, but some will be cut down, still conscious, and forced to watch as they are disembowelled and their entrails burnt before their very eyes. A few will be hanged in chains or placed in a gibbet until the flesh rots from their bones. Alongside these unfortunates march the spectators, the family and friends of the dead, and those who consider public executions to be first-rate entertainment. For centuries, hangings were holidays, offering all the fun of the Tyburn fair. The crowd gorged on gingerbread, roast pork and beer, before shouting 'Hats off!' and craning to see the condemned men kicking their way to death at the end of a short rope.

Barbaric by modern standards, public executions were a common sight up until 1868. In 1660, the diarist Samuel Pepys went to see Major-General Harrison hanged, drawn and quartered, and observed that he looked as cheerful as any man could in that condition. 'He was presently cut down, and his head and his heart shown to the people, at which there was great shouts of joy.' Pepys also witnessed the hanging of Colonel John Turner for burglary in 1664. After paying a shilling to watch, Pepys stood on the wheel of a cart, 'in great pain', as Turner tried to delay his death by delivering speech after speech. Turner was eventually hanged, 'flung off the ladder in his cloak' and Pepys went home to dinner 'all in a sweat'. Pepys also saw a number of gibbets. During a country ride, he and a female companion 'rode under the man that hangs upon Shooter's Hill; and a filthy sight it was to see how his flesh is shrunk to his bones'.

The 1752 Murder Act allowed judges to make an example of murderers by ordering that their corpses should be displayed on a gibbet. Thus, in the 1770s, up to one hundred gibbets stood on Hounslow Heath, so that, according to the poet Robert Southey, 'from whatever quarter the wind blew, it brought with it a cadaverous and pestilential odour'. The Sunday after the highwayman Lewis Avershaw was gibbeted on Wimbledon Common in 1795, the city was deserted as Londoners flocked to view the corpse. For months after, this grisly spectacle was a popular outing.

Taking Tyburn and the history and abolition of capital punishment as its major theme, this book visits the major landmarks of London's underworld. In the course of this journey, I introduce the reader to Newgate Gaol, described by the barrister Henry Fielding as 'London's prototype of Hell', and its equally famous neighbour, the venerable Old Bailey. There is the chance to canter across the moonlit Common with the highwaymen, learn the secrets of top pickpockets in the Victorian West End, and venture into the dark and deadly territory of Whitechapel on the trail of Jack the Ripper. From time to time, the narrative will be interrupted, just as London has been, by insurrection, from the Gordon Riots of 1780 which saw Newgate Gaol burnt to the ground, to the disturbances of August 2011.

The horrific history of capital punishment includes an extraordinary cast of characters, from the celebrated Newgate escapee Jack Sheppard to the evil thief-taker Jonathan Wild, from the mild-mannered Doctor Crippen to the glittering ash-blonde Ruth Ellis, the last woman to be hanged. This tour of the capital's underworld is not for the faint-hearted. Beneath the veneer of sophistication and culture lurks a lawless London, a substratum of passion, darkness and despair. The legacy of this lingers on in the incipient melancholy of the London street, the abiding sense of mystery and unsolved crimes, of footsteps echoing in the distance, the flick of a cape, the discovery of a battered corpse lying in a pool of blood. Murderers cast a long shadow. Even today, serving police officers post in chat rooms, speculating on the true identity of Jack the Ripper and other unsolved crimes. Who can forget the image of Lady Lucan, staggering out of her Belgravia home with a massive head wound, after her husband Lord Lucan had apparently murdered their nanny, Sandra Rivett, mistaking her for his wife? Or the glittering, violent career of the Kray twins – local heroes, celebrity socialites and ruthless murderers?

Everyone in London has their own tale to tell of near-misses and narrow escapes. When the estate agent, Suzy Lamplugh, went missing in 1986, her car was found outside the house where I lived. My flatmate, who knew Suzy from the West London social scene, took it personally. I also recall the sense of outrage when the television presenter Jill Dando was shot dead on her own doorstep, just a street away from ours.

My own interest in crime began early, after I raced through the original Sherlock Holmes stories then read my way through my parents' extensive collection of Penguin thrillers. Rather more unsuitably, I picked up Colin Wilson's *Encyclopaedia of Murder* at the age of twelve and scared the life out of myself. To my mother's horror, I was transfixed by this graphic catalogue of true-life crime, but my interest was creative and forensic rather than ghoulish. I was intrigued not only by crime itself, but by the killers' motivations, and the strong conviction that above all the victims should not be forgotten. Years later, after exploring the darkest aspects of London's history, this fascination still endures. The distinguished advocate Sir Edward Marshall Hall once said that when defending a client, and bringing the details of the case alive, he set out 'to create an atmosphere out of the vivid, living dream of someone else's life'. If I have managed to do this in *Underworld London: Crime and Punishment in the Capital City*, then I shall have succeeded.

1

CITY OF GALLOWS

Roots of the Tyburn Tree

The shadow of the noose looms large over London's history. Nowhere more so than at Tyburn, that desolate space beyond the city walls, where rebels, criminals and martyrs have been executed from time immemorial, as merciless governments strove to preserve an iron grip upon the populace. In the earliest years, offenders were hanged from the branches of the elm trees, until the development of purpose-built gallows, consisting of simple wooden structures with a transverse beam, from which the unfortunate prisoners dangled at the end of a very short rope.

Today, Marble Arch, surrounded by an endless flow of traffic, marks the spot where once the gallows stood. Eight hundred years ago, this windswept plain was silent, apart from the rustle of the elm trees and the caw of the carrion crow. Tyburn was located three miles north west of London for a reason. While the sight of a hanged man was believed to represent an effective deterrent, no citizen wanted to live alongside the reek of putrefaction. Tyburn also had its gibbets, metal cages in which the corpses of the hanged were displayed and left to rot. The mediaeval historian Matthew Paris recorded seeing two prisoners gibbeted, one already dead, the other still alive, condemned to die of exposure and starvation. Between executions, foxes, birds and badgers feasted on the 'friendless bodies of unburied men'[1] and scattered their remains across the heath.

On 6 April 1196, the stillness was shattered by the arrival of a roaring mob, and the pounding of hooves as a horse appeared in a cloud of dust over the horizon, dragging behind it the body of a man. This was the scene as William Fitzosbert, alias 'Longbeard', arrived at Tyburn to be executed for treason, the most grievous crime in the land. Plotting to overthrow the king and the state could only be punishable by death, and death of the most horrific and undignified kind. The sentence consisted of drawing, hanging and quartering, a barbaric practice which involved being dragged or 'drawn' to the gallows, then 'hanged by the neck and let down alive' before being disembowelled (another form of 'drawing' when the intestines were 'drawn' from the body), burnt alive, beheaded, and hacked into four parts or 'quarters'. Finally, the mutilated head and 'quarters' were put on display in prominent positions, such as Tower Bridge or the Temple Bar, *pour décourager les autres*.

Fitzosbert had already been stripped to the waist, bound hand and foot with rope, tied to the tail of a horse, and then 'drawn' or dragged from the Tower of London, a distance of over five miles. Many prisoners died of 'drawing' long before they reached the gallows.

As Fitzosbert was untied and hurled at the foot of the gallows, where a thick chain was placed around his neck preparatory to hanging, he must have reflected on the unhappy series of events that had brought him to this pass. For Fitzosbert had been a privileged man, even if the 'Fitz' in his name denotes that he was a 'bastard', born out of wedlock, to the affluent Osbert family. Fitzosbert, who was raised by his older brother and followed him into the family tailoring business, should have led a long and uneventful life, without troubling the history books. But Fitzosbert was the original bearded agitator.[2] Despite the Norman fashion for a clean shave and cropped hair, Fitzosbert had retained the waist-length beard he had grown when serving on the Third Crusade. Indeed, Fitzosbert's beard became a symbol of political resistance as he encouraged his Saxon supporters to follow his example, making them as unlike the Norman ruling class as possible.

Fitzosbert prided himself on challenging the authorities, denouncing the government from St Paul's Cross, a prototype of Speakers' Corner located in the precincts of St Paul's Cathedral, where craftsmen and labourers flocked to hear him.[3] Fitzosbert's moment of glory finally arrived as a result of the imposition of a tax to secure the release of King Richard I, who had been kidnapped by Duke Leopold of Austria on his return from the Crusades. The Duke demanded £100,000 (around £20 million today) for his release. 'Some citizens claimed, with considerable justification, that the Mayor and Corporation of London had assessed themselves and their friends lightly for the tax and passed the greater part of the burden on to their poorer neighbours.'[4] In a bid to stop the tax, Fitzosbert sailed to France, where the king was held hostage, and explained his grievance to the king in person. Richard gave him assurances that he and his fellow Londoners would not be heavily taxed to raise funds for the ransom. Fitzosbert returned to London, where the authorities were waiting for him. A well-loved demagogue of the people he may have been, but Fitzosbert was not so popular with the Mayor of London and his aldermen, who were terrified that Fitzosbert would incite a tax riot. The government, headed by the Justiciar Hubert Walter in the absence of

Richard I, shared their fears. Apprehensive that trouble in the City might spread to the outlying countryside, the authorities decided to move against him.

Barricading himself into his headquarters with a band of loyal supporters, Fitzosbert prepared for a long siege. But the authorities surrounded him, fearing that London would go up in flames. During the fighting that ensued, Fitzosbert killed one of the king's men. Fitzosbert might have seized this opportunity to parade through London with a dripping sword, followed by hundreds of rebels. Instead, he was so horrified by the fact that he had killed a man that he fled to the nearby church of St Mary-le-Bow for sanctuary. Many of his supporters deserted him, and a mere nine men and his 'concubine' accompanied him into the church where he prepared to wait it out. Hubert Walter, the Justiciar, was faced with a dilemma. Should he defy ecclesiastical law and send in his men to arrest Fitzosbert and his supporters, with the attendant violence and possible killing, on holy ground? Or should he play a waiting game, until Fitzosbert ran out of food and ammunition and gave himself up?

The resourceful Hubert Walter formulated a plan. He ignored the time-honoured right of sanctuary and instructed his men to kindle a fire around the walls of the church. Coughing and spluttering, with streaming eyes, Fitzosbert and his followers were forced to abandon their sanctuary or choke to death on the fumes. One long-term consequence of this tactic was that the tower of St Mary-le-Bow collapsed in 1271, as a result of the fires lit to smoke Fitzosbert out.[5] As they emerged into Bow Lane, Fitzosbert was attacked and wounded by the son of the man he had killed. Fitzosbert and his men were arrested, and Fitzosbert was tied up, fastened to a horse's tail and dragged to the Tower to await trial for treason and the inevitable sentence of death.

And so Fitzosbert found himself at Tyburn, standing with

a chain around his neck, awaiting the remainder of his sentence, which entailed being 'hanged by the neck and let down alive', then disembowelled while still conscious. He would then be faced with the grisly prospect of watching his own intestines burnt in front of him, before his head was cut off.

There are conflicting accounts as to how Fitzosbert responded to his final ordeal. Over one thousand years later, historians cannot agree on the exact circumstances of his death. According to the thirteenth-century Benedictine monk, Matthew Paris, a massive crowd turned out to pay their last respects to this people's champion who had incited riots against an unfair tax. The Elizabethan historian John Stow, however, wrote that Fitzosbert died ignobly, blaspheming Christ, and calling 'upon the devil to help and deliver him. Such was the end of this deceiver, a man of an evil life, a secret murderer, a filthy fornicator, a polluter of concubines, and a false accuser of his elder brother, who had in his youth brought him up in learning and done many things for his preferment.'[6]

Whatever the truth of his final moments, Fitzosbert's execution was notable for two reasons. His death was the first recorded execution for treason at Tyburn, and it was also the first occasion upon which a victim of Tyburn had become a martyr. According to Matthew Paris, after Fitzosbert had been hanged in chains, his gibbet was carried off and treated as a holy relic by his supporters. 'Men scooped the earth from the spot where [the gibbet] had stood. The chains which had held his decomposing body were claimed to have miraculous powers.'[7] Fitzosbert was vindicated, having 'died a shameful death for upholding the cause of truth and the poor'.

Fitzosbert's status as a secular martyr did not prove popular with the authorities. The pilgrims who came to worship at Fitzosbert's 'shrine' were driven away by Hubert the Justiciar, who had instigated the action against him. But

Fitzosbert had his posthumous revenge. Two years later (1198), the monks of Canterbury complained to the Pope about Hubert's conduct, claiming that he had violated the peace of the church of St Mary-le-Bow by forcing out Fitzosbert and his supporters. In response, the Pope put pressure on Richard I and Hubert was dismissed from his post as Justiciar.[8]

Fitzosbert's status and crime made him eminent enough to enter the record books, while the thousands of humble thieves who perished at Tyburn were regarded as so unexceptional that they did not deserve a mention. Hanging had been introduced by the Anglo-Saxons during the fifth century as a punishment for murder, theft and treason. While William I repealed the death penalty, it was reinstated by Henry I in 1108. As Fitzosbert's fate demonstrates, hanging served as a means of social and political control. According to the great Edwardian historian of Tyburn, Alfred Marks, 'the country swarmed with courts of inferior jurisdiction, each with the power to hang thieves'.[9] The law of the day had nothing to do with dispensing justice, and existed merely to defend property, which was regarded as more valuable than human life. The right to erect a gallows was granted to some surprising places, including monasteries. Despite the fact that England was nominally a Christian country, the church had no reservations about capital punishment, with St Paul and Thomas Aquinas enlisted in its defence.[10] The treatment of criminals was governed not by the compassionate doctrines of the New Testament, but by the implacable concepts of the Old. Wrongdoers were publically punished, so that their agonies would be witnessed by as many people as possible, both for the retributive satisfaction and the deterrent effect.[11]

Although the priesthood were forbidden to shed blood, they were not banned from requesting their bailiffs to hang criminals. The Abbot of Westminster owned sixteen gallows in Middlesex in 1281, and the practice extended to convents. Geoffrey Chaucer's tender-hearted prioress, Madame Eglantyne, who was said to weep at the sight of a mouse caught in a trap, would nevertheless have had a gallows on her property, upon which, at the hands of her bailiff, she would have hanged thieves.[12]

The gallows was a familiar sight throughout the land. One popular anecdote tells of a foreign traveller, who, having survived shipwreck, scrambled ashore on the English coast and found himself gazing up at what appeared to be a massive shrine. Crossing himself he fell to his knees, grateful to have arrived in a Christian country. But the structure he was kneeling before was in fact a gallows.[13]

The very first recorded execution at Tyburn was that of John Senex, in 1177. Senex, a nobleman, had been the ringleader of a gang that perpetrated a series of burglaries on private houses in London. By 1236, when Henry III had ordered the King's Gallows to be erected at Tyburn, it had become the place for men of rank to be executed, usually for treason. A notable case was that of William Marsh, who was not only drawn and hanged but quartered. Marsh, son of the viceroy of Ireland, was accused in 1235 of murdering Henry Clement, a messenger who interceded between the Irish and the king. Although he protested his innocence, Marsh was already under suspicion for the attempted assassination of the king. His assets were seized and he went on the run, eventually joining a gang of brigands on the island of Lundy, off the English south-west coast. Turning to a life of piracy, Marsh gave himself up to plunder and rape, as he and his gang descended suddenly on parties of unsuspecting travellers. Henry III put a price on Marsh's head, and he was eventually betrayed by his comrades and ambushed by the king's men, who brought him back to London and threw him into the Tower in 1242,[14] with instructions that he 'should be safely contained in the direst and most secure prison in that fortress, and so loaded with irons' that there could be no risk of his escaping.[15]

On 25 July Marsh and sixteen of his henchmen went on trial at Westminster and were condemned to death by the king with immediate effect. Marsh was drawn from Westminster to Tyburn, and hanged from a gibbet. When his body was stiff it was cut down and disembowelled, and the bowels were at once burnt on the spot. And then, according to the chronicler, 'the miserable body was divided into four parts, which were sent to four of the chief cities, so that this lamentable spectacle might inspire fear in all beholders'.[16]

Some fifty years later, the execution of Sir Thomas De Turberville for treason on 6 October 1295 is notable for the degree of humiliation the prisoner endured as he travelled to

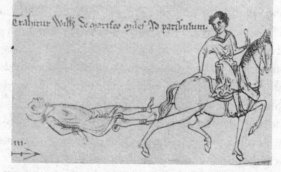

Execution for Treason: William Marsh is dragged to Tyburn gallows, where he will be hanged and eviscerated. 1242.

his death. De Turberville had been captured during the war with France and released on condition that he became a spy and conspired with the French to invade England and support the cause of William Wallace, the Scottish patriot. Detected in the act of writing to the Provost of Paris, De Turberville was tried and condemned. The unusual manner of his execution was described as follows. 'He came from the Tower, mounted on a poor hack, and shod with white shoes, his being covered with a hood, and his feet tied beneath the horse's belly, and his hands tied before him.'[17] Riding alongside De Turberville were six torturers dressed up as devils, who hit him with cudgels and taunted him. Sitting on the horse with De Turberville was the hangman himself, grasping the horse's bridle. De Turberville was led through London to Westminster Hall in this manner, where Sir Robert Brabazun pronounced judgement upon him, sentencing him to be drawn and hanged, 'and that he should hang so long as anything should be left whole of him'.[18] De Turberville was drawn on a fresh ox hide from Westminster to Cheapside, and then to Tyburn. The purpose of the ox hide was not humanitarian. Instead, this method was adopted so that the prisoner would not die before reaching the gallows.

De Turberville's death was barbaric, even by the standards of the day. The fate that awaited William Wallace, the Scottish patriot, was even worse. Wallace (1272–1305) went on trial at Westminster Hall in 1305, although the trial itself was a travesty, and Wallace was forced to wear a crown of laurels as a mockery. He was condemned to be hanged and drawn for his 'robberies, homicides and felonies', and, 'as an outlaw beheaded, and afterwards for your burning churches and relics your heart, liver, lungs, and entrails from which your wicked thoughts come shall be burned . . .'[19] Wallace's execution included one refinement. 'The Man of Belial', as the chroniclers refer to him, was hanged on a very high gallows, specially built for the occasion, let down alive, then disembowelled before being beheaded and then undergoing the further indignity of ementulation or *abscisis genitalibus*.[20] In other words, Wallace's genitals were cut off his body and burnt.[21] Finally, because all Wallace's 'sedition, depredations, fires and homicides were not only against the King, but against the people of England and Scotland', Wallace's head was placed upon Drawbridge Gate on London Bridge, where it could clearly be seen by travellers on land and water, and his quarters were hung in gibbets at Newcastle, Berwick, Stirling and Perth, 'to the terror of all who pass by'.[22] A year later, on 7 September, the head of Simon Fraser, another Scots rebel, was placed on Drawbridge Gate alongside that of his leader.

Brutal and barbaric as these methods of execution may appear to the modern reader, they were consequence of an unstable political climate. And as kings were believed to be divinely appointed, treason was regarded as a crime against God. They are perfect examples of the punishment being designed to fit the crime. But while the majority of convicted criminals awaited a predictable fate on the gallows, early records also yield some curious anecdotes, such as the fate of the ringleader of the first great robbery in the annals of London crime, and his cruel and unusual – but very apposite – punishment.

In 1303 the biggest robbery for six centuries was carried out in London, the amount involved being £100,000, or £20,000,000 in today's currency. The target for the robbery was the palace of King Edward I, which at that period was located next to Westminster Abbey and housed the king's treasury. In addition to valuable ceremonial regalia, there were funds amounting to £100,000, destined to finance Edward's ongoing war with Scotland. When Edward I left Westminster for Scotland on 14 March 1303, a gang of thieves broke into the treasury, scaled a ladder by the Palace gate, broke open the refectory door, and 'carried off a considerable amount of silver plate', as well as jewels and coins.[23] When officers arrived to investigate they found broken boxes, scattered jewels and the king's signet ring, bearing the privy seal, rolling about on the floor. There was no sign of the treasure.

As soon as the robbery had been discovered, forty-one friars and thirty-four monks were rounded up and sent to the Tower of London. It soon emerged that this audacious robbery was the earliest 'project crime' in London, an inside job plotted by William the Sacrist, the churchwarden, and Richard de Podlicote, keeper of the Palace of Westminster, and both their servants.[24]

Months earlier, the monks had planted a crop of hemp in the cemetery plot in the cloisters, creating a thick bed of vegetation. It was here that they stashed their ill-gotten gains, which were later removed by another monk, Alexander of Pershore. Alexander placed the treasure in baskets, and rowed off with it to King's (now Westminster) Bridge. Eventually, ten monks and one cleric were arraigned but they refused to be tried by secular judges. They were remanded to the Tower, but the secular judges 'condemned the Sacrist of Westminster for receiving and concealing jewels of our lord the king',[25] There is no record of the sentence handed down to Richard de Podlicote or William the Sacrist. Indeed, there was not a word as to their fate for centuries.

It was not until 1863, when the architect Sir Gilbert Scott was working on the restoration of St Margaret's, Westminster, that he became fascinated by the discovery that certain doors giving access to the king's treasury appeared to be covered, inside and out, with skin. Scott submitted a sample to an eminent scientist of the day, a Mr Quekett of the Royal College of Surgeons, who, Scott regretted to tell us, pronounced it to be human skin. There had been vague anecdotes about these doors having been covered with 'the skins of Danes' at some grisly point in the abbey's history, but Dean Stanley (the dean of Westminster Abbey) stated that the skin was that of 'a fair-haired, ruddy-complexioned man' and concluded that this was all that remained of William the Sacrist. Scott concluded that the human skins were 'those of persons executed for sacrilege, intended as a means of terrifying less hardened depredators'. A cruel and unusual punishment indeed.[26] The fate of Sir Richard, meanwhile, remains a mystery.

The gallows at Tyburn did not stand idle over the following century. While hundreds, if not thousands, of unrecorded executions took place on this spot, the next notable victim was Roger Mortimer, Baron of Wigmore and Earl of March and effectively king of England for three years between 1327 and 1330.

In February 1327 the unscrupulous and ambitious Mortimer had joined forces with Queen Isabella to depose and murder her husband, Edward II. Isabella, living up to her name as 'the she-wolf of France', proved as ruthless as Mortimer. More than anything, Isabella wanted to see her husband dead so that she could rule in his stead, with Mortimer at her side. Edward II, a flamboyant homosexual with little interest in government, was murdered at Berkeley Castle on the orders of Mortimer, in a particularly grisly fashion – suffocated with a mattress while a red-hot poker was rammed up his anus. By 1329, Isabella's son, Edward, had formed a powerful alliance to overthrow Mortimer, and Mortimer was eventually seized at Nottingham Castle, brought to London and committed to the Tower. On 29 November, Mortimer was condemned to death at Westminster, in the presence of the entire parliament. Despite pleas from Queen Isabella to her son to spare Mortimer's life, Mortimer was drawn to Tyburn, 'and there hanged on the common Gallowes'.[27] Mortimer was left to hang for two days before his body was cut down and buried in Greyfriars Church.

The execution of an innocent man or woman is one of the

most grievous consequences of capital punishment. One of the earliest examples of a miscarriage of justice was recorded in the *Chronicle of the Grey Friars* in 1386. It concerns the landlord of the Cock in Cheapside, who was 'mortheryd in hys bedde be nyght'.[28] The victim's wife was found guilty of killing her husband and sentenced to the mandatory punishment for husband murder or 'petty treason', which was to be burnt to death at Smithfield. Three of the servants, who were implicated in the murder, were drawn and hanged at Tyburn. According to Marks, this was a terrible judicial error. The landlord's wife was innocent, and the actual perpetrator was a thief who 'came in at a gutter window' in the night and who later confessed to the murder when he was at the gallows, waiting to be hanged for another crime.[29]

One of the most extraordinary cases – which led to its protagonists' deaths at Tyburn and Smithfield respectively – came in 1441, when Roger Bolingbroke, an astrologer and magician, was charged with attempting to kill King Henry VI by sorcery, at the instigation of Eleanor Cobham, Duchess of Gloucester. Eleanor's intention was to see Henry VI dead so that her own husband, the Duke of Gloucester, could take the throne. The plotters set about their nefarious task with the aid of Margery Gourdemaine, 'the Witch of Eye' (Ebury, a village near Westminster), and Canon Thomas Southwell of St Stephen's Chapel, Westminster. While Margery worked on her magic potions, Southwell attempted to 'consume the kings person by way of Negromancie' by saying black masses in Hornsey Park, and Bolingbroke sat in a special chair decorated with magical symbols and willed the king to die.

Despite the fact that these spells were manifestly unsuccessful, Bolingbroke and Southwell were arrested and charged with treason, while Dame Eleanor fled into sanctuary at Westminster, which was taken to be an admission of guilt. Thomas Southwell boasted that he would never live long enough to be executed, and indeed, he was found dead in the Tower. The trial of the remaining three plotters at the Guildhall features in Shakespeare's *Henry VI Pt 2*, with their sentences providing some insight into the way that social class affected punishment. While 'the witch in Smithfield shall be strangled on the gallows', Dame Eleanor escapes capital punishment on the grounds that she is 'more nobly born', but she is condemned to spend the rest of her life 'in banishment' on the Isle of Man.[30] The reference to the witch being strangled on the gallows alludes to the practice of garrotting the more fortunate prisoners before the fire was lit, so that they would be dead before the flames consumed them. Bolingbroke, being a nobleman, was drawn from the Tower to Tyburn where he was hanged and quartered, proclaiming his innocence with his dying breath and begging for God's mercy.

Bolingbroke and his comrades suffered the predictable fate for conspiracy and witchcraft. While Margery was consigned to the flames for 'witchcraft', a specious crime for which thousands of women were murdered over the centuries, Bolingbroke met his death at Tyburn, like so many men before him. Far more rare are references to the death of women at Tyburn, as the following intriguing entry in the *Chronicle of the Grey Friars* reveals:

> **1523.** And this yere in Feuerelle [February] the xxth [20th] day was the lady Alys Hungrford was lede from the Tower vn-to Holborne, and there put in-to a carte at the church-yerde with one of hare seruanttes, and so carred vn-to Tyborne, and there bothe hongyd; and she burryd at the Grayfreeres in the nether end of the myddes of the churche on the northe syde.[31]

Upon reading this one immediately wonders who this mysterious lady could have been, and what she could have done to deserve such a fate. Stow provides some clues in *A Survey of London,* in which the great historian refers to a monument in Greyfriars Church commemorating one 'Alice Lat Hungerford, hanged at Tiborne for murdering her husband'. The Victorian antiquarian John Hardy became so fascinated with this case that he decided to investigate the fate of 'Lady Alice' more closely. Hardy concluded that whatever the lady's motive for murdering her husband, it seemed unlikely to have been greed. An inventory of her assets, which were forfeit to the Crown, included an extraordinary collection of valuable property including plate, jewels and sumptuous hangings.

Hardy published his findings in *The Antiquary* in December 1888. He revealed that the lady's name was not Alice at all, but Agnes, and she had married Sir Edward Hungerford in 1518. Sir Edward's family seat was Farleigh Castle, near Bath, and he owned a magnificent house in London, while the name lives on in Hungerford Stairs, by the Thames, and Hungerford Bridge. In December 1521, Sir Edward made a will in favour of his wife. When he died six weeks later on 24 January 1522, he freely bequeathed the residue of his estate to Agnes, including all goods, jewels, plate, harnesses 'and all other moveables [furniture] whatsoever they be'.[32] One wonders why Agnes would want to kill such a generous husband, a man considerate enough to leave her such wealth, when she already enjoyed a lavish lifestyle as his wife while he was alive?

The answer is simple. The husband who died, and who Agnes was accused of murdering, was not Sir Edward Hungerford. It emerged that Agnes had been married before, to a John Cotell of Somerset. Digging through the court records, John Hardy discovered that on 25 August 1522, two yeomen appeared in court in the county of Somerset charged with murdering Cotell three years previously on the orders of Agnes Hungerford. These two men, William Matthew and William Ignes, both from Wiltshire, were indicted for attacking Cotell at

Farleigh Castle. The pair set upon Cotell and 'then and there feloniously did throttle, suffocate, and strangle' him with his own scarf. In order to dispose of Cotell's body, they placed it in the kitchen furnace, where it was consumed by fire.[33]

This case raises many questions. Agnes obviously had a considerable position of power at the castle. Burning one's first husband's body in the kitchen fire was guaranteed to set tongues wagging among the staff. How had John Cotell come to be at the castle? Had he heard that Agnes had married again, and come to Farleigh Castle demanding an explanation, or threatening to blackmail her for bigamy? Or had young Agnes, employed upon the estate, caught the eye of rich old Sir Edward, who had arranged to have Cotell murdered so that he could marry Agnes? Was Sir Edward ruthlessly securing the hand of an attractive but innocent young woman, or was she herself complicit in her first husband's murder? The fact remains that for three years nothing was said about the death of Agnes' first husband, though there must have been gossip and speculation. Perhaps the powerful Sir Edward protected her while he was still alive. It was just seven months after he died that Agnes went on trial for 'petty treason', the murder of her first husband. Agnes was subsequently charged with providing shelter, comfort and aid to her servants, and all three were hanged at Tyburn on 20 February 1523.

Whilst Tyburn had become infamous as an execution ground for criminals and traitors, another faction to be put to death here were the religious dissenters. The first religious martyrs were the Jews, during the thirteenth century. Jewish immigration to England came with William I, when he brought Jews over after the Conquest on the grounds of financial expediency. Although the Christians were forbidden by canon law to practice usury, the Jews suffered no restrictions. Banned from entering medicine or the law, money lending was the only profession open to them. But as they prospered, the Jews endured terrible hatred from the gentiles. In 1189, a series of riots saw the entire Jewish population of London fleeing for protection to the Tower.[34] In 1255, eighteen Jews were accused of the ritual murder of a seven-year-old boy, Hugh of Lincoln. This 'blood libel', which was nothing more than anti-Semitic propaganda, saw the eighteen men hanged at the Tower.

In 1275, Edward I's Jewish Statute insisted that the Jews abandoned usury and learned a trade. Unable to practise as moneylenders, many Jews turned to a form of forgery known as 'clipping the coin'. This consisted of filing the edges off legitimate coins and melting them down to produce higher-denomination counterfeit money. The Jews became so proficient at 'clipping the coin' that there were fears that the entire financial system would collapse. However, they paid dearly for their skill. As the king controlled the Royal Mint, and therefore all the money in England, 'clipping the coin' constituted a form of treason. As a result, in November 1278, the entire Jewish population of England, around 600 people, was rounded up, charged with fraud and taken to the Tower.[35] Two hundred and eight Jews of both sexes were hanged, many at Tyburn. Those who survived were banished by King Edward in 1290.

The next persecuted minority consisted of the Lollards. This group (the word 'Lollard' derives from the Dutch, *lollen,* to 'mutter') were precursors of the Protestants. They followed the preaching John Wycliffe (c.1320–84), a priest and teacher who helped translate the Bible into English and criticized the authority of the Pope, who promptly launched a Papal Bull against him. The Lollards were regarded as heretics on the grounds that they disregarded the sacraments and encouraged the laity to preach, and they represented such a threat to the established church that, in 1401, an act was introduced entitled *De Haeretico Comburendo* or 'On the Burning of Heretics'.

This act permitted sheriffs and Justices of the Peace to burn suspected heretics to death. This punishment gave rise to the popular misconception that the name 'Tyburn' derived from the fate of the Lollards, as in the observation that: 'Tieburne, some will have it so called from Tie and Burne, because the poor Lollards for whom this instrument was first set up, had their necks tied to the beame, and their lower parts burnt in the fire'.[36] In fact, many Lollards also perished at Smithfield, and the name 'Tyburn' derives from the Saxon 'Teo-burna' or 'Two Brooks', referring to the two streams that converged at this location.[37]

The third category of martyrs to die at Tyburn were the Roman Catholics, executed upon the orders of King Henry VIII following the Reformation of 1534, when Henry severed relations with the Pope of Rome and appointed himself Defender of the Faith and head of the Anglican church in England. Among the unfortunate was one Elizabeth Barton (1506–34), later christened 'the Holy Maid of Kent'. Elizabeth, a nun, suffered from *petite mal,* a mild form of epilepsy, and was credited with seeing visions during her trances. In 1534, Elizabeth prophesied that if Henry VIII married Anne Boleyn, the 'Bullen whore', he would no longer be king of England and would die shortly afterwards. As a result of this prediction, Elizabeth Barton was arrested for treason, imprisoned in the Tower, and hanged at Tyburn on 20 April.[38] Elizabeth's head was later placed upon a spike on London Bridge, making her the only woman to be granted that grisly distinction.

As for the king, he survived for another fifteen years, during which he continued to stamp out support for the Roman Catholic cause with a series of high-profile executions at Tyburn. One of the most graphic instances was the execution of three Carthusian priors. On 4 May 1535, Father Robert Lawrence, prior of Beauvale, Father Augustine Webster, prior of Axholem, and Father John Houghton, prior of the Charterhouse in London, were dragged from Newgate to Tyburn. Father Houghton was cut down while still breathing and dragged to one side, where his garments were torn from his body and his genitals sliced off and roasted on a spit in front of him. Despite the fact that he was being disembowelled and his entrails burnt in a brazier, Father Houghton 'bore himself with more than human endurance, most patiently', to the astonishment of the crowd. Even as his heart was being torn out, the Father turned to his executioner and enquired, 'Sweet

Jussit amor pietasq́; facram me tangere dextram.
Cede loco pollex; cedere iuſſit amor.

Executions at Tyburn, c. 1607. Criminals, traitors and martyrs met a grisly end at this infamous execution ground.

Jesu, what will you do with my heart?'[39] These were his final words. His head was cut off, his body quartered, and his right arm was taken back to the Charterhouse where it was nailed to the door as an horrific warning. The remains of his fellow Carthusians were thrown into cauldrons and parboiled, and later displayed in different parts of London. In all, 105 Catholic martyrs died at Tyburn. Many were subsequently canonized, and they are commemorated at Tyburn Convent. This Benedictine convent, founded in 1901, stands on the spot where so many met their deaths, known and unknown.

This completes the first visit to Tyburn. Now it is time to travel to another sinister landmark on the historical map of London. To the Tower, that great castle of darkness from which so few escaped with their lives.

2

CASTLE OF DARKNESS

Torture and Death in the Tower of London

No history of crime and punishment in London would be complete without a visit to the Tower. This magnificent edifice has reared above the city since 1079, serving as a terrible warning to those who challenge the authority of the crown. Five miles from Tyburn, the Tower dominates the south-east stretch of old London Wall, forming another landmark on the city's bloody map. For generations, the Tower represented law and order, an important visual reminder in the years before the existence of a standing army and a professional police force. A royal palace, a fortress and a prison, the Tower exuded a powerful mystique that fascinated and repelled.

This chapter is the story of murder most royal, of famous and infamous who spent their last days here. The prisoners in the Tower were men and women of the highest rank, who met their fate on Tower Green, or Tower Hill. Then there were those who spoke out against monstrous tyranny, and endured agonies of torture before being dragged to Tyburn and Smithfield. To step inside these high walls on a cold, grey morning, with the mist rising from the river, is to feel the shades of the prison house closing around one and to understand how those two words, 'the Tower', could strike fear into the bravest heart.

As any modern visitor soon realizes, the Tower of London consists not of one tower, but of many, gradually added over the centuries as the Tower expanded into its various roles as palace, royal mint and prison. The oldest tower was 'the White Tower', so called because it was painted white in the thirteenth century. The White Tower was erected upon the site of an existing Roman fortification, chosen for its elevated, well-drained position above the tidal River Thames, and protected by the massive defensive wall which the Romans had built to protect Londinium. Beginning work under the guidance of Gundulf, Bishop of Rochester in 1077, the Normans exploited this existing fortification and created additional walls to enclose the site. Within the site, they built the White Tower, an immense, square castle with turrets 36 x 32.5 m (118 x 106 ft) across and, on the south side (where the ground is lowest), 27.5 m (90 ft) tall. The second largest structure of its type known to have been built, the White Tower is still remarkably well preserved and remains the most complete eleventh-century palace in Europe.

Slammed down upon the London skyline in 1079 like a massive fist, the Tower demonstrated the power and might of the new Norman government, and it served three purposes. As a palace, with state rooms, lodgings, a chapel, kitchens and even a latrine, it was fit for a king. But the Tower was also a fortress, with a moat surrounding it, an entrance well above ground and walls up to 4 m (15 ft) thick, making it virtually impregnable.[1] And as the Normans struggled to control England and her unruly cousins in Scotland and Wales, the Tower performed another role: it operated as a prison for men or women of rank. The prisoners fell into three categories: powerful men who had offended the king, prisoners of war, detained awaiting ransom, and potential troublemakers whose continued liberty was undesirable for political reasons.[2]

The first prisoner in the Tower to appear upon the records was Bishop Ranulf Flambard (1060–1128), chief tax collector under William Rufus. When William died, his brother Henry I incarcerated Flambard in 1100 on the grounds of extortion, a move calculated to win favour with the barons.[3] The conditions in which the bishop was held were not uncongenial; he was allowed his own servants and could use his ill-gotten gains to purchase food and drink, which were brought in to him by collaborators.

The bishop could also afford to purchase his freedom. A rope was smuggled into the Tower in a butt of wine, and a horse stood ready beneath the wall. On 2 February 1120 the bishop threw a feast for his jailors, ensured that they were hopelessly drunk, then slipped away to another room where he tied up the rope, squeezed his bloated body out through the window, and made his way to freedom, becoming not only the first recorded prisoner at the Tower, but the first man to escape from the fortress too. The bishop evidently led a charmed life; after taking refuge in France, he made his peace with Henry I and returned to England, where he was restored to his bishopric and died peacefully in 1128.

In 1244, Gruffydd ap Llewlyn, a Welsh rebel imprisoned by Henry III, attempted to emulate the bishop's death-defying feat. Despite being kept in reasonable conditions, enjoying good food and regular visits from his wife, Llewlyn decided after two and a half years of imprisonment that he would try to escape by a similar method, knotting together his sheets, bedcovers and every hanging he could find to make a rope.

Unlike the bishop, Llewlyn did not climb out of a window.

Instead, he went up on to the roof of the White Tower, fastened one end of his improvized rope to the parapet and began to lower himself over the side. He had scarcely started when the rope gave way and he plummeted ninety feet to his death. According to a contemporary writer, 'his head and neck were crushed between his shoulders, a most horrid spectacle'.[4]

Another famous escapee was Sir John Oldcastle, the first prisoner to be held in the Tower for religious dissent. Sir John, who was the model for Shakespeare's Falstaff, was revealed to be a Lollard when some of his old books were found in a second-hand shop in Paternoster Row. King Henry V, Sir John's former boon companion, risked his own reputation to protect his old friend, but as Sir John refused to deny his beliefs, he was inevitably gaoled. He managed to escape from the Tower on 19 October 1413, with the help of his co-religionists, but instead of fleeing abroad, Sir John squandered his opportunity for freedom by mounting an ambitious coup against his former protector, Henry V. The plot hinged on Sir John and his comrades gaining access to the king disguised as a company of entertainers on Twelfth Night. Characteristically brave but reckless, this plan was soon foiled and Sir John was recaptured and hanged at St Giles's Fields. According to John Foxe, writing in his *Book of Martyrs,* Sir John made a good end:

> He was brought out of the Tower with his arms bound behind him, having a very cheerful countenance. Then he was laid upon a hurdle, as though he had been a most heinous traitor to the Crown, and so drawn forth into St Giles Field, where they had set up a new pair of gallows.

After praying to God to forgive his enemies, and exhorting the huge crowd to follow the scriptures, 'he was hanged up there by the middle in chains of iron, and so consumed alive in the fire, praising the name of God so long as his life lasted'.[5]

The Tower had always been a place of terror, but it was towards the end of the fifteenth century that the fortress really developed its bloodstained reputation, as a result of the bitter family feud between the two factions of the Plantagenet family, commonly known as the 'Wars of the Roses'. The first victim of the power struggle between the two houses of York and Lancaster was Henry VI. When Edward IV seized power from Henry in 1461, Henry and his queen, Margaret, fled into Scotland. But they were recaptured four years later and Henry was confined to the Wakefield Tower. Gentle, ascetic Henry, with his religious fervour and scholarly ways (he was responsible for founding Eton College and King's College, Cambridge), had never been an effective ruler. Long considered to be insane, his symptoms consistent with a modern diagnosis of schizophrenia, Henry adapted to imprisonment better than many, and there is no suggestion that he was subjected to a particularly Spartan regime. If Henry was seen shuffling unshaven in ragged garments, this was more likely to have been a consequence of his austere lifestyle rather than a form of punishment.

The deposed Henry VI was permitted to attend Mass every day in the Wakefield Tower, to receive visitors, to study and to read. He appeared to be relieved that he no longer had to deal with the burdens of office. Edward IV, for his part, had no interest to serve by ill-treating the former king. However, in 1470, after a successful coup by the Duke of Warwick, 'the Kingmaker', and Edward's younger brother, the Duke of Clarence (both former supporters of Edward who had switched sides), Henry was briefly restored to the throne after being paraded through the streets from the Tower to St Paul's before his applauding subjects.

Edward IV soon regained the upper hand, however, and Henry was sent back to the Tower where, on 21 May 1471, he was found dead in the oratory of the Wakefield Tower, 'stykked with a dagger' while he knelt at prayer, according to Polydore Vergil, Henry VII's official historian.[6] Vergil attributed the crime to Edward's youngest brother, Richard, Duke of Gloucester, the first in a grisly series of charges laid against the future King Richard III as he carved his bloody path towards the throne.

The next victim was George, Duke of Clarence, brother of Edward IV. Although Clarence had supported the coup of 1470 that had briefly restored Henry VI to the throne, Edward had forgiven him, and continued to tolerate Clarence despite the fact that Clarence resented Edward's power and influence, insulted Edward's queen, Elizabeth Woodville, and continued to plot against him. Edward's generosity finally reached its limit in 1477, when he summoned Clarence to Westminster and had him arrested for treason and sent to the Tower. There he was detained for seven months while Edward waited for some sign of remorse from his weak and disloyal brother.

But Clarence remained defiant, and was condemned to death by the House of Lords in 1478, who ruled that he should be executed privately in the Tower. According to Polydore Vergil, Clarence was drowned in a butt of Malmsey wine, which seems an extraordinary method of execution. One explanation could be that Clarence's body was removed from the Tower in a barrel of wine after his death; another is that Clarence, a notorious drunkard, had asked to be despatched in this fashion with characteristic bravado.

William Shakespeare, upholding the Tudor view of history, accused Richard, Duke of Gloucester, later Richard III, of murdering Clarence. But, it has to be said, that although Clarence left the world in an unconventional manner, his execution had been authorized by Parliament and was perfectly legal, if shrouded in secrecy.[7] It is a similar veil of secrecy that surrounds the disappearance of the sons of Edward IV, the little princes Edward and Richard, who were sent to the Tower in 1483.

Edward IV died suddenly on 9 April 1483, and was immediately succeeded by his twelve-year-old son, Edward. However, Richard Duke of Gloucester, Edward IV's brother, swiftly seized control. Edward's widow, Elizabeth Woodville, fled into sanctuary at Westminster Abbey, and Richard appointed himself Protector.

Fearing that her son would not inherit the throne, Elizabeth Woodville plotted with William Hastings, the Lord Chamberlain, to overthrow Richard. But Richard, who by this stage was referring to himself as 'the Protector', learned of the conspiracy and summoned Hastings and his confederates Lord Stanley, Bishop Morton and the Archbishop of York to the Tower. Assuming that they had been summoned to a meeting of the Privy Council, the four men appeared promptly, only to be arrested on the orders of the Protector. Stanley, Morton and the Archbishop were immediately imprisoned in the Tower, but Hastings suffered a different fate. As Richard commented tersely that he could not sit down to dinner 'until he had seen his head', Hastings was led out on to Tower Green. A priest was sent for so that Hastings could make his final confession, and then, a piece of timber for repair work being conveniently to hand, Hastings laid down his neck and was beheaded, the first person to be executed on Tower Green.[8]

Having set a brutal example by executing Hastings, Richard the Protector promptly claimed the throne on the grounds that Edward IV's marriage to Elizabeth Woodville had been bigamous and that Edward's sons, who were living in the Tower in its capacity as a Royal Palace, were therefore bastards. While Richard appointed himself King Richard III, twelve-year-old Prince Edward and nine-year-old Prince Richard remained in the Tower, ostensibly for their own protection. From this point, their fate becomes a matter of conjecture. At the end of 1483, an Italian visitor who had been in London during that year noted that after Hastings had been removed, all the deposed young king's servants were denied access to him. He and his brother retreated into the inner apartments of the Tower and their appearances at the windows became rarer and rarer, day by day, until they ceased to be seen altogether. A doctor from Strasbourg reported that the young king, like a victim prepared for sacrifice, sought remission of his sins by daily confession and penance, because he believed that death was facing him:

> I have seen many men burst forth into tears and lamentation when mention was made of him after his removal from men's sight; and already there was a suspicion that he had been done away with. Whether, however, he has been done away with, and by what manner of death, so far I have not at all discovered.[9]

The 'inner apartments' are probably a reference to the White Tower, an area of the Tower to which few had access. Given the fate of Henry VI twelve years earlier, it is understandable that the populace would fear for the young princes. Rumours were circulating in the taverns of London that the princes were dead from July onwards, when an attempt to overthrow Richard, place Elizabeth Woodville upon the throne and rescue the little princes met with failure. By October, the general assumption was that they had been murdered and their remains interred somewhere in the Tower.[10] But who knew where the bodies were buried?

In 1674, some 191 years later, a complex of mediaeval buildings along the front of the White Tower was demolished. Part of this complex consisted of a stair turret giving access to the original entrance. Ten feet below the foundations of this staircase the workmen found a wooden chest containing the skeletons of 'two striplings', or young male children. These were assumed to be the remains of the princes, and buried in Westminster Abbey.

In 1933 the bones were examined by forensic experts, who concluded that the remains were those of the princes. Subsequent doubts have been raised but it is unlikely that the bodies of any other children would have been concealed in such a fashion at about the same time that the boys disappeared.

If the princes in the Tower were murdered, then by whom, and upon whose orders? The evidence is wholly circumstantial. Henry VII claimed to have received a confession from one of Richard III's trusted aides, Sir James Tyrell, before the latter was executed for treason in 1502. This flimsy claim was seized upon by pro-Tudor propagandists Sir Thomas More and Polydore Vergil, who were intent upon casting Richard III as the villain of the piece.

Later historians, eager to make the case for Richard III as a much-maligned monarch, attributed the murders to the Duke of Buckingham, a loyal supporter of Richard III who later deserted him; other writers claimed that the princes had been murdered on the orders of Henry Tudor, later Henry VII, as a method of discrediting Richard and removing any opposition to Henry's claim to the throne.

We shall never know the fate of the little princes, or who was responsible for their deaths. The Tower will never reveal this particular dark secret. But had the princes survived, they would almost certainly have endured the brief lives and early deaths experienced by their cousins. From 1483 onwards, the Tower's history becomes stained with tragedy, 'when the prisons were constantly filled and the scaffold deluged with blood'.[11]

This is the period when the ranks of servants at the Tower included jailers, torturers and an executioner, when all the terrible machinery of so-called justice could be made ready at a moment's notice, and when the steps of Traitors' Gate were worn down by the feet of those who climbed them. It was here that Henry Tudor, once he had defeated Richard III at the Battle of Bosworth Field in 1485, held court, and filled the Tower's prisons with his enemies, real and imaginary.[12]

In his position as founder of the new Tudor dynasty, Henry VII was confronted with a succession of rebels and pretenders to the throne. One such was Lambert Simnel, c. 1477–1525, who impersonated the Earl of Warwick and led a rebellion against Henry VII until the genuine Earl of Warwick was produced (while Simnel was parading around the country claiming to be him, the genuine Earl of Warwick had been imprisoned in the Tower). Simnel actually received a lenient sentence, being set to work in the royal kitchens – Henry VII shrewdly realizing that humiliation was more effective than martyrdom.

This tactic did not extend to the unfortunate Perkin Warbeck (c.1474–99), a young man 'of visage beautiful, of countenance demure, of will subtle',[13] who claimed to be Richard, Duke of York, the younger of the missing princes. Warbeck claimed that he had been spirited out of the country in 1483, and a young stable lad had taken his place, while he had been raised anonymously in France as 'Perkin'.

Henry VII could not suffer the young man to live. If Warbeck were to be the son of Edward IV, last of the Plantagenets, he represented a threat to the newly established Tudor throne. Even as a pretender, Perkin Warbeck was capable of summoning sufficient support to destabilize the monarchy and seize power. Warbeck was arrested and taken to the Tower of London before being drawn to Tyburn along with his supporters. Lost king or no, Warbeck made a good death of it, according to the Tudor historian Edward Hall, who tells us in his *Chronicle* of 1542 that 'Perykn standing on a little skaffolde, read his confession, and took it on hys death to be true ... asked the king forgiveness and dyed patiently.'[14]

The horrors which resulted from Henry VII's battle to enforce his position as monarch were as nothing compared with his son's reign of terror. Henry VIII's escalating rage and syphilitic paranoia guaranteed a death sentence for any man or woman who thwarted him, either on the grounds of religious convictions or treason. Many of these individuals met their deaths on Tower Hill, an execution ground established by Edward IV when he had built a permanent gallows on this former rubbish tip. This desolate spot, a 'liberty' or open space outside the Tower and beyond the jurisdiction of the Mayor and Aldermen, became one of the most grisly locations in London, where those who had defied the king met their deaths in an appalling public spectacle.

Among those made an example of under Henry VIII's regime were the Duke of Buckingham, who had a plausible case for opposing Henry's monarchy, and Sir Thomas More, the statesman and theologian who could not bring himself to support Henry's Reformation of the Church. When Sir Thomas mounted the scaffold in 1553, his parting words were: 'See me safe up, for my coming down I can shift for myself.'[15] Thomas Cromwell, Henry's secretary, fell out of favour in 1540, following Henry's disastrous marriage to Anne of Cleves, which Cromwell had brokered. Cromwell went to his death on Tower Hill on 28 July, to die horribly at the hands of a 'ragged, butcherly miser, which very ungodly performed the office'.[16]

Tower Green, by contrast, was a relatively private execution site. Tower Green lies next to the chapel of St Peter ad Vincula, and was where Lord Hastings had been summarily executed on the orders of Richard III. Tower Green was the execution site of Henry VIII's second wife, Anne Boleyn, beheaded for treason on the grounds of adultery in 1536. Despite her youth and innocence, Anne went to her death with impeccable poise, even joking to her executioner that his task would not take long as she had 'a little neck'. Executioners could by no means be relied upon to despatch their victims swiftly, but Anne seems to have been fortunate in her headsman, an experienced man brought over from France, who severed her head from her little neck with one blow of his sword.

Margaret Pole, Countess of Salisbury, did not demonstrate such commendable *sang froid* when she was put to death for treason in 1541. Although Margaret was the last member of the Plantagenet family, at seventy-one years old she scarcely represented a threat. Indeed, Henry's decision to have her executed rather than permanently imprisoned in the Tower gives some indication of his deranged mental state. The countess was a formidable woman who refused point blank to lie down with her head on the block, protesting that 'so should traitors do, and I am none!'[17] Instead of submitting to the headsman's axe, Margaret ran around the scaffold shrieking, dodging the executioner's blows, until, in a barbaric and shameful display, she was eventually hacked to death.

Henry VIII's fifth wife, Katherine Howard (born c. 1525), died on Tower Green in 1542, after Henry had discovered her affairs with the courtiers Francis Dereham and George Culpepper. It is said that Henry was so infuriated when he learnt of his wife's exploits that he would have run her through with his sword himself had he not been restrained by his aides. Katherine demonstrated a certain degree of bravado. So determined was she to appear at her best on the scaffold, that she demanded that an executioner's block be brought to her cell, so that she could perfect the appropriate pose. Katherine might not have been able to choose her executioner, but is said to have handed the headsman her golden chain with a request for an easy death. Katherine was buried in St Peter's ad Vincula, next to Anne Boleyn.

During their periods of imprisonment, state prisoners such as Anne Boleyn, Sir Thomas More and Thomas Cromwell experienced reasonably comfortable conditions. The Tower was luxurious compared with prisons such as Newgate and the Fleet. Eminent prisoners were permitted food, books, wine and adequate clothing, and it was customary for female prisoners to be accompanied by their ladies in waiting and servants. However, there was a far more disturbing aspect to life in the Tower if one refused to confess to one's crimes: torture.

Although England had its own form of brutality in the form of drawing, hanging, quartering and burning at the stake, and although prison conditions were barbaric for the common man, torture as such was rare, compared with conditions on the Continent. In 1215, Magna Carta had established that: 'No freeman shall be taken or imprisoned, or deceased or outlawed or exiled, *or in any way destroyed* [tortured] ... except by the lawful judgement of his peers or by the law of the land.'[18] However, torture could be condoned in exceptional circumstances, although these cases were rare, as permission had to be obtained from the Privy Council.

The existence of a torture chamber at the Tower of London is a powerful myth, derived from authors such as Harrison Ainsworth, who claimed in his novel *The Tower of London* (1840) that the torture chamber was located in the Constable Tower and consisted of a dank underground room filled with an impressive array of thumbscrews, gauntlets, collars, pincers, saws, chains and a rack. This was an exaggeration: there was no torture chamber as such. Instead, most instruments of torture were portable, and could be carried to the individual cells of those unfortunate prisoners upon whom they were employed. No ingenuity was spared in the creation of these barbaric instruments, many of which were named in honour of their sadist inventors.

Take, for instance, 'Skeffington's Gyves' or 'the Scavenger's Daughter', devized by Leonard Skeffington, the Lieutenant of the Tower during the 1530s. The 'Scavenger's Daughter' was 'in all respects the opposite of the rack, for while that draws apart the joints by the feet and hands tied, this, on the contrary constricts and binds into a ball'.[19] The device consisted of two iron bars that pressed the lower legs against the thighs and the thighs against the belly, so that the prisoner was effectively squashed inside a cage fastened with clamps, which could be tightened or released according to the whims of the torturer. This piece of apparatus was 'more dreadful and more complete than the rack' because the body was so cruelly bent that in some cases blood exuded from the tips of the hands and feet, or in other cases the pressure was such that the ribs burst and blood was expelled from the prisoner's mouth and nostrils.[20]

Then there was the rack, also known as 'the Duke of Exeter's Daughter' after Henry Holland, Fourth Duke of Exeter, who was credited with inventing it.[21] First mentioned 1446, the rack consisted of an open rectangular wooden frame, about seven feet long, raised about one to three feet from the floor on four or six legs. The victim was laid on the floor immediately beneath the framework and secured with ropes around his wrists and ankles to the windlass mechanisms at each of the narrow ends of the frame. Levels inserted into the sockets on the windlasses were then operated by jailors in opposite directions by means of which the prisoner was raised from the floor until level with the frame. At this stage, the sheer weight of the body simply induced pain to all four limbs; but any subsequent movement of the windlass levers would start to strain heavily on the shoulder and hip sockets until, as Thomas Norton, the Elizabethan rack-master was proud to boast when racking the Jesuit priest Alexander Briant in 1581, 'the prisoner was stretched twelve inches taller than God had created him'.[22]

Another method of torture consisted of manacles, which were fitted around the wrists, like modern handcuffs, but were much heavier. The method consisted of hanging the prisoner by the wrists from a beam, so that they stretched under their own weight. Another Jesuit priest, John Gerard, underwent such treatment in 1597, and remained permanently crippled from its effects.[23] Remarkably, Father Gerard nevertheless survived and went on to become one of the few prisoners to escape from the Tower, making his getaway in a boat with the help of his warder, Bennett.

While there was no specific torture chamber, certain dungeons served as instruments of torture in their own right. These included rat-infested caverns that filled with water when the Thames reached high tide, or Little Ease, a chamber in the cellar of the White Tower which was so small that the occupant could neither stand up to full height or lie down full length. As a place of punishment it could be made available on the orders of the Lieutenant and did not require permission from the Privy Council. Also in the White Tower was 'the Pit', a subterranean dungeon twenty feet deep and entirely without light, which may have been the remains of the old Norman well and into which prisoners could be hurled as into an oubliette.[24]

Under Henry VIII, torture was justified in the interests of national security. A staunch supporter of Rome before he chose to reform the Church, Henry VIII began his reign persecuting Protestants, such as the Lollards, and ended it with the Dissolution of the Monasteries and the extermination of the Roman Catholics. During the Reformation, any person who clung to their Roman Catholic faith and did not accept King Henry as the head of the Protestant church in England was considered to be committing treason. On these grounds, the Tower was constantly filled with prisoners, and the soil beneath the scaffold on Tower Hill was dyed with the richest and best blood in the land.[25] Notable victims included Robert Dalyvell, racked on the suspicion of being a Papist spy, and eventually released – but only after his ears had been cut off[26] – and Abbot Thomas Marshall of Colchester, who was arrested and interrogated for opposing Henry's marriage to Anne Boleyn.

Protestants might also find themselves accused of treason. One such, in 1546, was Anne Askew, an outspoken gentlewoman from Lincolnshire who had become good friends with Henry's sixth wife, Catherine Parr, and sympathized with Catherine's Protestant beliefs. Two courtiers, Archbishop Gardiner and the Duke of Norfolk, seized on Anne as a means of discrediting Catherine Parr for their own purposes, and had Anne arrested as a heretic, condemned to death by burning and sent to the Tower.

The intention was to frighten Anne into giving damning evidence against Catherine. Anne was questioned for hours by the Lord Chancellor, Thomas Wriothesley, and the Chancellor, Richard Rich, but refused to bear false witness against Catherine or recant her Protestant sympathies. In a desperate bid to scare Anne into a false confession, they sent for the lieutenant of the Tower, Sir Anthony Knyvett, and asked him to have the rack prepared in the basement of the White Tower. The racking of a woman was unprecedented, and Sir Anthony was assured that Anne would require no more than a light 'pinching' to make her talk.[27]

But Sir Anthony was wrong. Anne Askew was born to the role of martyr, and endured patiently as she was stretched on the rack and the screw was turned. Wriothesley and Rich resumed their interrogation, but still she said nothing. Further pressure was applied, but Anne still refused to discredit Queen Catherine or renounce her beliefs. When Sir Anthony demanded that Anne be released, the Chancellor told him not to interfere. Sir Anthony pointed out that what they were doing was illegal, and carried out without the consent of the Privy Council. Wriothesley ordered him to continue with the torture, in the king's name. When Sir Anthony refused, Wriothesley and Rich took off their gowns, rolled up their sleeves and continued with the racking themselves, while Anne prayed quietly and patiently, and 'abode their tyranny, till her bones and joints were almost plucked asunder'.[28]

When Anne was eventually released, she fainted, and never regained the full use of her limbs. As soon as he left the White Tower, Sir Anthony hurried to see the king at Westminster and told him what had happened. Although Henry's response is not on record, we do know that within days the attempt to discredit Catherine Parr had collapsed, and she was not quietly executed on Tower Green. Anne Askew saw her martyrdom through to the bitter end. Refusing to recant, so badly crippled that she could not walk, Anne was carried to Smithfield in a chair, where she was burnt to death.[29]

Henry VIII's reign of terror was continued by 'Bloody' Mary Tudor (1516–58), a fanatical devotee of the Roman Catholic Church, who rejected Henry's break with Rome and was eager to make England a Catholic country once again. A weak and unstable monarch, Mary was easily led by her councillors, who manipulated her to their own ends and persuaded her to sign the warrant for the execution of her rival, Lady Jane Grey. Although very much in keeping with the Tudor tradition of eliminating all opposition, this was a brutal and unnecessary gesture, as the sixteen-year-old Jane was no more than a political pawn, placed upon the throne for a mere nine days in July 1553, following an unsuccessful coup. A show of mercy would have brought dividends to Mary, and she did offer Jane a fragile opportunity of survival if she agreed to convert to Roman Catholicism. But Jane refused to abandon her Protestant faith, and Mary was convinced by

Archbishop Gardiner that it would be best to execute Jane and Jane's young husband, the Earl of Dudley.[30]

Execution day dawned on the morning of 12 February 1554, leaving Jane and her husband with no doubt as to the outcome of events. On execution days, prisoners and staff alike heard the carpenters hard at work, the noise of their saws rasping through the wood and their hammers echoing about the surrounding buildings as they nailed the planks to the posts. As Jane watched from her prison cell, her husband was led away through the gateway of the Bloody Tower.

Some time later, a cart returned through the archway, bearing the body of her husband, and his head, wrapped in a cloth. Soon afterwards, Jane herself went to the scaffold, accompanied

The execution of Lady Jane Grey at the Tower of London, as envisaged by Cruikshank.

by her weeping ladies-in-waiting and a Catholic priest, John Feckenham, who had made a last, unsuccessful bid to convert Jane to the Church of Rome. Jane was poised and calm until the last moment, when, blindfolded, she was unable to find the block, and stumbled about, crying out pitifully, 'Where is it? What shall I do? What shall I do?' It fell to Father Feckenham to guide Jane and help her to retain her dignity to the end.[31]

Weeks later, on 18 March, another young princess arrived at the Tower. As the 21-year-old Elizabeth Tudor stepped out of the boat and on to the steps of Traitors' Gate, making the same journey as her mother, Anne Boleyn, had done nineteen years earlier, it must have seemed to Elizabeth that she would soon join her illustrious predecessors on the scaffold. But within four years Queen Mary was dead and, in November of 1558, Elizabeth was crowned Queen of England. When she returned to the Tower as queen, Elizabeth touched the ground and said, 'Some have fallen from being princes of this land to be prisoners in this place. I am raised from being prisoner in this place to be the prince of this land. That dejection was a work of God's justice; this advancement is a work of His mercy.'[32]

Not only did Elizabeth I prove to be one of the few prisoners of the Tower to survive the experience, she consigned her enemies to the Tower in her turn. In 1586, Anthony Babington (1561–86) was seized and consigned to the Tower for his part in the eponymous plot that intended to assassinate the queen and replace her with Mary, Queen of Scots. Babington and his co-conspirators were subsequently hanged, drawn and quartered at Lincoln's Inn Fields in scenes considered disturbing even by hardened execution-goers.

Queen Elizabeth's sometime favourite, Sir Walter Raleigh (1554–1618), was twice sentenced to the Tower. In 1592 the queen had him imprisoned for six weeks for his affair with one of her ladies-in-waiting, Elizabeth Throgmorton. Raleigh was released in September but Elizabeth Throgmorton was held until the end of the year to ensure Raleigh's compliance.[33] In 1603 Elizabeth's successor, James I, sent Raleigh back to the Tower, on a charge of plotting an assassination attempt. Elizabeth Throgmorton, now Raleigh's wife, accompanied him in his imprisonment, where the conditions for an aristocratic family were tolerable enough and Raleigh remained productive. He wrote his *History of the World* (eventually published in 1628) and fathered a son, Carew, born in the Tower in 1604. Briefly released to lead an expedition into Venezuela, Raleigh could not escape his fate. Executed at Westminster when he returned to England, he died as bravely as he had lived. His last words, as he laid his head upon the block and the executioner raised the axe, were: 'Strike man, strike!'[34]

Every prisoner of consequence carved their names upon the walls of the Tower. Today, some of these inscriptions are still visible, serving as a lasting memorial. The Beauchamp Tower, where Philip Howard, Earl of Arundel, was held in 1572 before being beheaded for aspiring to marry Mary, Queen of Scots, includes the inscriptions *Dolor Patientia Vincitur* [Patience Will Triumph Over Sadness].[35] In the same tower appears an inscription from an Irishman, Thomas Miagh, tortured for spying in 1580. Having endured the horrors of Skeffington's Daughter and the rack, Miagh carved his own epitaph:

> Thomas Miagh which liethe here alone
> That fayne wold from hence begon
> By torture straunge mi trovth was tryed
> Yet of my libertie denied.[36]

Hugh Draper, imprisoned on charges of sorcery, left an elaborate carving and inscription on the wall of the Salt Tower in 1561, while on 10 September 1571 Charles Bailly offered the observation: 'Be friend to one. Be ennemye to none. The most unhappy man in the world is he that is not patient in adversities: For men are not killed with the adversities they have, but with the impatience they suffer.'[37]

Occasionally the mood of resignation breaks down, as in this anonymous carving, where a prisoner recorded that he had been: 'Close prisoner 8 months, 22 wekes, 224 dayes, 5376 houres'.[38]

On Tower Green, where once the headsman's axe rested in readiness upon the block, there is now a simple memorial to the prisoners who died at the Tower. Designed by the artist Brian Catling, this sculpture consists of two glass discs, one atop the other, with a glass pillow resting in the centre. Engraved around the upper disc is an epigraph in the spirit of those earlier inscriptions, carved upon the walls of the Tower during the desperate hours:

> Gentle visitor, pause awhile,
> Where you stand death cut away the light of many days,
> Here jewelled names were broken from the vivid thread
> of life,
> May they rest in peace while we walk the generations
> around their strife
> And courage under these restless skies.[39]

After taking a moment or two to pause and reflect on those who died here, it is time to move on, and travel up the Thames to the City, the mighty heart of London.

3

FRATERNITY OF VAGABONDS

London, Den of Thieves

Imagine, for a moment, flying over Jacobean London, from the bustling shops of Cheapside to the brothels of Petticoat Lane, then on to Whitechapel, to drink beer with Dutch sailors. Soar across the city, looking down over Billingsgate Market at its squabbling fishwives, and pampered aristocrats gorging on claret and oysters. And finally flutter down to the Strand, to witness the fops parading in their finery and the lawyers strutting up from Westminster Hall, clutching their wealthy clients like ivy clinging to a tree. Such was Ben Jonson's invitation to his audience in *The Devil Is an Ass* (1616) and Jonson knew his city better than most. As well as chronicling its nefarious underworld in a series of dramas, this playwright was a convicted criminal who had narrowly escaped the gallows after killing a man in a sword fight. Jonson owed his freedom to 'benefit of clergy', which stipulated that anyone literate enough to recite an excerpt from the

Bible was technically a priest and therefore immune to prosecution. This convenient legal loophole later became known as the 'neck verse'.

Jonson had first-hand experience of London's teeming lowlife of cheats, cutpurses, cony-catchers, roaring girls, pickpockets, counterfeit cranks, disgraced soldiers, thieves and whores, who spilled like human vermin through the chinks and gulleys between the cramped and narrow houses, to prey upon the law-abiding with a dazzling array of tricks and scams.

The glittering panoply of criminal behaviour at this period is a drama in itself, with its protagonists ranging from the elegant gentleman thief to the roughest, stinking lowlife, and locations extending from the hallowed precincts of St Paul's Cathedral to the bawdy anarchy of St Bartholomew's Fair, right up to the grim portals of Newgate Gaol which loomed nearby and marked the penultimate stage on the one-way journey to the execution grounds of Tyburn and Smithfield. This turbulent period is one of the most exciting, for it is at this point that the foundations of London's underworld were laid down for centuries to come.

Long before Jonson and his fellow writers, Green, Dekker and Nashe classified the knaves and villains, counterfeit cranks (fake invalids) and pedlars who flicker through their plays and pamphlets, London had developed an infamous reputation. The city had already become notorious as the crime-ridden capital of a blighted land, a reputation that had developed over previous centuries. As early as 1497, a Venetian diplomat had written home to his masters observing that no other nation in the world had as many thieves and robbers as England and that London was the worst place of all.[1] 'Few venture to go alone in the country, excepting in the middle of the day, and fewer still in towns at night, and least of all in London,' he wrote.[2] By 1516, Sir Thomas More noted that it had become commonplace to see twenty thieves hanged upon a single gibbet, while the breakdown of the old feudal system following Henry VIII's Dissolution of the Monasteries in 1536 brought thousands of uprooted labourers to the city, desperate for work, only to be sucked into a life of crime. As the Elizabethan historian William Harrison later recorded in his *Description of England* (1577), 'because they will not begge, some of them doeth steale, and then they be hanged'.[3]

The government had responded to the increase in crime by introducing draconian legislation. By 1540, during the reign of Henry VIII, crimes which carried the death penalty had risen from the original three (theft, murder and treason) to eleven: high treason including counterfeiting, petty treason, murder, rape, piracy, arson of a dwelling house or barn, highway robbery, embezzlement, horse theft, robbing churches and robbing a person in a dwelling house. In 1547, Edward VI's 'Act for the Punishment of Vagabonds' made it an offence to be a vagrant. Any unemployed man found wandering about was liable to be branded on the forehead with the mark of slavery and even subjected to having a ring of iron put about his neck, arm or leg.

Before this, another class of outsiders had already been persecuted under the 'Act Concerning Egyptians' (1530). The 'Egyptians' or gypsies had arrived in England during the reign of Henry VIII. This nomadic people constituted a 'spectacular class of vagrants, at once exotic and familiar, spectacular and outlandish with their faces painted red or yellow, fantastic costumes made up of embroidered turbans and brightly coloured scarves and clothes composed of shreds and patches, with bells tinkling around their ankles'.[4] Known as 'the offspring of Ptolemy' and the 'Moon Men', the gypsies were believed to be descendants of the ancient Egyptians, something they actively encouraged as Egypt was believed to be the land of all that was magical and mystical. They travelled from shire to shire reading palms and telling fortunes, and their reputation for supernatural powers provided some protection against persecution.[5] Such protection was needed, given that the Act Concerning Egyptians described them as 'wretched, wandering wily vagabonds' who committed 'many and heinous felonies and robberies to the great hurt and deceit of the people'.[6]

The Act, designed to expel all gypsies from England, seize their assets and bar further immigration, was ultimately unsuccessful, and the gypsies remained, leaving an ineradicable impression on two aspects of London life: underworld slang and place names. Existing thieves' cant mixed with Romany to produce a secret language, with terms such as *darkmans* (nighttime), *crackmans* (hedge), *figure caster* (astrologer), *greenmans* (fields), *merripen* (life and death), and *Romeville* (London) designed to confuse the outsider. And the old Romany names lingered on to mark the spot where their caravans had rested, such as Herne Hill and Gypsy Hill.

The law of the land was savage, and yet such was the desperation of the criminal underclass that the threat of execution was no deterrent. In a city of wealth beyond the dreams of avarice, crime flourished. And in noisy, dirty, dangerous London, where the rich and poor lived side by side, and where poverty and injustice rubbed shoulders with privilege, a bold new species was born. The urban criminal, characterized by a rebellious streak and contempt for authority.

London may have been the largest city in Europe but it was small by modern standards. Lying within the protective embrace of its ancient Roman walls, late sixteenth-century London was equivalent in scale to the 'Square Mile' of the City of London today. The wall still surrounded London on three sides, with the Thames marking the fourth boundary. Citizens and visitors made their entrances and their exits through the vast wooden gates of Aldersgate, Cripplegate, Moorgate and Bishopsgate, which were ceremoniously locked every evening. From dusk onwards, the streets were patrolled by the 'Bellman' or night watchman, equipped with a lantern, a dog, and a pike, whose task it was to call out the hour and warn residents to lock up their houses and protect themselves against fire and theft. Inside the city, the two main thoroughfares consisted of the Strand, lined with the mansions of the rich – such as Somerset House, Arundel House and Leicester House – and Cheapside, which was a broad street flanked by the handsome black and white half-timbered houses of affluent merchants. There were no other streets as such, merely narrow alleyways winding between overcrowded wooden houses, built so close together that, if he were so minded, a man leaning out of the upper window of one might reach over and shake hands across the divide with his neighbour. At ground level, the tapering thoroughfares were filled with rotting vegetables, animal carcasses, and the slops from chamber pots, tossed unceremoniously from bedroom casements.

Beyond the city walls, Hampstead and Highgate were still remote villages and Tyburn, with its gallows as a dreadful landmark, was the first stop on the road to Oxford, hence its modern name of Oxford Street. Moorfields, now the site of the Museum of London, was an open stretch of land where washerwomen spread out their sheets to dry. And through all this ran the River Thames, like a silver ribbon, busy with all manner of craft, from the modest boats of watermen, who ferried passengers back and forth from north to south bank, with their cries of 'Eastward Ho!' and 'Westward Ho!' to the royal barges shuttling between the Tower and the palaces of Whitehall and Hampton Court.

The responsibility for maintaining law and order within the city of London itself lay with the 'constables' of 'the watch', ordinary men who were co-opted into policing the city on an annual basis. Essentially, the city was 'policed by consent'.[7] When the shout of 'Stop! Thief!' went up, all able-bodied citizens were expected to join in a 'hue and cry' until the miscreant had either been arrested, and taken before the local Justice of the Peace, or had high-tailed it into one of the teetering rookeries where ne'er-do-wells would go to lay low until the pursuit had died down.

This somewhat arbitrary approach to policing London met with varying degrees of success. Certain parts of the city became 'no-go' areas controlled by a criminal underworld with its own security system and intelligence network, which was more sophisticated than the amateur police force or 'watch' intended to protect the city.[8] Amongst other activities, providing refuge for a man on the run became a vital function of the underworld underground. A thief fleeing for his life, with a hue and cry in hot pursuit, would always find shelter in the maze of winding lanes behind St Martin's Church or the ruins of the Savoy hospital, or take refuge in Damnation Alley, Devil's Gap or the exotically named 'Bermudas', the area now known as King's Cross.

The most notorious no-go area consisted of 'Alsatia', which lay between Whitefriars, a former Carmelite friary, and Carmelite Street, with the Thames to the south and Fleet Street to the north. This ancient citadel of vice and crime operated as a sanctuary on the grounds that it was a former monastery and therefore exempt from the jurisdiction of the City of London. As a result, it became a criminal ghetto. According to the historian Thomas Babington Macaulay, at any attempt to extradite a criminal, 'Bullies with swords and cudgels, termagant hags with spits and broomsticks poured forth by the hundred and the intruder was lucky if he escaped back to Fleet Street, hustled, stripped and jumped upon.'[9]

The failure of the authorities to control crime inside the city was compounded by the fact that they had no jurisdiction over crime outside the city. Districts such as Islington to the north, and Southwark, on the south bank of the Thames, accordingly became notorious dens of vice, swarming with taverns, bear gardens and brothels. London's criminal classes gravitated to these areas, living on their wits and emerging betimes to avail themselves of the glittering prospects. While criminality had always existed in London, the increased density of population meant greater opportunities for the urban rogue, with thieves thronging the alehouses and colluding with the landlords to relieve the unwary traveller of their worldly goods, and innkeepers encouraging professional thieves to use their premises, and 'fencing' (selling on) stolen goods. And so organized crime was born.

One good example of this was a notorious criminal known as 'the King of Cutpurses', Laurence Pickering, who held weekly thieves' kitchens at his home in Kent Street, Hackney, where robbers could swap tips, plan robberies and discuss which members of the watch were most likely to take a backhander. Like many a successful villain, Pickering was formidably well connected, possessing a reliable source in the form of his ostensibly respectable brother-in-law, William Bull, the Tyburn hangman.[10]

Stealing was a skill that had to be learned, and to this end many a prototype of Dickens' Fagin set up his own training school for pickpockets. Writing in 1585, William Fleetwood, Recorder of the City of London, described the activities of one 'Wotton', who had been a prosperous merchant but had fallen upon hard times. Wotton took on an alehouse in Billingsgate, to make ends meet, and when the alehouse was closed down by the authorities, he decided to open a school for thieves. Wotton invited all the best cutpurses in London to his alehouse, to provide professional training for aspiring young thieves. The instruction technique was as follows: two pieces of equipment were hung up, consisting of a pocket, and a purse. The pocket held a selection of counters, and was hung about with little bells, similar to the bells on hawks' feet. The purse, also decorated with bells, held silver coins. Any lad who could extract a counter from the pocket without ringing the bells was awarded the title of 'Public Foister', and if he could remove a coin from the purse without any noise from the bells, he was made a 'Junior Nipper'.

Other accomplishments learned at Wotton's academy included 'shaving' (which meant stealing a small item such as a sword or a silver spoon) and 'lifting' (robbing a shop, a term still in circulation today), a task best achieved with the collusion of two other thieves, one of whom would be wearing a heavy cloak which could be cast over the coveted objects. Aspiring criminals could also learn how to become a 'curber', with the aid of a long hook that folded down to resemble a walking stick, and which could be used to pull items of clothing from open windows. Small boys frequently started their careers as 'divers', wriggling through windows and passing objects down to their gaffers. An invaluable accomplice in these circumstances was a sympathetic serving wench, who could be prevailed upon to leave a window open for her 'hooker' and his 'diver'. If such inside help was not available, criminals trained in the 'black art' of picking locks would be called upon.[11]

Thieves newly graduated from this academy of crime had numerous opportunities to perfect their skills in Elizabethan London. The broad expanses of Cheapside and the Strand were thronged with affluent visitors, belts groaning with full purses, their persons adorned with flamboyant velvet cloaks, feathered hats and jewelled daggers, while the plethora of attractions provided many an opportunity to take advantage of an unfortunate traveller. Modern readers may be surprised to learn that the first of these 'crime hot-spots' was none other than St Paul's Cathedral, which by the reign of Elizabeth had become less a hallowed place of worship than a byword for iniquity. The cathedral dated from 1300 and consisted of a massive Norman cathedral, with a wooden spire, 160 metres (520 feet) high, which was struck by lightning in 1561. This wooden spire subsequently proved to be the downfall of the building during the Great Fire of 1666, when it was burnt to the ground. Standing at the western end of Cheapside and covering over twelve acres, St Paul's was already in an advanced state of disrepair by the age of Elizabeth I, thanks to the depredations of Henry VIII's assault on religious institutions, but the cathedral was still a major landmark in Elizabethan London, a tourist attraction, shopping centre and entertainment complex all rolled into one, operating rather as Covent Garden Piazza does today. And, like the Piazza, St Paul's attracted every type of con-artist, rogue and beggar in the city.

While preachers, rebels and self-appointed dissidents flocked to harangue the crowds at the outdoor pulpit of St Paul's Cross, the nave of the cathedral operated like a street market. Following the Dissolution of the Monasteries, the chantries and chapels had been given over to booksellers and printers, who published Protestant tracts, ballads, and broadsides. While tobacconists offered the intriguing tawny-brown weed from the New World to the curious, prostitutes plied their trade and unemployed servants perused the 'wanted' notices pinned on the cathedral doors.

St Paul's even operated as a horse fair, with all the dubious associations of financial double-dealing, conspiracy, brawls and even murder. Thomas Dekker exposed the chicanery of the second-hand horse trade in his *Lanthorn and Candlelight* (1608). A glossy-coated animal, he warned, had probably been painted to disguise the fact that it had been stolen, while sickness, such as the glanders, characterized by a runny nose, could be concealed by tickling the horse's nostrils with a feather dipped in mustard, which would prove so irritating that the horse would stand with its head held up for hours at a time. Lameness could be disguised by removing one shoe, and blaming the disability on the fact that the horse was missing a shoe, while a slow-moving animal could be systematically beaten for days so that its skin became so sensitive that the slightest tap would be sufficient to send it galloping away like Bucephalus with a young Alexander the Great upon his back.[12]

St Paul's Walk, the central aisle of the cathedral, was crammed with men and women from all walks of life, and every part of the country. With its vast confusion of people and stacks of fallen masonry, it resembled nothing so much as the Tower of Babel. Crushed together within this heaving, breathing mass one might meet the knight, the gallant, the upstart, the gentleman, the clown, the captain, the lawyer, the usurer, the citizen, the bankrupt, the scholar, the beggar, the idiot, the ruffian, the cheater, the puritan and the cut-throat. It was inevitably a magnet for 'nips' and 'foists' and 'cony-catchers' to hunt down their 'gulls'.

In an era when dress really did maketh the man, potential victims were easy to spot. The most obvious 'marks' were the ostentatiously wealthy, dressed in silk, gold and jewels and attended by three or four servants. A classic case concerns that of a magnificently clad country squire, who had come up to London to look for a wife, and who had invested the equivalent of £5,000 in a heavy gold chain so that he looked suitably prosperous. As he arrived at St Paul's, this splendid chain immediately attracted the attention of a gang, who formed a plan on the spot. The first thief, pretending to be an innocent well-wisher, advised the old gentleman that his chain made him vulnerable, and that he should take it off and hide it away at once, to avoid the possibility of being mugged. The gentleman did as he was instructed, telling the well-wisher that he would put the chain in the sleeve of his coat, as nobody would even consider looking for it there. Shortly afterwards, the old gentleman was making his way through St Paul's Walk when a fight broke out in front of him between two scruffy young men. When the old gentleman bravely attempted to do his civic duty and intervene, both men fled. But just as they ran off, a third party tripped the old gentleman up from behind, toppling him to the ground. As the old gentleman came to his senses and was helped to his feet, by yet another accomplice, he put his hand in his sleeve and discovered that his precious chain was gone. The old gentleman had been the victim of a formidably organized robbery.[13]

Another vulnerable group consisted of the naïve young country gentlemen sent up to London to study law at the Inns of Court. These 'gulls' were easily identified by their coats of homespun russet (coarse red cloth, the Tudor equivalent of tweeds), and their expressions of wide-eyed wonder as they gazed around the bustling environs of St Paul's. For an experienced cutpurse working alone, it was a simple matter to turn a young law student into a victim of crime as he paused to listen to divine service or devoutly bent his knee in prayer. Another effective strategy consisted of the thief collapsing at the feet of his prospect and cutting his purse strings when he bent down to help.[14]

Soft-hearted young men might also fall prey to the 'whip-jacks', vagrants who told hard-luck stories, claiming they had been left destitute after their house burnt down or they had lost everything in a shipwreck. Asking for a handout after such invented catastrophe was known as a 'demand for a glimmer'.[15] New young arrivals were also fair game for professional gamblers or 'courtesy men', who would lure them into a card game, allow them to win, praising their skill at gambling, and then rob them blind with the aid of false dice, designed to eliminate the element of chance in the game.

'Fullams' were loaded with lead to make them heavier, while 'bristles' had a hair set into one side, meaning that they would only land in certain positions. Sleight of hand also played a part here, with cunning gamesters stacking the cards in their own favour, with doctored packs designed to fall in a certain way. Many false dice and dodgy playing cards were manufactured in prisons, with the King's Bench and the Marshalsea providing the finest examples of workmanship.[16]

Any public gathering offered rich pickings for London's lowlife. The law courts themselves, where thieves and robbers went on trial for their offences, were not exempt. As the spectators concentrated on the technicalities of the trial, nimble-fingered 'nips' and 'foists' worked the crowd, escaping with purses and handkerchiefs even as the judge laid down the death sentence.[17]

Another common ploy was for a gang to team up with a street singer, who, between belting out ballads and broadsides, would entreat the crowd to protect their possessions. As people's hands instinctively flew to their pockets, sharp-eyed thieves quickly noted exactly where their valuables were stowed, 'either in sleeve, hose or at girdle, to know whether they be safe or no'.[18]

Not every visitor to London was quite as naïve as the old gentleman with his gold chain, or the country bumpkin still wet behind the ears. The educated, sceptical victim required a different approach, and it was here that another species of criminal came into his own. This individual was the cony-catcher, who, with his elegant clothes and urbane manner, possessed a devastating mixture of plausibility and insight into human nature. The cony-catcher was generally well educated – a university man. He might have expected to find preferment (gain a fellowship) at his college, or be taken on as the private secretary to a courtier. But, with no inheritance or appropriate employment, he was thrown back upon his own resources, with nothing to rely upon but his quick wits and social accomplishments. This young man (for they were, most of them, young, cony-catching not being an occupation in which one could expect to grow old) was the original 'gentleman thief' or 'Volpone', the 'urban fox' from Jonson's play of the same name. Slinking through the dangerous streets of Elizabethan London and lying in wait for their prey, these sharp professionals would watch their victims leaving Westminster Hall after a banquet, or roam up and down St Paul's, Fleet Street, Holborn, and the Strand, dressed like honest gentlemen, 'or good fellows, with a smooth face, as if butter would not melt in their mouths'.[19]

Cony-catchers did not get rich underestimating human frailty. They understood that every man had his weakness, with sentimentality, lust and hate being the uppermost. In the dusty precincts of St Paul's, a shrewd cony-catcher would instruct his sidekick to reel in the punters with the Elizabethan equivalent of dirty postcards, in the form of French illustrations to Aretino's erotic sonnets. Intrigued by this merchandise, unsuspecting men were issued an invitation to a brothel, with the bawds splitting the proceeds with the cony-catcher and the unfortunate punter ending up robbed and beaten in a back alley.[20]

In a credulous age, when educated men might pose as doctors or even magicians, it was easy for cony-catchers to pose as quacks and charlatans. They offered charms to win over the objects of unrequited love, or potions to destroy a man's enemies. They sold rings which they swore blind incorporated such a 'quaint device' that a wench only had to slip it on her finger and she would have no choice but to follow her suitor up and down the street.[21] Those tormented by a rival could purchase a 'burning glass', which, if they stood upon the roof of St Paul's and aimed it at their enemy, would cast the sun upon his face with such force that he would be struck dead more violently than if he had been hit by a bolt of lightning. If this did not have the desired effect, then there was even an early prototype of the letter bomb, which consisted of 'a letter full of needles, which shall be laid after such a mathematical order, that when he opens it to whom it is sent, they all spring up and fly into his body as forcibly as if they had been blown with gunpowder'.[22] With his cynical ability to read his victim's baser desires and his smooth, plausible manner, the experienced cony-catcher was in many ways a more fearsome adversary for an unwary traveller – the enemy disguised as a friend.

At the beginning of this chapter the reader was invited to imagine flying over London, taking a bird's eye view of the nefarious city with Ben Jonson as guide. Now, at the end of this journey, it is time to land at Smithfield, a ten-acre stretch of wasteland just outside the city wall. On its margins stood Newgate Gaol, St Bartholomew's Church, St Bartholomew's Hospital and the Charterhouse, and the lanes between these august institutions were crammed with pens full of livestock, for sale at the cattle market.

Smithfield is best known as the site of Bartholomew Fair, celebrated by Jonson in his play of the same name from 1614. This annual extravaganza of debauchery, dating back to 1133, was the only real city fair in Elizabethan England and reflected the noisy, chaotic life of Londoners at the time. The authorities greeted Bartholomew Fair with much the same horror that the residents of Notting Hill used to respond to the August Carnival, with real anxiety at the prospect of lawlessness and anarchy. The event offered endless opportunities for cutpurses, cony-catchers and mountebanks, and was almost impossible to police as it took place upon the 'liberty' of St Bartholomew's, land which belonged to the church before the Reformation but which was now beyond the City's jurisdiction.

Opening upon St Bartholomew's Day, 24 August, the fair took place during the 'dog-days', when Sirius, the dog star, was ascendant in the heavens, and believed to cause mad behaviour in dogs and people. Bartholomew Fair was ostensibly a trade fair for cloth merchants, though by Jonson's time it had expanded to provide every form of entertainment, from freaks of nature such as a bull with five legs and two pizzles, to a black wolf, a team of dogs performing a Morris dance, and a hare that played the tabor, thumping away on the drum with its powerful back legs. Then there were the viciously satirical puppet shows, the origins of our modern Punch and Judy, to be enjoyed while munching on roast pork, gingerbread and hot pies, all washed down with ale. Enjoyment came with the tag of *caveat emptor* or 'buyer beware'. Those 'golden' rings were made of brass and would turn your finger green in a week, while even the beer frequently contained unappealing additives such as spiders and snails.[23]

The fair was opened by the Lord Mayor of London every year, after he had taken a cup of sack (fortified wine) with the governor of Newgate. A German visitor, Paul Hentzner, recalled watching the fair being opened in 1600. The Lord Mayor, clad in his scarlet robes and golden chain, rode out of the city accompanied by twelve aldermen, and took up a position near one of the tents to watch members of the crowd engage in a wrestling match, with money for the winners being awarded by the magistrates. After this, a sack of live rabbits was released into the crowd, eagerly pursued by a number of boys, trying to catch them while making as much noise as possible. Hentzner and his friends became so absorbed in the scene that it was not until afterwards that one colleague, Dr Tobias Salander, realized he had been robbed of a purse containing nine crowns by an Englishman who had been standing close by.[24]

Given the gleeful lawlessness of the occasion, the authorities made some effort to impose order on the proceedings in the form of a 'fair court'. This was known as the court of 'Pie Powder', a corruption of *pedes pulverosi* or *pieds poudrés,* a reference to the 'dusty feet' of itinerant pedlars, but the court frequently proved ineffectual. Jonson depicted this court as presided over by Adam Overdo, a well-intentioned Justice of the Peace who attempts to fight crime by patrolling the fair in disguise. Overdo tracks down tricksters such as Joan Trash, the gingerbread woman, whose wares are composed of stale bread, rotten eggs and old honey. But Overdo himself is taken in, by Ezekiel Edgeworth, a bright young gentleman who turns out to be a cutpurse. Meanwhile, Overdo's own wife, who has been tricked into prostitution, is brought before him in a state of intoxication. Other recognizable London characters include Ursula the Pig Woman who sells roast pork and bottled beer from her booth, which doubles as a brothel, 'Punk Alice', a prostitute, and 'Zeal of the Land Busy', a Puritanical prig who denounces Bartholomew Fair as 'the shop of Satan'. For all his preaching, Busy is eventually revealed as a randy hypocrite who has consumed two entire roast pigs.[25]

The exuberant lawlessness of Bartholomew Fair represented just one aspect of Smithfield. This 'field of smiths, the grove of hobby horses and trinkets' as Jonson described in *Bartholomew Fair* had another, darker aspect. Jonson's audience knew that this foul stretch of wasteland had a far more sinister side. It was here that rebel Wat Tyler was stabbed to death by the Mayor of London, William Walworth, in 1381. By the Tudor period, Smithfield had become another of London's chief execution sites. In terms of the number who died there, it was the equal of Tyburn, and Newgate Gaol had become death row for heretics.

Henry VIII, a staunch supporter of Rome before he chose to reform the Church, began his reign persecuting those who preached against the Catholic faith and ended it with the Dissolution of the Monasteries and execution of the monks. While Henry VIII's most famous victims were, of course, Sir Thomas More and John Fisher, Bishop of Rochester, these were just two notables from a long list of martyrs. Among them was Richard Byfield, who was imprisoned for supporting Protestant doctrine. In 1532, he was led out to Smithfield to be burnt as a heretic. Although Byfield showed great courage and dignity, and 'went to the fire in his apparel manfully and joyfully', it took him over thirty minutes to die, 'for lack of a speedy fire'.[26] A similar fate awaited John Frith, a Cambridge man who had already fallen foul of the authorities for his support of Martin Luther. When Frith made the short walk from Newgate to Smithfield on 4 July 1533, he was accompanied by a naïve young tailor named Andrew Hewitt, who had fallen in with Frith and found himself convicted of heresy. Hewitt was tied up alongside Frith in order to balance the stake. Although the executioners had been at work since daybreak preparing the fire, a strong wind persistently flattened the flames, and both men died a protracted and agonizing death. To the end, Frith retained his dignity, and his calm voice could be heard attempting to reassure Hewitt above the crackle of the flames as poor Hewitt screamed in agony. An even more appalling fate awaited John Forest, a former chaplain to Catherine of Aragon. In 1538, after refusing to acknowledge Henry VIII as supreme head of the church, Forest was roasted to death at Smithfield, in a cage placed over a log fire. It took him two hours to die.[27] It was at Smithfield that 289 Protestants were burnt at the stake on the orders of Queen Mary, thanks to the zeal of Mary's ruthless enforcer, Bishop 'Bloody' Bonner, described by John Foxe in his *Book of Martyrs* (1563) as 'this cannibal in three years space three hundred martyrs slew, they were his food, he loved so blood, he spared none he knew.'[28]

More unusual crimes were dealt with by special legislation. Such was the fate of Richard Rouse, a cook accused of attempting to poison his master, John Fisher, the Bishop of Rochester. Rouse achieved the rare distinction of having an Act of Parliament passed against him in 1531. The story of Rouse's cruel and unusual punishment is told in the Act, 22 Henry VIII (1530–1), C9. On 17 February, during the seventeenth year of Henry's reign, Rouse, late of Rochester in the county of Kent, otherwise known as Richard Cook, 'of his moste wyked and dampnable dysposicyon' cast poison into a pot of porridge while it stood in the kitchen of his master, the Bishop of Rochester. Rouse was presumably motivated by religious hatred, as the bishop was a convinced Roman Catholic. But since the porridge was intended for the bishop's family, the entire household was poisoned. Sixteen people suffered severe poisoning, while Benett Curwen, a local gentleman, Alyce Tryppytt, a widow, and several paupers who had visited in search of alms actually died. As for the bishop, he had been too busy to eat all day and escaped entirely. Rouse was charged with high treason, a crime that parliament ordained should carry the most severe punishment. On 5 April 1531 a massive crowd gathered at Smithfield as Rouse was placed in an iron cauldron of cold water over a fire. As the cauldron heated up, Rouse was slowly and excruciatingly boiled to death.[29]

Newgate Gaol had seen all this, gazing down implacably over the burning heretics and revelling fairgoers alike. It is to Newgate, the next dark landmark on the map of criminal London, that I now turn.

4

SHADES OF THE
PRISON HOUSE

*From Newgate Gaol
to the Old Bailey*

By the reign of Queen Elizabeth I (1558–1603), London had eighteen prisons within the space of a square mile, of which the most infamous was undoubtedly Newgate Gaol, already a den of iniquity. An entry in an ancient book at the Guildhall refers to the 'foul, heinous jail of Newgate',[1] while by the Tudor period the gaol had become notorious as 'an abode of woe, a hotbed of vice and a school of crime'.[2] Beside Newgate sat the sessions house of the Old Bailey, dating from 1539 and so named because it was built upon the old fortified city wall. These two institutions, prison and court-house, would represent London's criminal justice system for centuries to come. In terms of human misery, Newgate had the same ghastly significance as Tyburn and Smithfield, while at the Old Bailey, ostensibly the repository of justice, thousands of prisoners became victims of the 'brutal methods of English criminal law' and the 'callous customs' of the period.[3]

While Newgate was London's most famous prison, many other prisons proved its equal in sheer human misery. The Clink, the Fleet, Bridewell and the Marshalsea loom large in the topography of London's underworld, and this chapter will explore them in all their horror and degradation. The high number of prisons in London was a result of the city's swelling population and the rising crime rate, and reflected the fact that London had been at the heart of the British legal system from Norman times. The great institutions of the legal profession were developed here, including the Houses of Parliament, the Royal Courts of Justice, the specific London courts in the form of Guildhall and the Lord Mayor's Court at Mansion House, as well as the Inns of Court where lawyers lived, trained and practised their profession.

English law had been influenced by two other legal systems, first that of the Roman invaders and subsequently French law as practised by the Normans. The law also operated in conjunction with the ecclesiastical authorities. 'The law was thought to have mystical significance' with judges regarded as 'priests of the law' and all judicial sentences as 'the judgement of God'.[4]

The earliest trials consisted of ordeals, such as trial by water. This involved throwing the accused into deep water. If he floated, without swimming, he was guilty, but if he drowned he was judged innocent. A variation of this practice consisted of plunging the arm of the accused into boiling water. Innocence or guilt was then determined by the condition of the wound. Trials by ordeal ceased in 1215 after Pope Innocent III declared that ordeals were not a demonstration of God's judgement. In the same year, clause 39 of the Magna Carta stated that: 'No freeman shall be taken, imprisoned, outlawed, banished or in any way destroyed [tortured], nor will we proceed to prosecute him, except by the lawful judgement of his peers and by the law of the land.'[5]

Being tried by one's peers was a new concept, but this clause helped pave the way for the first trials by jury four years later in 1219. Instead of being tried by ordeal, the prisoner was given the opportunity to be judged by their neighbours, local men of some standing in their community. In criminal trials they were known as 'local accusers'. Over the centuries, it was the jurors, and not the judges, who would decide the fate of the prisoner by returning the verdict of 'guilty' or 'not guilty'. In 1367 it was decided that the jury should consist of twelve men, and their decision or verdict had to be unanimous. As will become evident in subsequent chapters of this book, jury trials were frequently unsatisfactory, and subject to the capricious whims of powerful and often ruthless judges. Trials were very swift; evidence usually took the form of confessions, often extracted under torture, and juries frequently convicted on the basis of confessions.[6]

By the thirteenth century a prisoner or 'litigant' was permitted to appoint a legal representative, an agent or 'attorney'. As the law became more complex, the attorney required an increasingly complex body of knowledge; these men were often clerks of the court who acted for litigants in return for payment; they often possessed particular skills of advocacy or pleading or detailed knowledge of particular areas of the law. However only a wealthy person could afford to hire an attorney; the majority of common men and women had no such recourse, and were left to conduct their own defence, reliant on the character witnesses of friends and neighbours.

Although the former royal palace of Bridewell had been opened as a house of correction for vagabonds and whores in the sixteenth century, prisons were not designed for the rehabilitation of offenders. Nor was any distinction made between those remanded in custody awaiting trial and convicted prisoners awaiting execution. Instead, the prisons of London served to incarcerate anyone who had offended the authorities. Gaoling for debt had been common since the twelfth century. Hapless individuals, who would never satisfy their creditors, were locked up together with their entire families. In a microcosm of chaotic London, debtors, dissenters and dissidents were detained alongside rapists and murderers. And since prisons were run as businesses, the only class distinction once you were inside was how much 'garnish' you could offer your gaoler in return for provisions. Such was the corruption of the day that many guilty prisoners bribed their gaolers and delighted in an endless supply of roast meat and wine, while thousands of innocent captives languished in appalling conditions.

For an imaginative tour of London's prisons during the Tudor and Jacobean period, the 'water poet' John Taylor (1578–1653) serves as a useful guide. A prolific pamphleteer and waterman, also known as 'the Sculler', Taylor has been dismissed in some quarters as a 'literary bargee', but he spent forty years on the river and acquired an in-depth knowledge of London and its multifarious residents. In 1623, Taylor published a satirical survey of London's prisons entitled *The Praise and Virtue of a Jail and Jailers*, describing the horrors of the city's gaols and their wretched inhabitants:

> In London, and within a mile I ween [calculate]
> There are of jails or prisons full eighteen,
> And sixty whipping-posts, and stocks and cages,
> Where sin with shame and sorrow hath due wages ...[7]

Like the mythical Charon ferrying the dead across the Styx to Hades, Taylor regales his listeners with tales of London's darkest dungeons, providing a dour running commentary above the creak and splash of the oars as he rows along the Thames from the comparative serenity of the Gatehouse at

Westminster Abbey, where Sir Walter Raleigh spent his last night on earth, to the full horror of Newgate.

The Gatehouse, which strictly speaking falls outside the remit of the 'Square Mile', dates from 1370. The Gatehouse was built over two gates at right angles to each other, at Westminster Abbey. One gate looked north and included the Bishop of London's prison for convicted clerics, whilst the other looked west and included a gaol for lay offenders. Chiefly used for high-status prisoners such as royalty or prisoners of war, it offered 'good lodging-rooms and diet', which must have been some consolation to Sir Walter Raleigh in 1618, as he awaited his execution in Old Palace Yard.

Next on the itinerary is Bridewell, where, according to Taylor, 'Idleness and lechery is vext: for vagabonds and runagates [rogues] / For whores and idle knaves and suchlike mates.'[8] Bridewell was not intended to be a prison. Originally, Henry VIII had built a palace at Bridewell, at the spot where the Fleet River flowed into the Thames, in 1515, but the palace was little used. In 1553, Henry's son Edward VI granted the palace to the Corporation of the City of London to use as a House of Correction, designed to punish wrongdoers and teach beggars and vagrants the error of their ways. The opening ceremony on 16 December 1556 consisted of a woman being publically whipped, and then placed in a pillory at Cheapside, for the crime of abandoning her baby on the street.

The next stop on this grisly tour is the 'Compters', of which there were three in London: the Poultry Compter, taking its name from the Cheapside street market specializing in fowl, the Borough Compter, originally built within the precincts of the parish church of St Margaret's, Southwark, and mostly intended for debtors and petty offenders, and the Wood Street Compter. The term 'compter' derives from the 'counting' or keeping of official records, and Compters were sheriff's prisons, for all offenders against the City's laws. According to

Taylor, 'The Counter in the Poultry is so old / That it in history is not enrolled.'[9] The Poultry Compter actually dated back to the fourteenth century, was rebuilt in 1615, and enjoyed a particularly gruesome reputation, with its inhabitants described as 'ill-looking vermin, with long, rusty beards, swaddled up in rags'.[10]

The Wood Street Compter dated from 1555, taking in prisoners from the former Bread Street Compter, which had been closed down by the authorities in 1550. The Keeper of Bread Street Compter, Richard Husband, had been jailed briefly in Newgate for cruelty, but returned to his old ways when he was released, letting out his cells as cheap overnight accommodation for thieves and prostitutes. The historian John Stow, who was on the jury that tried Husband, observed at the time that gaolers such as Husband 'will deal hardly with pitiful prisoners'.[11]

One of the best accounts of prison life in Jacobean London was published by William Fennor, an Anglo-Dutch writer and rogue, whose pamphlet of 1617 recounts his experiences as a prisoner at Wood Street Compter. As Fennor tells it, he was walking down the street one autumn evening in 1616, when a merchant accidentally ran into him and knocked him into the gutter. Fennor was enraged and struck the merchant over the head with his sword. It was a blow that should have stunned an ox, but this tough tradesman was made of sterner stuff. He shrugged off Fennor's assault and ran away, while Fennor was arrested by a pair of constables and dragged off to Wood Street Compter.

Once he arrived, Fennor was offered three different types of accommodation, depending on how much money or 'garnish' he was prepared to pay to his keepers.[12] The choice consisted of the Master's Side, the Knight's Side, or a destination referred to ominously as the Hole. Flush with cash, Fennor opted for the Master's Side. Once his name had been entered on the prison register or 'black book', Fennor was conducted through a series of locked gates, and had to pay a shilling each time to the turnkey until he reached the Master's Side, where he had to produce another two shillings to gain entry, or forfeit his hat and cloak. Having spent the best part of ten shillings, Fennor was eventually conducted to a narrow cell festooned with cobwebs, lit by a guttering stub of candle. His bedding consisted of a straw mattress and dirty sheets, but at least there was the prospect of dinner to come, with claret, ale and even tobacco. However, these luxuries came at a price. As he sat down to eat, Fennor was informed that on this occasion he was not only expected to pay for his own dinner, but everyone else's, including all the prisoners on the Master's Side, and the keepers, right down to the vintner's boy who poured the wine.

For those who could afford to lodge on the Master's Side, conditions were relatively comfortable. A knight or wealthy yeoman who could afford to pay a weekly charge of ten shillings could enjoy beef on the bone, roasted veal, capon (chicken), claret and unlimited bread. On 'fish days', when notional fasting was observed for religious purposes, the wealthy prisoner still received two bowls of butter and three or four generous dishes of fresh fish. He could dine alone or with his friends, and be waited on hand and foot. After dinner, a further helping of 'garnish' ensured the prisoner would not be locked in his cell for the night. Instead, he could entertain his friends or enjoy a whore, brought in from a local brothel at his request. Gambling was so widespread that the Fleet Prison even had its own bowling alley.

Fennor remained on the Master's Side for three or four weeks, but, given that he needed to fork out 'garnish' on a regular basis, he soon ran short of funds and was transferred to the Knight's Side. Conditions here were tolerable, and a reasonable meal could be had for fivepence a time, but Fennor still had to pay for everything, from a cup of wine to a breath of fresh air. As shortage of funds dictated that Fennor's cell was located next to the stinking 'jakes' or latrine, regular access to an open window was a necessity.[13]

Happily for Fennor, he was released before he ran out of money altogether and could be consigned to the third and worst form of accommodation, known as the Hole. Here prisoners endured conditions of the most abject wretchedness, and up to fifty distressed inmates slept on bare boards, famished and 'languishing in great need, cold and misery'.[14]

Conditions were no better at the Poultry Compter, where the Hole was less than twenty feet square, but inhabited by over forty prisoners. Thomas Dekker, who spent seven years at the Poultry Compter for debt, recalled the pandemonium caused by snoring bedfellows and bellowing gaolers while drunken singing and laughter emanated from the Master's Side. Dekker's hair turned completely white while he was doing his time there.

Even if prisoners could endure the hardship and deprivation of the Hole, they were still likely to starve to death. With no funds set aside to provide food and drink, the prisoners were wholly dependent on charity or leftovers from the food confiscated from traders who had been caught giving short measure. Religious orders offered bread and meat, but the keepers inevitably took the choicest cuts, leaving the prisoners the remains – unsavoury scraps that had passed through unwashed fingers and been licked and rejected by dogs. Charitable donations, such as the £20 a year bequeathed by Robert Dowe in 1612, which was intended to pay off prisoners' debts, were pocketed by the keepers, while friends and relatives were reduced to tossing money through the bars of the Hole so that the prisoners could stretch their arms out through the gratings to buy food direct from the street vendors. When a prisoner died, the keepers' greed knew no bounds. According to Fennor, the Wood Street keepers were so rapacious that they refused to release one body for burial unless they received a handsome payment from the prisoner's relatives.

According to Taylor the Water Poet, the Fleet Prison dates from 'Richard's Reign the First', specifically 1197. The Fleet Prison was located on what is now Farringdon Street, and named after the Fleet River, which subsequently gave its name to Fleet Street. The Fleet was built on an island formed by the Fleet River and ditches, and by the fourteenth century these ditches were full of foul, stagnant water. In its early years, the Fleet was used for those in contempt of the Royal Courts, and, in Tudor and Stuart times, those convicted in the Court of Star Chamber. Distinguished prisoners included the Earl of Surrey in 1543 and William Herbert, Earl of Pembroke, in 1601. Conditions were tolerable for wealthy prisoners. As well as decent food, tobacco and whores, there was a tap room, racquet games in the courtyard and even a bowling alley.[15]

The Clink, 'where handsome lodgings be' as Taylor ironically comments, was of course anything but handsome. The prison's very name became synonymous with incarceration, the 'clink' referring to the rattle of the prisoners' chains. The Clink was the oldest prison in London, dating back to Saxon times when it originated in cells beneath the Bishop of Winchester's palace in Southwark. The Bishop's Palace was burnt down during the peasants' revolt of 1381, and in the rebuild that followed the men's prison was transferred to a vault underneath the palace's great hall. While gratings at street level allowed ventilation and enabled the prisoners to stretch out their hands for alms, the vaults were often flooded when the Thames reached high tide, and there was no latrine.

Although the majority of the Clink's population consisted of prostitutes and drunks, actors and writers joined their ranks with the development of the Bankside theatres. On more than one occasion the entire cast of one theatre was 'thrust into the Clink for acting obscenely',[16] while in 1554 the aristocrat Sir Francis Wyatt was committed to the Clink after an unsuccessful attempt to depose Queen Mary. Of London's other prisons, John Taylor refers to a 'hole or den for men' at St Katherine's Dock, a prison in East Smithfield which was little better, a 'gaol for heretics' at Three Cranes, Blackfriars, and two other gaols at Whitechapel and Finsbury. But these institutions pale into insignificance as John Taylor takes his leave at the final destination of this tour, described by the chronicler Raphael Holinshed as the 'most ugly and loath-some prison' of Newgate.

Originally taking its name from 'New Gate', one of the gates in the massive fortified wall that surrounded London, Newgate had been a gatehouse gaol since the reign of King John.[17] Five storeys tall and measuring 25 x 15 m (85 x 50 feet), it was an imposing building, with room for around 150 prisoners, although occupation was normally closer to 250.

Conditions had been dismal from the earliest years. In 1218, John's successor, Henry III, wrote to the sheriffs of London, 'commanding them to repair the jail of Newgate for the safe-keeping of his prisoners' and offering to contribute to the expense.[18] The repairs were clearly inadequate as by 1253 Henry III sent the city sheriffs to the Tower of London for a month because they had allowed a prisoner to escape from Newgate who had killed the queen's cousin.[19]

Since Newgate accommodated so many desperate criminals, many of whom were destined for execution, the escape rate was high. Methods varied from climbing out through the roof, rushing the gates or blowing a hole through the walls. In 1456, a crowd of prisoners crawled out onto the leads (roof tops) and held the sheriffs and keepers at bay until they were surrounded by a crack squad of constables and forced to give themselves up. Escape was relatively easy because the fabric of Newgate was in a constant state of disrepair – the walls were so weak and crumbling that they provided very little security.[20]

By 1341 the prospect of the gaol was already enough to inspire terror. The prison had become a repository for every class of offender, and King Edward III complained to the Mayor of London that the jail was 'so full of prisoners that they are continually dying of hunger and oppression'.[21] Newgate, like Tyburn, also provided the authorities with the opportunity to discourage potential malefactors with grisly exhibitions of justice in action. For example, on 10 July 1345, Sir John of Shoreditch, a member of the King's Household, was suffocated by four of his servants at his house in Ware. The servants confessed and were convicted of 'petty treason', the crime of killing their masters. Just eight days after the murder, on 18 July, they were drawn, hanged and quartered and their heads set up on poles at Newgate.[22]

Men were sent to Newgate for comparatively trivial offences. In 1287 Roger le Skirmisour was sent to Newgate for running a fencing school, which had been forbidden as it was thought to encourage sword fights. Even speaking your mind could land you in this most dismal of prisons. In December 1371 Nicolas Mollere, a smith, was sent to Newgate until such time as the sheriffs saw fit to release him for the offence of 'circulating lies'. Mollere, who was sentenced to the pillory, had claimed that Newgate was to be closed and all the prisoners sent to the Tower of London.[23] In 1378, a parish clerk was incarcerated for insinuating that John of Gaunt had Lollard sympathies.[24] Other offences which could land one in Newgate included cheating at dice, highway robbery and 'nightwalking', being out after the official curfew of nine o'clock.

Conditions became so overcrowded at Newgate that in

1382 Ludgate Prison was opened for 'respectable' criminals such as debtors or tradesmen convicted of fraud. However, Ludgate was closed in 1419 and its unfortunate denizens transferred to Newgate, where sixty of them promptly succumbed to 'brain fever', probably typhus, which would have flourished in Newgate's filthy conditions.

Newgate had reached such a distressing state by 1421 that Sir Richard Whittington, legendary Mayor of London, re-opened Ludgate Prison and left a substantial part of his estate to rebuild Newgate when he died in 1423. Work started almost immediately and the new prison, which was completed within a few years, stretched up from the Old Bailey in a northerly direction, forming an arch over Newgate Street. It was a much larger building than its predecessor, with a central hall, a chapel, day and night wards, and separate quarters for women. There were the inevitable dungeons, and more comfortable rooms for those prisoners who could afford to pay for them. Some effort was made to segregate the debtors and minor offenders from the more serious criminals, and in 1435, Thomas Knolleys, a grocer who had been Mayor of London in 1400, paid for the installation and upkeep of a water supply, and 'caused sweet water to be conveyed to the gates of Newgate and Ludgate for the relief of the prisoners there'.[25]

Despite these improvements, Newgate continued to be a byword for iniquity. One of its most ghoulish features was 'Jack Ketch's Kitchen', named after the legendary hangman. All the reassuring associations of the word 'kitchen' disappear when one learns what happened in there. This chamber was known as 'Jack Ketch's Kitchen' because 'it is the place in which that honest fellow boils the quarters of such men as have been executed for treason'. According to one eyewitness:

When we first came into Newgate, there lay (in a little by-place like a closet in the room where we were lodged), the quartered bodies of three men who had been executed some days before for a real or pretended plot, and the reason why their quarters lay there so long was that the relatives were all that while petitioning to have leave to bury them; which at length, with much ado, was obtained for the quarters but not for the heads, which were ordered to be set up in some part of the City. I saw the heads when they were brought up to be boiled; the hangman fetched them in a dirty dust basket, out of some by-place, and setting them down among the felons he and they made sport with them. They took them by the hair, flouting, jeering and laughing at them; and then, giving them ill-names, boxed them on the ears and cheeks. Which done the Hangman put them into his kettle, and parboiled them with Bay-salt and Cummin-seed, – that to keep them from putrefaction, and this to keep off the fowls from seizing on them. The whole sight (as well as that of the bloody quarters first and this of the heads afterwards) was both frightful and loathsome, and begat an abhorrence in my nature.[26]

In keeping with its barbaric reputation, Newgate endured a succession of cruel and sadistic gaolers. The records reveal a list of brutal administrators, beginning in 1290 with a keeper who was hanged for murdering a prisoner. In 1330 Edmund le Lorimer, Keeper of Newgate, was sent to the Fleet prison for torturing and blackmailing prisoners, loading them mercilessly with irons and subjecting them to excessive fees.[27] A few years later, one of his successors was dismissed for confining minor offenders in the dungeons and torturing them until they had given large sums of money. In 1447 the keeper, James Manning, left the corpse of one prisoner in the street outside his gaol, 'causing a nuisance and great danger to the King who was passing there'. Manning refused to remove the body and, following an exchange of 'shameful words' between Manning and the king's messenger, Manning and his wife were both jailed.[28] After one keeper was imprisoned for raping female prisoners, the Court of Aldermen set up a board of visitors who were instructed to make regular inspections of the jail.

Despite these measures, Newgate continued to be a byword for infamy, notorious for its appalling keepers. One such was Andrew Alexander, appointed during the reign of Henry VIII and obnoxious even by the standards of his day. Alexander charged 'garnish' to have chains and fetters removed, and anyone who could not pay him was consigned to the Hole. Alexander was particularly sadistic towards martyrs, and once left eleven monks chained, standing up, until they starved to death. When John Rogers, vicar of St Sepulchre's, was awaiting execution at Smithfield and wanted to share his food with his fellow prisoners, Alexander intervened and took it for himself. According to John Foxe in his *Book of Martyrs,* Alexander suffered divine retribution. In 1554, 'Alexander, the severe keeper of Newgate, died miserably, swelling to a prodigious size, and became so inwardly putrid that none could come near him.'[29]

It is from around this period, under Mary Tudor, that references to the sinister 'Black Dog of Newgate' start to appear, although the legend itself is much older. This terrifying and mythical beast appears to have emerged during the reign of Henry III, when London had been hit by a famine. The prisoners, already deprived of food, suffered more harshly than most.

When a portly German scholar was detained in Newgate on charges of sorcery, the prisoners could not contain themselves. They fell on the man, killed him, cooked him and ate him, pronouncing him to be 'good meat'. However, the prisoners soon regretted their actions. Shortly after the scholar had been killed and eaten, a hideous black dog – with eyes of fire and jowls dripping with blood – appeared in the dead of night and proceeded to exact a terrifying revenge. Some hapless prisoners were torn limb from limb by the ferocious beast, as their anguished screams echoed through the gaol, striking terror into the very souls of the other inmates. Others simply died of fright, when they heard its ghostly panting and its heavy paws padding towards them across the cold, stone floors. Those who survived the first nights of its lust for vengeance became so terrified that they killed their guards and escaped. But no matter how far they travelled, the beast hunted them down one by one.

Only when the murder of its master, the sorcerer, had been fully avenged did the Black Dog return to the prison's foetid dungeons, where it became a hideous harbinger of death, always appearing on the eve of executions or the night before a felon breathed his last. References to the Black Dog appeared for centuries afterwards, with chilling descriptions of a shapeless, black form seen slithering along the wall of Amen Court, near St Paul's Cathedral, then sliding down into the courtyard and melting away, its appearances accompanied by the sound of dragging footsteps and a nauseating stench, like the smell of death. It fell to one prisoner, Luke Hutton, to immortalize the beast in 1596. Hutton wrote about the Black Dog while he was imprisoned at Newgate, describing a shape-shifting monster that was sometimes gaoler, sometimes coney-catcher. At first the creature appeared in the shape of a man, but then transformed himself into a coal-black Cerberus (the dog at the gates of Hades), with eyes like torches, poisonous breath and smoking nostrils:

> His countenance ghastly, fearefull, grim, and pale,
> His foamy mouth still gaping for his prey:
> With Tigers teeth he spares none to assail,
> His lippes Hell gates, ore-painted with decay:

His tongue the Clapper, sounding wofull knell,
Tolling poore men to ring a peale in Hell.[30]

It was always said that the Black Dog appeared on the eve of
one's execution: a sighting of this dismal creature meant that
you were as good as dead. Whether Hutton chose to memori-
alize the creature in a final bid to gain immortality or actually
saw it is a matter for speculation. But one thing is for certain:
whether Hutton saw the dog or not, he was a marked man.
The 'neck-verse', normally guaranteed to secure release for an
educated man, did not save Hutton from the gallows.
Although he was released from Newgate, Hutton was subsequently hanged at York in 1598. Hutton, who had abandoned
writing for a more lucrative career as a robber, was typical of
a new breed of criminal, many of whom would end up in
Newgate en route to Tyburn. These characters, some of the
most famous criminals in the history of London, were the
highwaymen.

STAND AND DELIVER!

The Golden Age of Highway Robbery

As the trees rapidly disappeared behind them, the riders galloped across a broad tract of wasteland, interspersed with ditches and fences, over which their horses bounded as if well accustomed. At that moment, what with the fresh air, the fitful moonlight now breaking broadly out, now lost in a rolling cloud, the exciting exercise, and that racy and dancing stir of the blood, we cannot ignore the fascination of that lawless life. A fascination so great, that when one of the most noted gentlemen highwaymen of the day stood upon the scaffold with the rope about his neck, and the priest exhorted him to repent of his ill-spent life, the reply was defiant. 'Ill-spent, you dog! –'Gad! (smacking his lips) it was delicious!'[1]

This description, drawn from the 1830 novel *Paul Clifford* by Edward Bulwer-Lytton, epitomizes the romantic appeal of the highwayman, that swashbuckling, debonair character who has haunted popular culture for three centuries, but whose origins are lost in the mists of time. The earliest high-waymen were semi-mythical men such as Hereward the Wake who led a resistance movement against the Normans, and the legendary Robin Hood, the rebel nobleman banished to the greenwood by a savage king. Closer to our own times, the notorious figures of Claude Du Vall, Plunkett and MacLaine and Dick Turpin come bounding into view. These 'high Tobys' (robbers on horseback) were the most glamorous of English villains, celebrated in their day for their defiant courage and romantic appeal, living like legends and dying like heroes.

This chapter ventures out from the heart of London to the fringes of the underworld, to the shady groves where the robbers lie in wait, ready to ambush the stagecoaches of wealthy travellers and the post-chaises that delivered the mail. For centuries, London had been framed by woodland, and any person brave enough to risk the open road did so in the knowledge that mortal danger haunted the wayside. Travellers heading for the Great North Road had to traverse the wilds of Hampstead and Highgate. Bearing east meant riding through the gloomy depths of Epping Forest whilst the Dover Road took one through the aptly named Shooter's Hill. The route of the Great West Road to Bath and Exeter took a hazardous course across the leafy commons of Putney and Hounslow. Even within twelve miles of London, the roads were treacherous, their muddy surfaces full of potholes, while deep ditches ran either side. Every traveller had cause to dread the rustle of leaves as a masked gunman emerged from the undergrowth and levelled his pistol with that terrifying command: '*Stand and deliver – your money or your life!*'

The archetypal highwayman was the dispossessed aristocrat, turning his military skills to useful account as a courtly armed robber. Following the Reformation, many gentlemen lost their family estates and turned to robbery to survive. One of the earliest documented highwaymen was Gamaliel Ratsey (d. 1605), a gentleman's son from Lincolnshire. Name-checked by Ben Jonson in *The Alchemist*,[2] Ratsey was one of the first highwaymen to exhibit a whimsical, humorous approach to his calling. When it emerged that one of his victims was an undergraduate from Cambridge, he demanded a speech in Latin. Holding up an actor in Norwich, Ratsey asked him to perform a scene from *Hamlet*. Most significant of all, in the best Robin Hood tradition, Ratsey robbed only the rich. Ratsey's social conscience did not, alas, endear him to the judiciary. Betrayed by one of his colleagues, he was hanged in 1605.

A near-contemporary of Ratsey, John Clavell (1601–43), was more fortunate. From a distinguished Dorset family, he attended Brasenose College, Oxford, but not for long. He was sent down for stealing the silver, became a career criminal and was sentenced to death for robbery. It was only due to the intervention of his father that he was pardoned, and married an Irish heiress.[3]

The actual term 'highwaymen' entered the language in 1617, when William Fennor complained that Newmarket Heath and Royston Downs were so infested with highwaymen that the poor were unable to make their way home without being robbed.[4] Just as the Restoration had produced an early wave of gentleman thieves, the English Civil War (1642–9) saw the beginning of 'the golden age of highway robbery'. Royalist officers who had lost their estates to the Commonwealth put their skills of horsemanship and combat to the service of crime, leading gangs of robbers eighty strong through the chaos and anarchy of war-torn England. Among the most celebrated was Captain Philip Stafford (1622–49), one such Royalist officer whose estates had been sequestered. Stafford possessed many of the essential criteria for being a romantic highwayman; a dispossessed gentleman with an army background, he was a notorious jewel thief and seducer of women. Stafford was eventually arrested and sentenced to hang at Reading, setting an example of the heroic death that would be imitated for years to come. Defiant to the last, Stafford dressed in his finest clothes and, when the cart paused at a tavern on its way to the gallows, he took a pint of wine and laughingly told the innkeeper that he would pay for it on his way back. His funeral was attended by several fashionable people, including society ladies who wept copiously.[5]

Another legendary highwayman was Captain James Hind. Although not a gentleman by birth, Hind had a long and distinguished army career, fighting alongside Charles I, before turning to robbery during the Commonwealth. When he was tried by the Council of State in 1651, Hind admitted to being a highwayman, but it was for his Royalist sentiments rather than his crimes that he was subsequently drawn, hanged and quartered for high treason. Accounts of his exploits continued to be printed a century after his death.

Stafford and Hind fade into insignificance, however, compared with Claude Du Vall, the epitome of the romantic highwayman whose reputation was much embellished after death. So much so, indeed, that it is now difficult to separate the fact from the fiction. Alfred Marks, author of *Tyburn Tree,* observed that 'there have been other highwaymen before Duval [sic] and he was succeeded by others. But the great merit of Duval is that he gave a tone and dignity to the profession which it never wholly lost'.[6] This 'prince of highwaymen' was born in Normandy in 1643 and arrived in England during the Restoration as a footman to the Duke of Richmond. The Restoration of Charles II in 1660 ushered in a period of wild extravagance, and Du Vall soon proved himself as proficient in drunkenness and debauchery as his masters. Running out of money, he took to the road, operating between Islington and Highgate, north of London. Du Vall soon became one of the most famous highwaymen of his day, an imaginative and resourceful robber, as this anecdote demonstrates.

One evening, Du Vall arrived at the Crown Inn, Beaconsfield, to find celebrations in full swing. There had been a fair on the common that day, and now the young people were making merry in one room, while a haggard old farmer sat next door, nursing a tankard. He had sold several animals that day and his takings sat in a bag at his feet. Du Vall plied him with wine and encouraged him to join in the dancing, while he watched his bag. Gingerly, the old fellow climbed to his feet and went into the other room. Du Vall, meanwhile, did a deal with one of the grooms, offering him two guineas to assist with a robbery. Together, the two men seized a large mastiff dog and dressed it up in a cowhide, fastening the horns directly over the beast's forehead. With the help of a ladder, the pair managed to drag the unfortunate dog onto the roof and let it down the chimney, into the room where the party was going on. The scene may be imagined. Pandemonium broke out as the massive dog emerged howling from the fireplace: tables went over, drinks were spilt, a violin was smashed to pieces as the partygoers stampeded in all directions, convinced that the devil himself had come for them. Meanwhile, Du Vall slipped away under cover of the chaos, and was on the road to London, £100 the richer. By this time the ostler had released his dog from its disguise, none the worse for the experience. When they realized that the farmer's bag of money was gone, the assembled company came to the only conclusion that made sense: the devil had vanished into thin air, taking with him the money, as a punishment for the farmer's covetousness.[7]

Du Vall's most famous characteristic was his 'gallantry' towards the ladies. One evening, having learned that a knight and his lady were travelling through Holloway with £400 in their coach, Du Vall overtook them on the road with four or five accomplices. As the couple spotted several horsemen riding backwards and forwards beside the coach, they realized that they were about to be robbed. At this point the young lady, who was a spirited woman, pulled out her flageolet and began to play. Taking the hint, Du Vall took out a flageolet of his own and picked up the tune, riding along to the coach door. 'Sir,' he said to the knight, 'your lady plays excellently, and I make no doubt but she dances as well. Will you please to step out of the coach and let me have the honour to dance one courant with her on the heath?' 'I dare not deny anything, sir,' the knight readily replied, 'to a gentleman of your quality and good behaviour.' Immediately the footman opened the door and the knight emerged. Du Vall leapt off his horse and handed the lady down from the coach. Although he wore heavy French riding boots, Du Vall moved as gracefully as the best dancing master in London. As soon as the dance was over, Du Vall handed the lady politely back into the coach, but not before he had asked her husband to pay for the music. The knight took the hint and handed over £100, before the parties politely wished each other good night.[8]

Du Vall soon had a huge price on his head and escaped to France, where he might have lived on into a healthy old age, gambling and seducing to his heart's content. However, bravado dictated that he return to England, where he was arrested, drunk, at the Hole-in-the-Wall pub in Chandos Street. He was promptly committed to Newgate and condemned to death.

On 21 January 1670, Du Vall rode to the gallows. Hundreds of women, from great ladies to street prostitutes, witnessed his execution and then attended his funeral in Covent Garden, where he was buried under a white marble stone, bearing his coat of arms and the following epitaph:

Here lies Du Vall, reader, if male thou art,
Look to thy purse; if female, to thy heart.
Much havoc hath he made of both; for all
Men he made stand, and women he made fall.
The second conqueror of the Norman race,
Knights to his arms did yield, and ladies to his face.
Old Tyburn's glory, England's bravest thief,
Du Vall the ladies' joy! Du Vall the ladies' grief.[9]

Given his aristocratic connections and lack of violence, it is perhaps surprising that Du Vall did not receive a pardon. But, whatever his personal appeal, Du Vall's actions represented a real threat and the government could not be seen to condone his flamboyant flouting of authority. Highway robbery had increased steeply during the reign of Charles II, with a series of royal proclamations for the arrest of highwaymen being issued from 1668 onwards. Further proclamations followed in 1677, 1679–80, 1681, and 1682–3. In 1684 and 1684–5, more proclamations were issued, followed in 1687 by an Order in Council, which would pave the way for the Highwayman Act of 1694. A new proclamation came in 1690, with another notable execution when the notorious highwayman William Davis, commonly known as 'the Golden Farmer', was hanged in Fleet Street and his remains subsequently hung in chains on Bagshott Heath.

Endless proclamations failed to serve as an effective deterrent. In December 1691, sixteen highwaymen plundered £2,500 of the king's money from the Worcester stagecoach, and, in 1692, seven highwaymen robbed the Manchester carrier of £15,000 of royal treasure. In a more unusual form of robbery, one gang even stole an heiress. On 7 November 1691, Sir John Jonston and his gang kidnapped Mistress Mary Wharton, who was only thirteen years old and worth £1500 a year. The girl was bundled into a coach and carried off. When

Mary returned home a week later, she said that she had been married, against her consent, to a Captain Campbell, the brother of Lord Argyle. A proclamation went out ordering the arrest of the gang, and a week later Sir John was captured and committed to Newgate. On 23 December, he went up to Tyburn in a mourning coach and was executed. The final reference to Mistress Wharton appears three months later. '1692. March 19. On Thursday last Colonel Byerley was married to Mrs. Wharton, stole formerly by Campbell.'[10] Let us hope for her sake that this time she was happy.

After outrages such as this, the new monarch, William III, had no option but to take the toughest line against highwaymen, as the case of 'Captain' James Whitney illustrates. Whitney (b. 1660) was a man of humble origins who had promoted himself to the rank of captain. Intelligent and brave, Whitney commanded the respect of his gang, which roamed the countryside around his native Reading. But Whitney was inevitably a thorn in the side of the authorities and by 1692 there was a price on his head. On 20 December that year Whitney offered to bring in thirty horses with as many stout men if the king would grant him a royal pardon. The king refused, and Whitney was subsequently arrested in Bishopsgate, after being followed home to his lodgings by a Mr Hill. Whitney did not give in without a fight; he stabbed Hill with a bayonet, although the wound was not mortal, and defended himself for an hour before being arrested. Whitney was taken to Newgate and closely guarded, his legs weighed down with 40 lb of iron weights. Far from downcast, Whitney petitioned the king for a pardon, and ordered a rich embroidered suit and hat, worth £100, for his journey to the scaffold. Sentenced to death, Whitney was carted to Tyburn on 28 January 1693, only to be reprieved, and brought back to Newgate with a rope still around his neck, followed by a vast crowd of people. From Newgate, Whitney went by sedan chair to Whitehall, where he claimed that he knew of a plot to assassinate the king, and would reveal the names of the conspirators in return for a pardon. But in the end, it made no difference. Whitney was executed on 1 February at Porter's Block, near Cow Cross in Smithfield. 'He seemed to die very penitent,' wrote one chronicler, 'was an hour and halfe in the cart before turn'd off.' Perhaps he was waiting for another reprieve.[11]

The rise in highway robbery had caused such outrage that in 1694 the Highwayman Act was ushered in, raising the reward for capturing a highwayman from £20 to £40 per head. Villains were actively encouraged to impeach or 'peach' on their partners-in-crime, informing on them to the 'thief-takers' or bounty hunters who roamed the country, searching for wanted men. As highwaymen tended by nature to be boastful, gregarious and given to holding forth about their exploits while in their cups, arrests were easily made and thief-takers flourished. However, some prisoners were more recalcitrant, and for those who refused to inform or confess, torture remained the order of the day.

In February 1721, William Spiggot and Thomas Phillips were indicted at the Old Bailey for committing several highway robberies, but they refused to plead unless the goods taken off them when they were arrested were returned. As this was directly contrary to the Highwayman Act, the Court informed them that their demand could not be complied with. Spiggot still refused to plead guilty, and so the judge ordered that he should be sent to the Press Room at Newgate, to undergo *peine forte et dure* or 'pressing', a form of legally sanctioned torture, 'and shall there be laid on the bare ground without any litter, straw, or other covering, and without any garment about him except something about his middle. He shall lie upon his back, his head shall be covered and his feet shall be bare. One of his arms shall be drawn with a cord to the side of the room, and the other arm to the other side, and his legs shall be served in the like manner. Then there shall be laid upon his body as much iron or stone as he can bear, and more.'[12] This barbaric treatment, coupled with a diet of barley bread and stagnant water on alternate days, was designed to eke a confession or death.

When the prisoners arrived back at Newgate, Phillips had scarcely entered the Press Room before he agreed to return to the bar and plead guilty, but Spiggott continued to be obstinate and was put under the press. 'He bore three hundred and fifty pounds weight for half an hour, but then fifty more being

The torture of William Spiggot by 'peine forte et dure'
(pressing) in the Press Room at Newgate Gaol. 1721.

added, he begged that he might be carried back to plead, which favour was granted.'[13]

Before he was taken out of the press, Spiggot had fallen into 'a kind of slumber' and had hardly any sense of pain left. After his ordeal, Spiggot was very faint and almost speechless for two days. Eventually, he told the Ordinary of Newgate that his chief reason for enduring the press had been so that nobody might reproach his children by telling them their father had been hanged. But hanged he was, along with Phillips, at Tyburn on 23 February.

In an another bid to prevent highway robbery, and the poaching of deer and cattle, the government ushered in the 'Black Act' of 1723, which made it a capital offence to ride out with one's features concealed by a mask, or a kerchief tied over the face. Despite this threat, the following decades became the golden age of highway robbery, with the highwaymen becoming celebrities, feted and pampered by fashionable society hostesses. 'Tales of their cunning and generosity were in the mouths of everybody, and a noted thief was a kind of hero.'[14] Indeed, for many, the prospect of dying young served to enhance the romantic appeal. The brave and the reckless concluded that there was nothing to being hanged apart from 'a wry neck and a wet pair of breeches'.[15]

Whether they were gentlemen turned thieves, or ordinary men aspiring to the role of gentleman by becoming highwaymen, highway robbers certainly enjoyed a distinctive status in eighteenth-century London. Their 'wanted' posters became pin-ups; Moll Hackabout, the anti-heroine of Hogarth's *Harlot's Progress* (1732), sports a picture of a famous highwayman on the wall of her Covent Garden bedchamber. This fictional character is one of the most famous highwaymen of all, the infamous but irresistible Macheath, protagonist of *The*

Beggar's Opera, a topical satire by John Gay and John Rich. This 'Newgate pastoral' proved such a rip-roaring success when it first appeared in 1728 that it was universally agreed to have made 'Gay rich and Rich gay'. A parody of the overblown Italian operas popular at the time, set among the thieves and whores of Newgate, it featured the villainous but sexually compelling Macheath and his evil nemesis Peachum, based on the thief-taker Jonathan Wild. The fictional Macheath rapidly became the inspiration for real-life outlaws, who whistled his songs as they polished their pistols before 'going upon the Common'.

Macheath cast a long shadow. Decades later, in 1763, James Boswell tells of picking up a couple of girls on Covent Garden Piazza, and taking them to a private room in a tavern where a bottle of sherry was swiftly placed before them. 'I surveyed my seraglio and found them both good subjects for amorous play,' he wrote. 'I toyed with them and drank about and sung "Youth's the Season" [the song Macheath sings with his whores] and then thought myself Captain Macheath; and then I solaced my existence with them, one after the other, according to their seniority.'[16]

English travellers became so habituated to the constant threat of highway robbery that it was commonplace to carry ten guineas or so in a special pocket, which could be handed over when they were waylaid. According to one French visitor, the Abbe Le Blanc, the English took a pragmatic attitude to highway robbery and were almost proud of the robbers' exploits. Le Blanc relates the experience of an 'M. C.', who was ambushed near Cambridge by 'the celebrated Turpin'. When M. C. failed to 'stand and deliver', despite threats, the celebrated Turpin fired a pistol at him, but missed. Fearing a second shot, M. C. handed over his money, his watch and his snuff-box, leaving him just two shillings. Before he departed, Turpin asked M. C. to give his word of honour that he would not inform upon him or cause the justices to pursue him. When M. C. agreed, they parted politely.

Subsequently, M. C. ran into Turpin at the races, and he kept his word. He did not allow Turpin to be arrested, and, in return, Turpin gave him a good betting tip. M. C. accepted this with good grace and subsequently won. Whereupon Turpin, impressed with M. C.'s generous behaviour, paid back the money he had stolen and even expressed regret that, because of the trifling matter of the robbery, he did not feel that they could drink together.[17]

The legendary Dick Turpin was the most famous of all highwaymen, although he lays least claim to the title, having been a ruthless criminal who turned to the highway late in life, after an extensive career as an armed robber. Born in Essex in 1705, Turpin was apprenticed to a butcher but never completed his training. With his heavy-set build and brutal, pockmarked features, he was marked out early on as a man of violence.

After being caught out stealing his neighbour's cattle and selling the meat at market, Turpin went on the run and teamed up with William Gregory's Essex Gang. From their base in Epping Forest, the Essex Gang carried out a series of brutal armed robberies, targeting lonely farmhouses occupied by the frail and elderly. At Loughton in Essex they broke into the home of an elderly lady and Turpin had her thrown onto the fire when she would not reveal the whereabouts of her cash. In agony, she was forced to reveal the hiding place, and the gang escaped with over £400. In another robbery, a Mr Mason, the keeper of Epping Forest, was beaten unconscious and the gang escaped with 120 guineas that had been hidden in a punchbowl. Mr Mason's daughter, meanwhile, had a lucky escape. When she heard the gang breaking in through the front door, she ran out of the back door and hid in the pigsty.

The gang's most brutal robbery took place at the home of a Mr Lawrence at Edgware, near Stanmore, on 4 February 1735. Turpin's gang descended on the house at seven in the evening. When Mr Lawrence refused to tell the gang where the money was, Turpin pistol-whipped him on the bare buttocks, and dragged him around the house by his nose, and threw a kettle of water over him. William Gregory found the maid-servant hiding in the dairy, dragged her upstairs and raped her.

Once news of this particularly atrocious robbery reached the authorities a £50 reward was slapped on Turpin's head and a pardon was promised to anyone who informed on him. But this made no difference to the robbers, who continued their devastation as before, and, flushed with success, seemed to defy the law. After further robberies and the violent beating of a householder and her maid, the price on Turpin's head went up to £100. Two of the gang were arrested, tried, convicted and hanged at Tyburn, and their bodies hung in chains to rot.

Turpin fled north to Yorkshire, where he reinvented himself as 'John Palmer', a hunting, shooting, fishing country gent. He ran a horse-stealing operation on the side, and would perhaps have remained undetected had it not been for his poor impulse control. One afternoon, on the way back from a shoot, Turpin gratuitously blew the head off a neighbour's cockerel. This random act of violence proved to be his downfall. When the cockerel's furious owner tracked Turpin down, his true identity was revealed, and he was exposed as a thief and a killer. Sentenced to hang at York, Turpin redeemed himself with the courage shown at his execution. Before the hangman could complete his work, Turpin kicked away the ladder and leapt to his death.

Richard Bayes, an opportunistic hack, promptly rushed out a memoir of Turpin, portraying him as a hero in the mould of Claude Du Vall. Almost a century later, William Harrison

Ainsworth glamorized Turpin in *Rookwood* (1834) and provided Turpin with a mare, 'Black Bess', which carried him on a two-hundred-mile ride from London to York before collapsing and dying from her ordeal. Turpin never possessed such a magnificent beast. The story of 'Black Bess' derived from folklore about a highwayman and his loyal animal, perpetuated by Daniel Defoe. But the story took hold, transforming Turpin's reputation from that of pockmarked armed robber into a sympathetic anti-hero.

While Turpin represented the dark side of 'the gentleman of the road', James MacLaine (d. 1750) was one of the last embodiments of the gallant highwayman. Descended from a reputable Scottish family, young MacLaine was extravagant, gambling his way through his own fortune and that of his wife, a young heiress. Destitute after his wife died, MacLaine became so despondent he consulted an Irish apothecary named Plunkett for a pick-me-up. Plunkett soon realized that MacLaine was a valuable ally, handsome and fit, although something of a coward. Plunkett, for his part, was totally fearless and handy with a gun. Plunkett suggested they take to the road, and after a solemn agreement to abide by each other in all adventures, and to share their profits to the last shilling, the pair ventured out together.[18]

On their first *sortie* Plunkett and MacLaine held up a farmer on Hounslow Heath, taking £60 off him. As they both had extravagant tastes, this money was soon gone, and so they headed for the St Albans Road. Seeing a stagecoach coming towards them, the pair agreed to ride up to the carriage on opposite sides. But MacLaine hesitated, frightened, and when Plunkett finally ordered the driver to stop, MacLaine demanded money from the passengers with the utmost trepidation. When they got back to London, Plunkett accused him of being a coward, and told him that he was unfit to be a highwayman. This made such an impact on MacLaine that he rode out alone, robbed a gentleman of a large sum and returned and shared it with his companion.

Shortly afterwards, Plunkett and MacLaine robbed Sir Horace Walpole, the prominent author and MP, in Hyde Park. MacLaine's pistol went off, although Walpole was unscathed. When MacLaine read about the attack in the press, and realized who his distinguished victim had been, he penned an open letter to the *Daily Advertiser*, apologizing to Walpole and assuring him that the gunfire had been entirely accidental and that it was 'by no means Design'd Either to hurt or frighten you for tho' we are Reduced by the misfortunes of the world and obliged to have Recourse to this method of getting money Yet we have Humanity Enough not to take any bodys life where there is Not a Nessecety for it'.[19]

MacLaine even offered to return Walpole's valuables in exchange for forty guineas, rather than fencing them elsewhere, an offer that Walpole subsequently accepted. By this point, MacLaine had become quite the dashing young blade, posing as an Irish aristocrat to avoid inconvenient questions regarding the source of his wealth. Gracious and charming, he seemed destined to make a good marriage. But then, on the night of 26 June 1750, the pair overreached themselves.

Riding out together beyond Hounslow, Plunkett and MacLaine met the Earl of Eglinton in a post-chaise. MacLaine, going towards the coachman, commanded him to stop, but placed himself in a direct line in front of the driver, in case his lordship attempted to shoot him with a blunderbuss, for he was certain that the peer would not fire so as to endanger the life of the coachman. In the meantime, Plunkett forced a pistol through the glass at the back of the carriage, and threatened to shoot him unless his lordship threw away the blunderbuss. Eglinton realized that resistance was futile, and gave in, allowing himself to be robbed. Once the carriage had moved on, MacLaine retrieved the blunderbuss, which had fallen to the ground, and a frock coat.

A few days later, MacLaine tried to sell the frock coat to a tailor, a Mr Loader of Monmouth Street. Loader recognized the garments from a description circulated in a broadsheet, and followed MacLaine back to his lodgings with a constable; there, they found Lord Eglinton's stolen blunderbuss. MacLaine's arrest and trial caused a sensation. He was so popular in high

An anatomy class at the Surgeons' Hall showing
the dissection of a hanged man. Under the Murder Act,
the bodies of felons were donated to medical students.

society that many people sprang to his defence, and Lord Eglinton refused to give evidence against him in court. According to Horace Walpole, 'the first Sunday after his trial three thousand people went to see him. He fainted away twice with the heat of his cell.'[20] According to the *Newgate Calendar,* MacLaine was a model prisoner, but his courage deserted him at the end. Arriving at Tyburn, he looked sadly up at the gallows, and with a heartfelt sigh exclaimed: 'O Jesus!'

Under the provisions of the Murder Act 1752, MacLaine's body was handed over to the College of Surgeons for anatomy practice. His skeleton appears in the fourth plate of Hogarth's *Stages of Cruelty* showing an anatomy demonstration at the Surgeons' Hall.

Although the *Gentleman's Magazine* was complaining, in 1774, that highway robbery seemed to have become a recognized form of outdoor sport for young men, the 'profession' was actually falling into decline by the end of the eighteenth century.[21] This was largely thanks to the astonishing developments brought in by the Bow Street magistrates Henry and John Fielding, whose achievements will be discussed in a later chapter. For the time being, though, let me return to those gallant figures riding through the dusk at the beginning of the chapter. I left one of the 'noted gentleman highwayman of the day' standing on the gallows with the noose around his neck, and being urged, by the minister, to repent of his ill-spent life.

'Ill-spent, you dog! – Gad! (smacking his lips) it was delicious!'

'Fie! fie!' replies the priest. 'Raise your thoughts to Heaven!'

The gentleman highwayman is having none of this. In the face of death his last words are: 'But a canter across the Common–oh!'

His soul, we are told, 'cantered off to eternity'.[22]

6

THE BLACK PARADE

The Road to Tyburn

On the night before they died, Newgate's condemned prisoners were issued with a stern exhortation. The bellman patrolled the streets outside the gaol intoning this grim reminder of their fate:

> All you that in the condemned hold do lie
> Prepare you, for tomorrow you shall die ...
> And when St Sepulchre's bell tomorrow tolls
> The Lord above have mercy on your souls.[1]

After a sleepless night, riddled with desperate plans of escape and hopeless prayers for reprieve, the prisoners were bombarded by the noise of the bells of St Sepulchre's, which were only rung on hanging days, tolling out across the neighbourhood to remind one and all that death was imminent. The sound of the bells was met with 'dismal groaning and crying' from the condemned cells, swiftly followed by uproar, with fellow prisoners displaying their sympathy by weeping bitterly, cheering, cursing, and a few, a very few, praying.[2] The condemned men and women were about to embark on the three-mile journey from Newgate Gaol to Tyburn, along a route that twisted like a black ribbon through the streets of London.

Eight times a year, prisoners made this grim pilgrimage, witnessed by thousands of spectators wedged fast into every rooftop, window frame, balcony and tree. The horse-drawn carts were followed by a massive crowd which wove its way through the streets in a macabre carnival, growing ever greater, gathering into itself the young and the old, the rich, the poor, the halt and the lame until it became a many-headed monster, 100,000 strong, weaving drunkenly but defiantly to the gallows.

Without much provocation, the crowd was capable of shape-shifting into 'the mob', a large and powerful entity described by the novelist Henry Fielding as 'the fourth estate', prefiguring its modern meaning.[3] Public executions might have been designed to demonstrate the terrible power of the king, but when the mob turned out authority was mocked and criminals frequently transformed into heroes.[4] This noisy, anarchic crowd provided some comfort for the prisoners, even as the deafening roars drowned out the educated tones of the Ordinary as he urged his doomed flock to repent. And the many-headed monster could demonstrate sympathy, too, when needed. In 1777, while one Joseph Harris, a fifteen-year-old burglar, sat weeping in his cart, the crowd walked to the gallows alongside him, in silent commiseration.

This chapter returns to Tyburn, which has changed little since our first visit, in 1196. A permanent gallows, the infamous triple tree, had been erected in 1571. Since then, Tyburn had become the principal execution site in London. In the eighteenth century alone, 6,000 prisoners were sentenced to death at the Old Bailey. Of these, 1,600 were hanged (the remainder were either pardoned or transported to the penal colonies of the New World). The majority of those who died perished at Tyburn. This chapter follows in the footsteps of the crowd that accompanied the condemned on their last journey. It pays its final respects, and salutes the courage or considers the evil deeds of Tyburn's notorious dead.

The journey begins at Newgate, where conditions had not significantly improved since the Tudor period. Rebuilt after the Great Fire of 1666 to hold around 300 prisoners, Newgate's population was now closer to 800, with debtors' children adding to the ranks of miscreants, robbers and murderers. Wealthy criminals with access to funds could still enjoy reasonable conditions on the Master's Side, where their 'garnish' purchased food, wine and even feather beds. They were permitted to stroll in the Press Yard and receive visitors in the Stone Kitchen, where well-wishers might be entertained with wine from 2s. or brandy at 4d. a bottle. For the poor, the situation on the Common Side was as dire as ever. The cells had no heat or light, and were riddled with vermin; cockroaches crunched beneath the foot with every step. Newgate Gaol was so dark that 'links' or torches burnt all day, thickening the already foetid air with tallow fat and smoke. 'Gaol fever' or typhus flourished in these insanitary conditions; during one outbreak in 1750, which spread from the gaol to the neighbouring Old Bailey, forty-three people died, including two judges and the Lord Mayor of London. Little wonder that Daniel Defoe, who had been a prisoner there himself, described Newgate Gaol as 'an Emblem of Hell' in *Moll Flanders* (1722).[5]

Defoe's novel testified to the public fascination with Newgate, which had developed its own macabre charisma composed of 'the mesmerism of depravity and the morbid fascination of the gibbet'. Throngs of sightseers assembled daily outside the massive gates, just watching and waiting and seeping up the malevolent atmosphere of the gaol.[6] The criminals themselves had become celebrities, stars of ballads and broadsheets, leading Horace Walpole to despair of 'the ridiculous rage there is of going to Newgate and the prints that are published of the malefactors, and the memoirs of their lives'.[7]

The most famous example was Jack Sheppard, a true son of Newgate whose story illustrates the black parade from gaol to gallows like no other. Jack Sheppard was a young burglar whose *pièce de résistance* was not stealing, but escaping. Jack Sheppard features prominently in this chapter, but the stories of other felons, from the most prolific to the hapless, are intertwined with his. Like the carts that rumbled out of the Press Yard on hanging days, bearing a miscellany of offenders from devil-may-care highwaymen to forlorn young pickpockets, this chapter carries the last sightings of a motley crew, from much-loved Jack Sheppard to the despised 'Thief-Taker General of England' Jonathan Wild.

A carpenter's son from Spitalfields, Sheppard intended to follow the same trade as his father before falling into bad company with 'Edgworth Bess', a handsome receiver from Drury Lane. Sheppard absconded from his master and took on a different type of apprenticeship with the robber Joseph Blake, also known as 'Blueskin' on account of his swarthy complexion. First arrested in August 1723, Sheppard was imprisoned in St Giles's Roundhouse but managed to escape through the roof. Shortly afterwards, he was arrested again, along with Edgworth Bess, whilst trying to steal a gentleman's pocket watch in Leicester Square. The couple were remanded at the New Prison in Clerkenwell awaiting trial, only to make spectacular escape by securing a sheet to the bars of their cell window, climbing down twenty-five feet to the ground, and then scaling the twenty-two-foot high doors by hanging on to the locks and bolts. This exploit made Sheppard particularly popular with women, as he could so easily have left Bess to her fate.

Sheppard was back in gaol by 30 August, sentenced to death for housebreaking. Committed to the condemned hold at Newgate, he managed to escape through a hatch in the door, aided and abetted by Edgworth Bess. After going on the run, Sheppard was recaptured a week later in Finchley. By this time, the keeper of Newgate had learnt from his mistakes. Sheppard was incarcerated in a strong room known as 'the Castle', loaded with irons and chained to the floor. Over the following days, dozens of sightseers trooped in to pay tribute to the famous thief. James Thornhill (father-in-law of William Hogarth) drew his portrait and his memoirs were ghost written by his publisher, John Applebee. Sheppard entertained his visitors with a rich stream of anecdotes, pausing only to beg visiting aristocrats to petition the king for a pardon.[8]

At some stage of the proceedings, a helpful visitor dropped a tiny nail. This was all Sheppard needed to work on the great 'horse padlock' that shackled him to the floor, and he whittled away at his manacles while the keepers' backs were turned, waiting for his moment. Sheppard's chance came on the afternoon of Wednesday 14 October. Blueskin had been arrested by the thief-taker Jonathan Wild, and put on trial at the Old Bailey. Condemned to death, Blueskin asked to speak to Wild in confidence, begging him to get his sentence commuted to transportation. When Wild told him this was impossible, Blueskin grabbed Wild by the neck and slashed his throat. Wild would have died instantly had it not been for his thick muslin stock; as it was, he suffered severe injuries.

In the pandemonium that followed, the guard on Sheppard was dropped, leaving him free to escape. With windows opening onto a sheer drop, and the door of his cell locked,

The villain Blueskin attacks Thief-Taker General Jonathan Wild outside the Old Bailey after being condemned to death.

Sheppard's only recourse was to the fireplace. He was not the first to attempt this hazardous form of exit; rumours abounded that desperate men had tried to escape from Newgate through the labyrinth of chimneys, and had been trapped, suffocated and killed in the attempt. But Sheppard kept his nerve and crawled upwards through choking clouds of dust, emerging at last into the room above his cell.

But Sheppard was far from free. Over the following hours, he systematically picked his way through a series of heavily locked chambers, until he emerged onto the leads. Springing across to the roof of a neighbouring house, Sheppard sneaked into an attic bedroom and lay low, until the family had settled down for the evening and he could creep downstairs. Just as he was setting foot on the top step, the clink of his chains gave him away. The mistress of the house cried out, alarmed: 'What's that?' 'It's only the dog,' replied her husband, reassuringly, and Sheppard stole past the door and escaped into the street, a free man once again.[9]

But not for long. Unable to resist the opportunity to boast about his exploits, he was recaptured a week later, drunk in an alehouse, and taken back to Newgate. And yet even when execution day dawned, on 16 November 1724, Sheppard had not given up hope. Alerted by his bravado, a young under-sheriff named Watson decided to search him before the cart left the Press Yard. Sheppard had concealed a penknife in his coat pocket, intending to cut through the ropes which bound him and escape into the crowd at a suitable moment.

Eventually the procession set off, with Sheppard seated on his own coffin, a halter around his neck and his arms tightly bound. Two officers sat either side of him, and the cart was flanked by horse-guards. These in turn were surrounded by javelin-men walking four abreast and constables of the watch securing the perimeter. Outside St Sepulchre's, the cart paused so that the sexton might exhort everyone present to pray for the poor sinners; his sentiments were almost drowned out by the noise of the crowd – the shrieks, yells, groans and cheers – as the guards struggled to clear the way. Over 100,000 people had turned out to follow Jack Sheppard to Tyburn, and the route was jammed in every direction. As the cart made its ponderous way down Snow Hill and crossed the Fleet Ditch by a stone bridge, every window, from ground floor to garret, was filled with spectators, while more were crowded onto the roofs, all calling out encouragement and expressions of sympathy. Young girls in pretty dresses and prostitutes in their finest gowns strewed his path with flowers and pelted him with bouquets. As the procession toiled slowly up Holborn Hill, a dreadful scream rang out. It was Edgworth Bess, come to witness Sheppard's last journey; with the scream she fainted dead away, but was caught by a group of well-wishers.

At St Giles, the procession halted outside the Crown Inn, so that the condemned man might enjoy his last refreshment on earth. The soldiers and javelin-men dismounted and drank too, while Sheppard was offered 'the St Giles's bowl', full of ale, which he downed in one, much to the delight of the crowd. The tradition of the St Giles's stop was a merciful one, allowing many a prisoner to go almost unconscious to the gallows.

The journey resumed and entered its final stages along Tyburn Road, with the crowd filling the street from side to side and the windows and rooftops black with sightseers, and out into open country. The crowd dispersed across the fields, leaping over, sometimes running through, the hedges, rushing towards the gallows as fast as their legs could carry them. As the cart arrived at the foot of the gallows, the crowd emitted a collective gasp of anticipation. Sheppard, from his position in the cart, had his back to the infamous 'triple tree', the triangular gallows standing eighteen foot high, but he would have seen a sea of heads, and the crowd milling around the scaffold in a frenzy of expectation. Tyburn Fair, a 'free market for outlaws, whores, and rogues of the meaner sort',[10] was in full swing, with buxom women elbowing their way through the crowd, baskets of gingerbread and meat pies on their arms; others carried frothing tankards of ale, while another category offered simply themselves. Child pickpockets scampered through the melee, while thugs and rogues scuffled in the dust. The more discerning visitor could avoid the contamination of *hoi polloi* by purchasing a 'Tyburn ticket', which bought him a ring-side seat in 'Tyburn pews', erected near the gallows.

Sheppard had visited Tyburn in the past, but as a spectator, not as the main event. Now, taking in this tumultuous scene, he remained calm, aware that he still had the opportunity to cheat death. It would not have been the first time. In 1705, a housebreaker named Smith was cut down after being reprieved. Smith had been hanging for seven minutes but was revived after a bronchotomy and made a full recovery.[11] In 1651, one Anne Greene was executed in Oxford for killing her newborn child, although it was doubtful whether the child had actually been born alive. After hanging for half an hour, Anne was cut down and found to be unconscious but still living. Dr Petty, the Oxford professor of anatomy, revived her, and within a month Anne had made a full recovery. She went off to her friends in the country, taking her coffin with her.[12]

Sheppard was convinced that he too could make a great escape. As he stood in the cart with the noose around his neck and the clergyman encouraging him to say his final prayers, Sheppard's eyes searched the crowd for his publisher, John Applebee, who had planned in advance to cut Sheppard down the instant he was hanged and whisk him away. A surgeon had been retained, ready to resuscitate him. Before Sheppard could spy Applebee, the hood was placed over his head, and the crowd roared 'Hats off!', not from respect but so that their headgear would not spoil the view. There was a sudden dreadful silence, like the calm before a thunderstorm, as a constable struck the horse's flank a sharp blow, the cart moved towards the fatal tree and Sheppard was 'turned off'. After a collective intake of breath, the crowd emitted a blood-curdling shriek, as Sheppard was launched into the air and left dangling. But instead of his neck being broken, as intended, he was choking to death on the end of the rope. Twitching and circling in the death throes, 'stretched', 'nubbed', 'dancing the Tyburn jig'. This sight proved too much for Sheppard's family, who rushed forwards and grabbed his short legs, wet with urine, trying to break his neck and put him out of his misery.

When Applebee and his men eventually fought their way forward and tried to cut Sheppard down, they were mistaken for body snatchers and a dreadful tug-of-war ensued. Matters were made worse by hordes of trophy hunters. Some jostled forward to clip a lock of Sheppard's hair or pluck a ring from his finger, while superstitious gamblers tried to grasp fibres from the rope, believing it would bring luck at the gaming tables. Then came the sick, the maimed and the diseased, eager to touch the body of the hanged man with its miraculous properties. During this struggle, the unfortunate Sheppard expired. Eventually, his body was cut down and taken to the Barley Mow pub in Long Acre, for the wake, and he was buried in the churchyard of St Martin-in-the-Fields.

Despite his grisly last moments, Jack Sheppard died a hero, and his legend lived on. A century later, the social investigator Henry Mayhew noted that, among the London poor, children were more familiar with the adventures of Jack Sheppard than they were with the Bible. Newgate ballads and broadsheets were handed down from one generation to another, the story becoming increasingly embellished with the retelling. But if Sheppard was a hero, his story also had to have a villain, and that villain was Jonathan Wild, the self-styled 'Thief-Taker General of England and Ireland', who followed Sheppard to the gallows six months later.

'Thief-takers' were effectively bounty hunters, tracking down criminals in exchange for rewards. Escalating levels of crime had led to the government offering substantial rewards for the arrest and conviction of serious criminals, such as highwaymen and coiners. In addition, many victims of crime would offer rewards for the return of their stolen goods. The advent of daily newspapers meant that information about these rewards was circulated on a regular basis. Jonathan Wild had thoroughly developed all aspects of the thief-taker's trade and dominated London's criminal underworld in the early 1720s. By arresting Jack Sheppard and the villainous Blueskin, he was much praised for making the streets of London safe for the emerging middle classes, and by 1723 he was petitioning the Lord Mayor to give him the Freedom of the City of London.

But Wild was himself a crook. Totally corrupt, he had been committed to the Wood Street Compter in 1704, which had proved to be the making of him. In this academy of crime, Wild built up the extensive web of criminal contacts who were to provide his substantial income for the next twenty years, and met his match in the form of Mary Milliner, a prostitute and receiver. The pair set up home together when they were released in 1708, and Wild went into business in Newtoner's Lane, Covent Garden, where he effectively devised a new method of organized crime: Wild's 'corporation of thieves' employing legions of criminals, from highwaymen to pickpockets. Specialist teams robbed shops and churches, while protection rackets extorted payment from taverns, inns and brothels. Even highwaymen had to pay protection money, or risk being captured. Wild preferred to recruit convicts who had illegally returned to England after being transported, since they could not give evidence against him if they were caught. Wild had complete and utter power over them, because if they rebelled, he could hang them. At the height of his career, Wild offered immunity to his henchmen in return for absolute loyalty.

Criminals sneaked into Wild's offices with details of robberies and stolen goods. For a fee, Wild reunited the victims of robberies with their stolen property while gaining vital information that would allow his men to organize another robbery. Wild even engaged craftsmen to remove the hallmarks or owners' names from the watches, rings, silver plate and other valuables so that they could be sold on without being traced. This system worked flawlessly until 1717, when the Solicitor General, Sir William Thompson, ushered in an Act of Parliament which made it a capital offence to take a reward under the pretence of assisting the owner to recover their stolen goods. 'Jonathan Wild's Act', as it became known, was designed to put an end to at least one aspect of Wild's nefarious business. Wild was ultimately caught out when, in 1725, he was paid by the owner for the return of some lace that Wild had arranged to have stolen, worth just £40. Wild was arrested and went on trial at the Old Bailey. Despite the fact that his reputation was in tatters as crime after crime was revealed, Wild conducted his own defence and pleaded for clemency on the grounds that he had sent at least sixty criminals to the gallows and secured the imprisonment and transportation of many more. But Sir William Thompson, who was sitting as judge, sentenced Wild to death on 17 May 1725.

Wild was taken to Newgate, where news reached him that Mary Milliner had attempted to kill herself, but failed. Wild was a broken man. On 24 May, the night before he was due to hang, Wild took an overdose of laudanum, but not a sufficient quantity to end his life; and when his fellow prisoners saw that he had attempted to dodge the gallows, they dragged him to his feet and walked him up and down until he had regained consciousness and vomited. By the time Wild entered the cart in the Press Yard, he was deathly pale and almost unconscious, which was perhaps just as well, considering the reception he received from the mob. Not for Wild the paths strewn with flowers and genial condolences that met young Jack Sheppard. 'The populace treated this offender with remarkable severity,' noted *The Newgate Calendar*, 'execrating him as the most consummate villain that had ever disgraced human nature,' and pelting the semi-comatose Wild with sticks and stones, excrement, dead dogs and cats. 'Rough music' (pots and pans beaten with sticks), whistles and catcalls accompanied him on the journey to Tyburn, where he appeared to have revived.

When the executioner allowed Wild time to sit in the cart and compose himself, and prepared to hang a coiner, Ralph Harpham, first, the crowd went mad. They threatened to attack the executioner if he delayed any longer. Judging it prudent to comply, the hangman cut Harpham down and turned his attention to Wild, at which the clamour ceased.[13] Wild's body was cut down quickly before the surgeons' men could seize it and buried in St Pancras Churchyard. A few days later the coffin was dug up, and found later in Kentish Town. His body had disappeared. An unidentified body washed up on the banks of the Thames near Whitehall soon afterwards, and the extremely hairy chest led some to believe that it was Wild. An ignoble fate indeed for the former 'Thief-Taker General of England and Ireland' and a suitable reminder as to how the mighty are fallen.

So far, this narrative has concentrated on the men who were hanged at Tyburn. But women too were subject to the death penalty. Between 1703 and 1772, ninety-two of the 1,242 people hanged in London were female. The lower numbers testify to the fact that fewer women than men become involved in criminal activity, but the harsh sentencing of the era reflects the fact that those women who fell from grace were treated with equal, if not greater, severity than their male counterparts.

In 1726, Catherine Hayes was executed at Tyburn for the murder of her husband. While this was a grim enough occurrence, it was scarcely unusual. Murder carried the death penalty, and the murder of one's husband was classified as 'petty treason', the husband at that time standing in relation to his wife as the king did to his subjects. But the appalling reality of this sentence was, of course, that the punishment for treason consisted of more than a trip to the gallows. In the case of a man, it meant that the prisoner was drawn, hanged and quartered. Since quartering was regarded as an inappropriate punishment for a woman, involving as it did a display of nudity, the sentence for a woman convicted of treason was to be burnt at the stake.

The mysterious sequence of events that ended with Catherine Hayes' execution began on 5 March 1726. As dawn broke over Westminster, a severed head was discovered floating in the dock near the Horse Ferry. The head was that of a man, aged around thirty, with brown curly hair; his skull had been fractured in two places, and there was a large cut on his cheek. A bloodstained bucket was found nearby, and a number of bargees said that they had seen a couple of ruffians bring the bucket to the waterside, throw the head into the dock and run away. Despite an extensive search, the constables of the watch could not find a body. There was only one solution. The head was placed on a wooden pole in St Margaret's churchyard, in the hope that someone would identify it. After two false leads, when it was believed the head had been that of a gang member murdered by his accomplices, and when a woman came forward claiming it was that of her husband (it wasn't; he was alive and well and living in Deptford), the constables had a breakthrough on 26 March when a headless corpse was discovered in a pond near Tyburn Road. According to *Mist's Weekly Journal,* the body was 'much mangled and bruised'.[14] Not only did *Mist's* identify the corpse as that of one John Hayes, but they also had a scoop. Hayes' wife had been arrested for murder, along with her lover, and committed to Newgate.

By 2 April 1726, Catherine Hayes, a shopkeeper, had confessed to the murder of her husband, aided and abetted by not one but two lovers: Thomas Wood, a butcher, and Thomas Billings, a tailor, who were both also sent to Newgate. Wood and Billings claimed that the murder had been instigated by Catherine, who had offered them to kill her husband. The men had challenged John Hayes to a drinking contest, and when he slumped unconscious to the floor, they smashed his head in with an axe. The plan was to remove the body in a trunk, but when the trunk proved too small for the purpose, they dismembered his body, put the head in a bucket and removed his remains under cover of darkness.

Thus far, the case seemed a typical if lurid example of murder, driven by the traditional motives of love, lust and lucre. The fact that Hayes had not one but two lovers to assist her added a little spice, but then the *Mist's Weekly Journal* revealed on 9 April that Thomas 'William Billings, the person that beat out Mr Hayes's brains with a hatchet,' was not only Catherine's young lover but her illegitimate son.[15] Now the heady mix of greed and desire was swelled by incest. It emerged that Thomas Billings was Catherine's long-lost son, conceived when Catherine was in service to Hayes' father in Worcestershire. Thomas had come to lodge with Catherine and her husband John in London, and their relationship had subsequently developed. In the sensational language of the tabloid press, 'Billings was her own son, got by Mr. Hayes's father ... So that Billings murdered his own brother, assisted in quartering him, and then lay with his own mother, while his brother's mangled limbs were under the bed.'[16]

Catherine denied any part in the murder of her husband, although she claimed that he had been abusive, beating and starving her. This might have met with a sympathetic reception had not Catherine developed a reputation as a harridan, with endless witnesses prepared to testify to her hatred of John Hayes and her constant desire to kill him off like an unruly dog. On 30 April, all three were sentenced to death at the Old Bailey, with Catherine facing the traditional punishment of being burnt at the stake – but with an exquisite refinement. In order to 'strike a proper terror in the spectators of so horrid a crime', she was to be burnt alive, 'without the indulgence of being first strangled, as has been customary in like cases'.[17] When the sentence was handed down, Hayes collapsed in the dock and fainted clean away.

On 14 May 1726, Catherine Hayes stood in the Press Yard of Newgate ready to join the traditional convey of death. Three carts left Newgate that morning. In the first cart were three 'sodomites' whose crime was considered so heinous that they took precedence over the usual aristocrats of the gallows, the highwaymen in the second cart. In the third cart stood Catherine Hayes' son, Thomas Billings, with three burglars. Thomas Wood had died of gaol fever ten days earlier. The journey was briefly enlivened when two of the highwaymen, John Map and Henry Vigus, made a bid to escape, but they were seized immediately.

Catherine Hayes did not travel to Tyburn by cart. Instead, she was drawn to Tyburn on a hurdle, where she endured the additional torture of watching her own son hanged before her eyes. She did not live to see his remains cut down and hung in a gibbet on the Paddington Road.[18]

Enticed by watching a woman burn, an even greater crowd than normal had assembled. Additional 'Tyburn pews', which had been shoddily erected nearby, collapsed under the combined weight of over 150 spectators, killing around a dozen people. Some parts of the platform remained standing, and the mob gathered on it in large numbers, but after about half an hour, this too gave way, and several more people were hurt.[19]

After order had been restored, Hayes was fastened to the stake by an iron collar around her neck, and an iron chain around her body. There was also a halter around her neck, which the executioner could have pulled tight if he wanted to end her suffering. The kindling was placed around her, and lit with a torch, as Hayes begged, for Christ's sake, to be strangled. The executioner relented, and tried to pull the halter tight; but the flames were so fierce that they burnt his hands, and he lost his grip. Hayes uttered three dreadful shrieks as the flames engulfed her on all sides. In a final attempt to put her out of her misery, the executioner threw a piece of timber

Catherine Hayes is burnt to death at Tyburn for 'petty treason' after conspiring to murder her husband.

at her, which fractured her skull and dashed her brains out. In three or four hours she was burnt to ashes.[20]

When another female killer, Sarah Malcolm, was accused in 1733, she suffered a similar level of vilification, even though the evidence linking her to the Inns of Court murders was largely circumstantial.

Born in County Durham in 1710, Sarah Malcolm was raised in Ireland. She was an educated woman, from a respectable family, but when her father moved to London, Sarah's life began to unravel. She fell in with a disreputable woman named Mrs Mary Tracey, and Mary's brothers, James and William Alexander. After a spell as a barmaid at the Black Horse in Temple Bar, Sarah became a laundress at the Inner Temple Inns of Court. Sarah's clients included Mrs Lydia Duncomb, a wealthy old lady, Mrs Duncomb's invalid companion, Mrs Harrison, and their young servant girl, Ann.

At midday on 5 February 1733, Mrs Duncomb's neighbour, Mrs Love, arrived for lunch. Receiving no reply, and worried that some harm had come to the old lady, Mrs Love and another neighbour, Mrs Rhymer, persuaded a young laundress to climb into Mrs Duncomb's chambers from a neighbouring garret, and help them gain admittance. This was a precarious enterprise as the chambers were on the fourth storey, but the girl agreed. When the door was finally opened, the first object that the horrified neighbours set eyes upon was: 'the poor unhappy young Maid murder'd! inhumanly murder'd! and lying weltring in her own Blood, and her Throat cut from Ear to Ear!' The tragic spectacle did not end here. They then found Mrs Duncomb strangled in her bed, and her good friend murdered in the same manner. Three hundred pounds' worth of money, plate and jewellery was missing, including a silver tankard.[21]

News of a brutal triple murder at the heart of the legal establishment caused consternation. The very nature of living in the Inns of Court involved trust, with the tenants obliged to entrust their keys, their property and even their lives to others. Collective suspicion fell immediately upon the servants. The following day, Sarah Malcolm's landlord approached the watch and said that he had found a bloodstained shirt and apron, and a silver tankard, hidden in Sarah's commode. Sarah was arrested, along with Mary Tracey and the two Alexander brothers.

Sarah Malcolm was indicted for the murders and the robbery, but was tried for murder only, at the Old Bailey on 23 February 1733. Sarah mounted her own defence, admitting to participation in the robbery, which in itself brought a capital sentence, but denying any knowledge of or part in the murder of the three women. Sarah claimed that the blood on her clothes was menstrual blood, and not that of the victim Ann Price, and the tankard had belonged to her father. The blood on the tankard came from a cut on her finger. But the jury found Sarah guilty of murder in just fifteen minutes and she was sentenced to death.

In Newgate, 'the Irish laundress' became a celebrity criminal, visited by William Hogarth among others. Hogarth, who painted Sarah's portrait, had no doubt as to her guilt, and said he found her 'capable of any wickedness'.[22] Sarah maintained her innocence and showed tremendous courage at her impending fate, but she was particularly distressed that she would not be executed at Tyburn. Instead of dying among strangers, Sarah was hanged in Fleet Street, near the Temple Gate. Following her execution, the other three suspects, Mary Tracey and the Alexander brothers, were released without charge. Dreadful as Sarah's fate was, she escaped a worse death. Had she been an indentured servant to Mrs Duncomb, her mistress's murder would have been classified as petty treason, for which the sentence was being burnt to death.

If gender was not a sufficient cause for leniency in sentencing then neither was social rank. In an earlier age, it seems unlikely that Laurence Shirley, Earl Ferrers, would have been executed in 1760 for killing a faithful family servant, John Johnson. In days gone by, perhaps this aristocrat, who had the blood of the Plantagenets running in his veins, would have escaped justice and the fatality passed off as a tragic accident. But with the 1752 Murder Act designed to 'put down murder', justice had to be seen to be done, to the highest as well as to the lowest in the land.

A violent drunk with a reputation for cruelty, Earl Ferrers once beat a footman to a pulp for serving him bad oysters. The attack was so severe that the man was rendered incontinent for years afterwards. Ferrers' treatment of his wife was so abominable that she sued him for divorce, an almost inconceivably elaborate procedure in those days that required an Act of Parliament. When Lady Ferrers demanded half of his estate, at Staunton Harold, Leicestershire, John Johnson, the Ferrers' trusted retainer, was appointed to administer Lady Ferrers' affairs. Ferrers took an acute dislike to Johnson, denouncing him as a swindler. Matters came to a head one afternoon when Ferrers summoned Johnson to Staunton Harold Hall, ordered him to kneel, and shot him. Johnson died the following morning, and a drunken Ferrers, armed with a blunderbuss and a brace of pistols, was captured by one of his tenants. Far from being frightened, the young man, a collier named Curtis, quietly talked the earl down and persuaded him to give himself up.

Ferrers was driven to London in his landau under an armed guard. As an aristocrat, he was spared the horrors of Newgate and committed to the Tower, where he boasted that, if executed, he would at least be despatched with a sword like his ancestor, Robert Devereux, the Earl of Essex (1567–1601). When Ferrers went on trial at the House of Lords on 16 April 1760, he put in a plea of insanity, but this failed to convince his fellow peers, and Ferrers eventually confessed that he had been reduced to attempting to prove himself a lunatic in order that he might not be regarded a murderer. The greatest shock came when the death sentence was passed and Ferrers was informed that he would be hanged at Tyburn, like a common criminal.

Ferrers' last journey was spectacular, with the disgraced earl appearing in the white silk suit, richly embroidered with silver, which he had worn to his wedding. He travelled to the gallows in his own landau, preceded by a body of horse guards and mourning coaches crammed with aristocratic friends and civic dignitaries. The procession moved so slowly that the journey from the Tower to Tyburn took two and three-quarter hours, but Ferrers remained quite calm, remarking that the journey was worse than death itself and he supposed so large a mob had gathered because the people had never seen a lord hanged before. The traditional stop at St Giles was denied to him, on the grounds that to pause for a glass of wine would delay the proceedings even further.

When the landau arrived at Tyburn, Ferrers maintained his composure. As a concession to his noble birth, the gallows had been decorated with black mourning cloth and a special scaffold had been built, described by Horace Walpole as 'a newly-invented stage, to be struck from under him'.[23] Ferrers was to experience the latest innovation in the executioner's art: a trapdoor designed to make death instantaneous by ensuring that his neck was broken by the fall. After reciting the Lord's Prayer with the chaplain, Ferrers prepared to submit to his fate. As a peer, he was entitled to be hanged with a silk rope, though whether this was the case is a matter for conjecture.

What is not a matter for conjecture, sadly, is what happened next. Instead of falling open at the moment of execution, the trapdoor remained steadfastly shut. In Walpole's words, 'As the machine was new, they were not ready at it; his toes touched it, and he suffered a little, having had time by their bungling to raise his cap.'[24] Far from being launched into eternity, the earl was left to dangle; he even freed a hand and managed to pull off the hood covering his face. Swiftly, the executioner drew Ferrers' hood down again, and the bystanders pulled at his legs, 'so that he was soon out of pain, and quite dead in four minutes'.[25] The body was left to hang for a full hour, before being taken to Surgeons' Hall to be anatomized. According to Walpole, the mob tore the black fabric off the gallows for use as relics, but 'the universal crowd behaved with great decency and admiration'.[26]

Many of the anecdotes that emerge from this period in London's history of crime appear bleakly comic. Such was the fate of Hannah Dagoe, an Irish woman sentenced to death for robbing her employer in 1763. Hannah, who had stripped her mistress's house of its possessions, was sentenced to death at the Old Bailey. A strong, masculine woman with a filthy temper, Hannah was the terror of her fellow prisoners, and actually stabbed one of the men who had given evidence against her. Hannah's stubborn streak of defiance really began to assert itself during her journey to Tyburn. Showing little concern for her impending fate, Hannah ignored the Roman Catholic priest who was trying to administer the Last Rites, wriggled free of her bonds and began to strip off her clothes, much to the delight of the mob, which cheered her on. Eager to cheat the hangman of one of his perks, the garments of the deceased, Hannah removed one item after another and flung them into the crowd. By the time the procession arrived at the scaffold, Hannah was virtually naked. As her cart was drawn under the gallows, Hannah seized the executioner and punched him so hard that he nearly fell over. Eventually, after a struggle, the hangman got his noose around Hannah's neck, but she was determined to deny him his moment of triumph. Before the signal was given, she threw herself out of the cart so violently that she broke her neck and died instantly.

By contrast, the crimes of Elizabeth Brownrigg were so shocking that the midwife had become a universal hate-figure by the time of her execution at Tyburn in 1767. Even by the standards of the day, the vicious treatment Brownrigg dispensed to her young charges made a powerful impression on the public, and the response to her crimes was one of universal loathing.

Brownrigg had not always been a cruel, sadistic woman. Originally, she had a reputation for being skilful and humane to the women in her care. When she approached the Foundling Hospital and asked to take on young girls as apprentices, the trustees were happy to comply. But it later emerged that she treated these girls with unimaginable cruelty. They were stripped naked, horsewhipped, forced to sleep in the coal-hole and sexually exploited by the men of the family. One girl escaped and complained to the hospital, but no further action was taken until another girl, fourteen-year-old Mary Clifford, was rescued after a neighbour found her emaciated and bleeding in the yard. When Mary died of her injuries, Mr and Mrs Brownrigg and their son went on trial for murder. Only Elizabeth Brownrigg was found guilty of the 'wilful murder' of her apprentice although it was established that at times other members of the family had joined in the beatings. No adequate explanation has ever been given for Elizabeth Brownrigg's sadistic impulses. The *Gentleman's Magazine* published a full account showing the 'hole' in which the girls were confined, and the kitchen in which one of the girls is shown tied to a beam to be flogged.

Brownrigg was executed on 14 September and her body carried to Surgeons' Hall to be anatomized. Afterwards, 'her skeleton has since been exposed in the niche opposite the first door of the Surgeons' Theatre, that the heinousness of her cruelty may make the more lasting impression on the minds of the spectators'.[27]

In stark contrast, Mary Jones, executed in 1771, was clasped to the collective bosom of the Tyburn crowd and embraced like a martyr. Mary Jones was between nineteen and twenty-six years old and happily married when her husband was press-ganged and forced to join the navy. Mary was left with no money, no food, no home, and two small children. Refusing to turn to prostitution, Mary, who had been honest all her short life, attempted to steal some muslin from a draper's shop on Ludgate Hill. Arrested before she had completed the theft, Mary was taken to court, and, as it was her first offence, she might well have been pardoned. But, when Mary received the guilty verdict, she lost her temper, and turned on the judge and jury, accusing them of being 'a lot of old fogrums!'[28] This outburst cost Mary her life, although her neighbours from Red Lion Street, Whitechapel, rallied to her defence with a petition. A pardon denied, Mary set out on the cart from Newgate with one of her children still at her breast, and 'met death with amazing fortitude'. Sir William Meredith, one of the earliest campaigners for the abolition of capital punishment, later observed that 'I do not believe that a fouler murder was ever committed against law, than the murder of this woman by law.'[29]

Mary, and many others like her, was a victim of 'the Bloody Code', one of the most savage systems of laws and punishments ever devised. Under the Bloody Code, the number of capital offences in England had risen from fifty in 1688 to 160 by 1765. Theft of any item worth more than a shilling (twelve pence in today's currency) carried the death sentence. Hence the observation that one 'might as well be hanged for stealing a sheep as for a lamb'. As the government's attempts to enforce the rule of law became increasingly brutal, even those guilty of what we would now term 'white-collar crimes' were not exempt. In 1776, the Perreau twins, Robert and Daniel, who ran an upmarket apothecary's shop in Golden Square, forged documents to obtain a bank loan. Although it was suggested at their trial that the forgery was actually carried out by Robert's mistress, a Mrs Rudd, the twins were found guilty and sentenced to hang. A petition signed by seventy-eight influential tradesmen, bankers and merchants was not sufficient to convince the king that the sentence should be commuted to transportation and the twins went to Tyburn. In death, they were not divided: the young men fell from the gallows with their four hands clasped together.[30]

Even men in holy orders were not exempt, and the days of being acquitted with a recital of the 'neck verse' were long since over. In 1777, Dr William Dodd, a popular clergyman, found himself on the scaffold for the crime of forgery. Dodd had been one of the king's chaplains and a fashionable young preacher before falling into debt. At some point, his situation became so desperate that 'he even descended so low as to become the editor of a newspaper'. Dodd fell even lower: he forged the signature of his patron, Lord Chesterfield, to a cheque for £4,200. The forgery was discovered, and Dodd made partial repayment and guaranteed to pay back the remainder. When Dodd was sentenced to death on 26 May 1777, he delivered a rousing speech, written for him by his supporter, Dr Samuel Johnson. Johnson subsequently claimed the eloquence was all Dodd's own. 'Depend upon it, Sir, when a man knows he is to be hanged in a fortnight, it concentrates his mind wonderfully.'[31]

Everything possible was done to save him. Newspapers were full of letters and editorials voicing support for him, and a petition, twenty-three pages long, was sent to the king. The king agonized over the sentence, before concluding: 'If I pardon Dodd, I shall have murdered the Perreaus.'[32] On

June 27 the fatal procession set out from Newgate, followed by 'perhaps the greatest concourse of people ever drawn together by a like spectacle'.[33]

The last hanging at Tyburn took place in 1783, but not as a result of penal reform or enlightened attitudes towards capital punishment. Instead, public executions were moved to the exterior of Newgate Gaol as a concession to genteel sensibilities. The authorities had been attempting to move the gallows from Tyburn for decades. Back in 1719, one writer noted that: 'the famous and ancient Engine of Justice called Tyburn is going to be demolished' and moved to Stamford Hill, 'the Reason given is said to be, because of the great Buildings that are going to be erected in Maribone-Fields'.[34] This came to nothing, but as the impressive Palladian mansions spread west from Mayfair towards Hyde Park Corner, it became obvious that the last thing the fashionable new residents wanted to see was an unruly drunken mob fighting and cheering its way towards the gallows. The last man to hang at Tyburn was John Austin, who had been convicted the preceding Saturday of robbing and wounding John Spicer. According to the chronicles, Austin behaved with great composure, requesting the populace to pray for his departing soul. Austin 'died hard': 'The noose of the halter having slipped to the back part of his neck, it was longer than usual before he was dead.'[35]

Transferring public executions to Newgate meant the end of the processions that had been a feature of London's life for six hundred years. Many people, including Dr Johnson, did not approve. 'All the business of the world is to be done in a new way,' he blustered. 'Tyburn itself is not safe from the fury of innovation!' When told that this represented an improvement, Johnson replied, 'No, Sir, it is not an improvement: they object that the old method drew together a number of spectators. Sir, executions are intended to draw spectators. If they do not draw spectators, they don't answer their purpose. The old method was the most satisfactory to all parties: the public was gratified by a procession: the criminal was supported by it. Why is all this to be swept away?'[36]

'All this' was not swept away. Although the gallows at Tyburn was demolished, public executions continued to enthral Londoners for almost another century, drawing massive crowds, and the appetite to witness capital punishment continued unabated. The judiciary continued to inflict the Bloody Code upon those who offended against the law, while a new development meant that the gallows was never short of victims. This was the founding of London's professional police force, bringing with it two memorable names which would dominate the landscape of crime for generations to come: Bow Street and Scotland Yard.

7

THE LONG ARM
OF THE LAW

From Bow Street to Scotland Yard

The story of London and crime so far has concentrated on villains, prisons and executions. Now, moving through the eighteenth century, we arrive at the first great landmarks of law enforcement: Bow Street Magistrates' Court, with its famed Bow Street Runners, and Scotland Yard, home of the Metropolitan Police. This chapter traces the evolution of London's crime-fighting force, from De Veil's Covent Garden mansion to the founding of the Metropolitan Police.

These institutions did not spring, fully formed, into being. Instead, these legendary crime-fighting bodies emerged gradually from the barely suppressed anarchy of Hanoverian London. First Thomas De Veil founded Bow Street Magistrates' Court, and then the Fielding brothers created its eponymous 'Runners'. Towards the end of the eighteenth century, the visionary reformer Patrick Colquhoun lobbied for the establishment of a professional, city-wide police force, but it would not be until 1829, after the Bow Street Runners foiled the Cato Street conspiracy, that Sir Robert Peel's Metropolitan Police was finally unleashed against London's 'dangerous classes'.

Thomas De Veil (1684–1746) was Bow Street's presiding genius. A former army officer turned magistrate, De Veil had only to look out of the windows of his house at 4 Bow Street to witness the groundswell of felony that lapped about its walls. De Veil's house was set on the borders of Covent Garden, the fashionable hub of vice from which taverns, theatres, coffee houses and brothels radiated outwards like the spokes on a wheel. Every other house in the street was a gin shop or a brothel, and within a short walk of Inigo Jones' magnificent piazza stood the stinking tenements and thieves' kitchens of Seven Dials.

Chaotic, violent Hanoverian London was almost impossible to police. The writer Fanny Burney complained that she could not take a walk before breakfast 'because of the danger of robbers' and dusk was generally known as 'the footpad hour'.[1] The teeming rookeries of Seven Dials and Saffron Hill were villains' strongholds, a labyrinth of secret passageways riddled with booby traps. Any constable of the watch foolhardy enough to give chase into the tottering ruins might find himself stumbling headfirst into a cesspool or set upon by an army of thugs. Drink had always played a prominent part in the underworld, but now the traditional flagons of ale and sack had been forsaken and London was floating on a tide of gin, the cheap but potent liquor sold at 15,000 drinking establishments throughout the city, where the public could be 'drunk for one penny and dead drunk for tuppence'.[2] Once they had recovered, drinkers had to go and find the wherewithal to do it all again, which inevitably meant crime.

Such law enforcement as there was consisted of parish constables, and 'Charlies', a corps of night watchmen introduced by Charles II. Positioned in little sentry boxes by the side of the road, the elderly and infirm Charlies attracted much ridicule, particularly from the Mohocks, upper-class hooligans who delighted in rolling the sentry boxes over, with the Charlies still inside.[3]

Given the failure of the watchmen and the unreliability of volunteer constables, parishes began to hire paid constables instead, but many such constables developed too close a relationship with the underworld they were supposed to police, and were prone to corruption.

If the constables did succeed in making an arrest, the felon was taken before a magistrate or 'Justice of the Peace' who would then pass sentence or, if the crime was serious enough, remand them in custody until they could be tried at the Old Bailey.

As the authorities came to understand that London required a more efficient method of dealing with crime, 'rotation offices' or magistrates' courts opened in the capital. These were offices where Londoners could be certain to find a magistrate at fixed hours. Anyone witnessing a felony was legally obliged to apprehend those responsible for the crime, and to notify a constable or Justice of the Peace if they heard that a crime had taken place.

Unfortunately, Justices of the Peace could prove to be as venal as the offenders who appeared before them and were often men of corrupt morals, incapable of inspiring respect and quite indifferent about the efficiency of their subordinates. While there was no shortage of reputable country gentlemen in the shires, content to serve as Justices of the Peace without financial gain, in London the duties of a magistrate were so much more arduous that the candidates were seldom men of distinction and frequently people whose motive was to exploit rather than serve the public. Although the justices were not paid, they were entitled to certain fees, and many were referred to scathingly as 'trading justices' who lived on their expenses.[4]

Sir Thomas De Veil joined the ranks of the magistrates in 1739, and opened his own magistrates' court at 4 Bow Street in 1740. A former army officer from a Huguenot family, De Veil was an authoritative, energetic and intelligent man, who had previously dispensed legal advice from an obscure corner of Whitehall known as 'Scotland Yard'. As befitted a former army officer, De Veil was not lacking in physical courage. He survived at least one murder attempt after breaking up a criminal gang, and faced down a violent rabble that tried to torch Bow Street during a gin riot in 1743. De Veil had been involved in the legislation to curb the consumption of gin by imposing a massive 5 per cent increase in duty, which earned him the undying hatred of the London mob. De Veil was immortalized in a ballad as a hero who 'cool and dauntless saw the Bow Street fray, and taught rebellious lackeys to obey'.[5]

However, for all his hatred of gin, De Veil was no stranger to the bottle himself, as illustrated by Hogarth in *Night* (1738). Hogarth, who despised De Veil for being a Freemason and a hypocrite, depicted the magistrate being escorted home from his Masonic lodge so hopelessly drunk that he was oblivious to the chamber pot being tipped over his head or the gin riots raging in the background. De Veil's other appetites included 'a most irregular passion for the fair sex'. He kept a small room directly behind the bench for swift couplings between cases, and, according to his obituary in the *Gentleman's Magazine,* 'he served himself by means of his office with a variety of women'.[6] If an attractive young woman appeared in the dock, De Veil would ask in a kindly way if her lodging was far from Bow Street, and if a sedan chair might halt outside without suspicion. On hearing a positive response, De Veil would drop the charges.[7]

Following the death of De Veil in 1746 a magistrate named John Poulson held office until 1748, when the Bow Street practice was taken over by a barrister named Henry Fielding, an attractive and gregarious man, 'overflowing with wit, mirth and good humour'.[8] Today, Henry Fielding is best remembered as the author of hearty picaresque novels such as *Joseph Andrews* (1742) and *Tom Jones* (1751) but at the time he was better known as a satirist. In *Jonathan Wild* (1743), Fielding drew a sardonic parallel between the disgraced thief-taker and the notoriously corrupt prime minister, Robert Walpole. Jonathan Wild proved to be more than a literary inspiration. Fielding, who had attended Wild's hanging in 1725, was determined to reform the climate of sleaze that had allowed Wild to flourish and the culture of fear that left private individuals afraid to come forward as prosecutors, meaning that no proceedings could be taken against the criminal.

Henry Fielding was appointed to the bench on 25 October 1748; six weeks later, he was dispensing justice in Bow Street. Living with him at the same house was his half-brother, John Fielding, who had been blinded after a naval accident at the age of nineteen. Despite his blindness, John Fielding was also a respected magistrate, known as 'the blind beak of Bow Street' because he could recognize over 3,000 individual criminals by the sound of their voices. John Fielding's original and witty personality used to attract audiences to listen to his examinations of prisoners, and the figure of the blind magistrate, with a bandage over his eyes and a cane in his hand to wave before him when he left the bench, came to be as familiar to high society as it was to the poor wretches who appeared before him.[9]

To be a magistrate in eighteenth-century London was no easy task. The Fieldings handled up to fifty hearings a week, and attended frequent all-night sittings, in the foetid, soot-blackened courtroom. On one occasion, forty-five people were arrested following a raid on a casino in the Strand, all of whom had to be committed immediately.[10] Henry Fielding's new career offered little in the way of financial recompense in return for the long hours. Although his fees were supposed to amount to some £1,000 a year, much of this had to go to his clerk. However, between the two of them, the brothers made the name Fielding synonymous with peacekeeping for a generation of Londoners, and ushered in a number of innovations that played a vital part in the development of criminal intelligence.[11]

The first of these innovations was an effective weapon against the highwaymen who laid siege to the carriages, post chaises and mail coaches travelling in and out of London. Henry Fielding enlisted the support of twenty country gentlemen with houses within twenty miles of the capital. These individuals were asked to donate two guineas to a common pool and to send Fielding a messenger on horseback with written details of any crime committed in his area, including, if possible, an accurate description of the thief and the horse he was riding, together with the name of the victim. On his way to London, the messenger was to warn all innkeepers, stable boys and turnpike keepers against harbouring the fugitive, supplying him with a horse or letting him pass. The messenger was to return with a note from the magistrates proving that he had performed his task, and for this he was paid out of the pool. The information and description of the highwayman was then published in the *Public Advertiser* (the forerunner of the *Police Gazette)* and, with its pictures of known offenders, constituted an early form of the criminal records department. Even if the highwayman got safely away to London, he was at the mercy of the thief-takers. And, since highwaymen tended to be flamboyant young men, prone to bragging about their exploits in the taverns, it was only a matter of time before they were identified and arrested. The result of Fielding's scheme was the 'Mounted Patrol', which reduced the rate of highway robbery in three months. Unfortunately, soon after Fielding's death, the Mounted Patrol was disbanded, and highwaymen immediately took to the road again. It was not until 1806 that the Mounted Patrol was revived, eventually becoming the mounted division of the Metropolitan Police.[12]

The Fieldings believed that they could deter criminals by increasing the certainty that they would be detected and prosecuted, and that by supervizing their activities, they could improve the reputation of thief-takers, who they believed were essential in the fight against crime. These officers, who liked to refer to themselves as 'principal officers' of Bow Street, were more commonly known as 'the Bow Street Runners', although Londoners also, in a more irreverent fashion, referred to them as the 'Robin Redbreasts' or the 'Raw Lobsters' on account of their distinctive red waistcoats.

Alongside the problem of widespread criminality, another form of lawlessness threatened the capital in the form of civil unrest. During the eighteenth century London saw three serious disturbances of this kind: the riots which broke out after the 1736 Gin Act, the Spitalfields Riots of 1765 and the Gordon Riots of 1780. Existing legislation in the form of the Riot Act (1715) meant that magistrates could order 'riotous assemblies' of more than twelve people to disperse within the hour or be charged with capital felony. Dispersing the crowd became the responsibility of the army, but the troops were placed in an unenviable position. A soldier who overreacted and opened fire on the mob, killing or seriously injuring a rioter, faced a court martial, as did the magistrate.

Reluctance to invoke the Riot Act in June 1780 led to shocking scenes when the Gordon Riots raged through London for days. Over 400 people were killed, the Bank of England was attacked, and 150 houses and shops were destroyed, causing £70,000-worth of damage to property (£6.5 million at today's prices) and £30,000-worth of personal injury claims (c. £3 million

Newgate Gaol in flames during the Gordon Riots.

today). Events culminated with the destruction of Newgate Gaol by fire and the release of its prisoners.

Events had unfolded peacefully at first, with little indication of the anarchy that would follow. On 2 June 1780, Lord George Gordon (1751–93), leader of the 'Protestant Association', arrived in London with his band of 40,000 supporters, to petition Parliament against the 1778 Catholic Relief Act. Gordon and his followers feared that, given sufficient power, the country's Roman Catholic community would overthrow the crown and put the country under the control of the Pope, hence their blue cockades and slogan of 'No Popery!' After their bid to overthrow the bill was dismissed by MPs, the protest started to get out of hand. Ranks swelled by another 20,000 people, ranging from ruffians and apprentices to prostitutes and anonymous 'gentlemen' who may well have been *agents provocateurs,* the rioters rampaged through London, raiding and burning Roman Catholic churches and businesses in Holborn, Covent Garden and Leicester Square. The mansions of Tory aristocrats such as Sir George Savile, a Papist sympathizer, were destroyed. Fearing for their lives, even the Jewish merchants deemed it expedient to hang out 'No Popery!' signs.

After three of Gordon's men were arrested and taken before the aged Sir John Fielding, Bow Street Magistrates' Court was attacked. According to a Bow Street Runner named Macmanus, the mob arrived at around nine, armed with clubs and shouting 'Damn you! We will have it down!'[13] The Runners chained and bolted the doors behind them and escaped through the back. Some hours later, Macmanus returned, armed with a pistol, to discover the windows broken, the wooden shutters and wainscoting torn down and fires in the street where the mob had set fire to the furniture. Meanwhile, the landlord of the Brown Bear, opposite, was trying to placate the rioters with free gin, but the liquor only served to intensify their rage. Although all the goods and chattels were taken out and burnt, 4 Bow Street was not destroyed beyond repair.[14]

At around eight o'clock on the evening of 6 June, a mob rampaged down Holborn bellowing 'Ahoy for Newgate!' and converged on the house of the keeper, Mr Richard Akerman, clamouring for the release of the three prisoners who had been arrested on 2 June, the day the riots broke out. Akerman and his family were forced to flee to safety across the rooftops, after which Akerman demanded that the Lord Mayor, Richard Kennett, read the Riot Act and send in the troops, but the magistrates refused, fearing that such an action would further inflame the mob. In the meantime, Newgate Gaol went up in flames, accompanied by the screams of terrified prisoners. The rioters quickly set about freeing them, breaking down doors and leading them out, still in their chains.

Spurred on by the symbolic gesture of destroying London's Bastille, the rioters smashed open the gates of the New Prison and Clerkenwell Bridewell, burned down the Fleet and the King's Bench, and attacked the Bank of England and the Houses of Parliament. At this point, realizing that the riots were becoming uncontrollable, the Lord Mayor called out the City Militia and the Honourable Artillery Company and gave the order to fire. About 10,000 troops descended on the rioters, killing over 300 and arresting 450. Twenty-five rioters were hanged, the majority of them less than eighteen years old. Horace Walpole observed bitterly that 'the bulk of the criminals are so young that half a dozen schoolmasters might have quashed the insurrection'.[15]

In the following days, many of the prisoners who had been freed from Newgate gave themselves up, tired, hungry and destitute. They were confined to the Compters, while plans went ahead for the complete reconstruction of Newgate Gaol. Lord George Gordon, who had instigated the riots, was arrested and detained in the Tower of London, before going on trial for treason. Gordon was acquitted but ironically he ended his days in Newgate in 1793, after being sentenced on a charge of seditious libel.

It took three years to assess the full impact of the Gordon Riots upon London. The damage to property ran into billions by today's standards, and the majority of the victims were the landed gentry, manufacturers and tradespeople. As insurance companies examined their policies to see if they could avoid paying out for 'civil commotion', well-to-do Londoners came to realize that the ancient parochial system of peace-keeping would always be ineffectual in dealing with violent and widespread disorder.[16] If the army was powerless to stop riots, and the constables of the watch were useless, there was only one solution. What was needed was a professional police force to act in collaboration with existing constables and watchmen to prevent crime and to 'put down' such acts of sedition before they became so destructive and dangerous. In 1785 the government attempted to pass a bill creating paid police commissioners throughout the metropolis. Their task would be to supervize a professional police force in London. The bill failed because the Lord Mayor opposed any infringement of his jurisdiction in the City of London and the magistrates saw police commissioners as a threat to their authority.

In 1797 the magistrate and statistician Patrick Colquhoun (1745–1820) argued the case for a professional force. 'It is an honourable profession to repel by force the enemies of the State. Why should it not be equally so to resist and to conquer these domestic invaders of property, and destroyers of lives who are constantly in a state of criminal warfare?' he demanded.[17] Colquhoun's detractors argued that a paid force would be regarded as 'anathema to the vast majority of the population', conjuring up the vision of governmental repression and a quite unwarranted interference with the liberties of the subject. Conversely, there was also a very real anxiety that, in the wrong hands, a professional police force would not serve the ends of the establishment but would be used against them, in a repetition of 'The Terror' when scores of people were seized and executed by the secret police in post-revolutionary France.[18]

Undeterred, Colquhoun persisted with his campaign and in 1798 he collaborated with a group of docklands merchants to form the Thames River Police, to protect the valuable cargoes coming in to the Pool of London, and opened the world's first police station, at Wapping. But it would take a sensational series of murders, an audacious assassination attempt and another riot before a city-wide force could come into being.

*

By 1811, the Ratcliffe Highway, near Wapping, was one of the worst streets in London – a dirty, dusty thoroughfare on the shore of the Thames, lined with taverns, brothels and cheap hotels. Close at hand was the grim spectacle of Executioner's Dock, where pirates and all manner of seafaring villains had undergone the traditional punishment of being chained to a post and left to drown. Shoehorned in between these dens of iniquity were the shabby genteel – the grocers, bakers, fish-mongers and tailors who struggled to make an honest living amid the depravity. Timothy Marr, who had opened a draper's shop at 29 Ratcliffe Highway, was a typical resident. A former merchant seaman who had served on the *Dover Castle* between 1808 and 1811, Marr lived behind his shop with his young wife, Celia, and their three-month-old son. Marr's apprentice, James Gowan, aged thirteen, and a servant girl, Margaret Jewell, also lived at number twenty-nine.

At midnight on Saturday, 7 December 1811, Marr finally shut up shop for the evening and instructed young Margaret to go out and buy oysters. When Margaret returned half an hour later, the shop was in darkness and she could not get in. After the watchman had hammered on the door to no avail, a neighbour, a Mr Murray, offered to investigate. When he walked round to the rear of the house, he found the back door wide open. Raising his candle, Murray encountered a scene of horror. The apprentice, James Gowan, lay dead, his head smashed in so violently that the walls were spattered with his blood and brains. Near Gowan was the body of young Celia Marr, blood seeping from her battered skull. Murray wrenched open the front door and raised the alarm with a cry of 'Murder! Murder! Come and see what murder is here!' By this time a small crowd had gathered in the street outside and as someone held up a lantern, the body of Timothy Marr was discovered, also battered to death. Margaret Jewell had been reduced to hysterics, and it fell to another woman to shriek: 'Where's the baby?' They found the child still in his cradle.

His throat had been cut and his head almost severed from his body.

When Charles Horton, of the Thames Police Office at Wapping, arrived to investigate, he found a ripping chisel at the scene, but it appeared to be perfectly clean. The actual murder weapon, a 'maul' or shipwright's hammer, was discovered upstairs, covered in blood and hair, and engraved with the initials 'J. P.' The discovery of two sets of bloody footprints, leading away from the back door, suggested that the perpetrators had been interrupted attempting a robbery. Marr's savings, £152, were still intact in a drawer, and he had £5 on his body when he died.[19]

As news of the terrible events spread throughout the East End, the street outside was crammed with sightseers, eager to satisfy their ghoulish curiosity. The bodies went on display as was the custom, and the Marrs were subsequently buried in a single grave at St George's-in-the-East, the church where only two months earlier young Timothy Marr had been christened.

Panic gripped the neighbourhood and a reward of five hundred guineas was offered for apprehending the killer. This was an unprecedented sum in an age when a working man was lucky to earn more than £1 a week. The incentive worked: the landlord of the Pear Tree public house, Robert Vermilloe, came forward to identify the owner of the maul as John Petersen, a merchant seaman and one of his lodgers. Vermilloe was in Newgate Gaol for debt, and must have welcomed the opportunity to claim the reward money. Another resident, Cornelius Hart, claimed ownership of the ripping chisel, saying he must have mislaid it when visiting Marr.

Before the Thames Police Office could act on this information, Wapping was shaken by another gruesome multiple murder. On 19 December a watchman patrolling New Gravel Lane was astonished to witness a half-naked man scrambling out of an upstairs window at the King's Arms Tavern shouting, 'Murder! Murder!'[20]

When the watchman and constables from the Thames Police Office forced their way into the King's Arms they discovered the body of the publican, John Williamson, hanging from a ladder in the cellar and the bodies of his wife, Elizabeth, and their servant, Bridget Harrington, in the kitchen. All three had been brutally battered and their throats had been cut. The murderer appeared to have escaped across open land at the rear of the premises, with Williamson's watch and other valuables. Apart from the lodger who had climbed out of the window, the only other survivor was Kitty Stillwell, the Williamsons' fourteen-year-old granddaughter, who had slept through the entire incident.

Wapping was again thrown into a state of panic, and several arrests were made. These included another resident of the Pear Tree, a sailor named John Williams. Williams was arrested on 21 December after a tip-off from Vermilloe, who stated that Williams had served with Marr on the *Dover Castle* and had a grievance against him. A ladies' man with no previous history of violence, Williams was an unlikely suspect for seven of the most brutal murders in London. The evidence against him was entirely circumstantial, consisting of the fact that the shirt he was wearing was torn and bloody, and that he was carrying an unusual amount of money. However, Williams was remanded in custody to Cold Bath Fields prison, and scheduled to appear at Shadwell Magistrates' Court on 27 December. In a shocking twist, a constable arrived on the morning of 27 December to inform the court that Williams had hanged himself in his cell.[21]

After a swift conferral, the magistrates decided to go ahead and hear the evidence of the other witnesses and by the end of the day had concluded that Williams had been the murderer and had acted alone. All of the evidence that pointed towards others being involved seems to have been conveniently ignored. That evening the Shadwell magistrates informed the Home Secretary, Mr Robert Ryder, that John Williams had murdered the Marr family and the Williamson family and had cheated the hangman by taking his own life in prison rather than face the consequences.

The Home Secretary accepted this verdict and decided to conclude the whole ghastly business by having Williams' body paraded through Wapping to prove that he no longer represented a threat. To avoid any danger of rioting, the Thames Police, the Bow Street Mounted Patrol, local constables and the watchmen were ordered to oversee the event. On New Year's Eve 1811, at half past ten in the morning, the procession set off from St George's Watch House, with Williams' body propped up on the back of a cart. The maul and the ripping chisel with which he had apparently committed the murders were displayed beside his head, while a wooden stake lay at his feet. As a crowd some 10,000-strong looked on, the procession wound down the Ratcliffe Highway, and halted outside the Marrs' shop, where a constable turned Williams' head so that he appeared to be gazing at the ghosts of his victims. A similar vigil was held outside the King's Arms, before the procession made its way along Ratcliffe Highway, up to the crossroads where Cannon Street meets Cable Street, where Williams' body was thrown into a narrow grave and the stake was driven through his heart, hammered in with the bloodstained maul. At that moment, the crowd, hitherto peaceful, let out a stream of shouting and curses.

Williams made a convenient scapegoat, offering the authorities the opportunity to reassure Londoners that law and order had been restored. But the circumstances surrounding his death remain mysterious. Witnesses from Cold Bath Fields prison said that on the night before he hanged himself, Williams did not appear to be distressed. Indeed, he was looking forward to

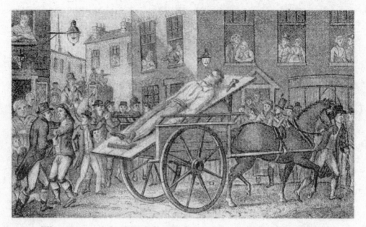

*The corpse of the Ratcliffe Highway Murderer John Williams
is paraded down the Ratcliffe Highway before being buried
with a stake through his heart.*

a visit from his fellow lodgers at the Pear Tree, Cornelius Hart
and John Petersen, who seemed very concerned for his welfare.
It is also curious that given Williams was in manacles, he actually managed to hang himself from a beam in his cell.

The temptation to speculate as to the real course of events
is difficult to resist. In their case study, *The Maul and the Pear
Tree,* the distinguished crime writer P. D. James and the police
historian T. A. Critchley concluded that Williams had become
involved in the robberies through the influence of his shady
fellow lodgers, and then been silenced to prevent him from
incriminating them. This made Williams himself the eighth
victim of the Ratcliffe Highway murderers, his death repre-
senting an attempt to silence him and prevent him from
incriminating other gang members.[22]

The horror and outrage generated by the Ratcliffe
Highway murders contributed to the demand for a city-wide
police force, although there were still libertarian protests from

the House of Lords. For instance, in a high-handed dismissal of the murdered proletariat, Lord Dudley reflected, 'Although they have an admirable police force in Paris, they pay dear for it. I had rather half a dozen people's throats were cut every few years in the Ratcliffe Highway than be subject to domiciliary visits, spies and the rest of Fouché's contrivances.'[23]

Fouché's contrivances would become indispensible over the following decades. By 1820, an unpopular Tory government under Lord Liverpool was facing potential anarchy, fuelled by widespread resentment of the Corn Laws, which had caused soaring food prices and famine. Disillusioned veterans, unemployed after the end of the Napoleonic Wars, proved fertile recruits to radicalism, and the authorities struggled to maintain order. A political meeting at Spa Fields in the East End descended into a riot in 1817 with twelve men killed by troops. In 1819, a rally at St Peter's Fields, Manchester, developed into the Peterloo Massacre when troops killed fifteen people during a cavalry charge. As political tensions escalated with the death of King George III in January 1820, the radicals saw the opportunity to seize power.

Following the teachings of Thomas Spence (1750–1814), radical groups consisted of individual cells rather than an overall organization. One such cell consisted of Arthur Thistlewood (1774–1820), a veteran of Spa Fields and Peterloo, and his comrades William Davidson, son of the Attorney General of Jamaica and a black slave, and James Ings, Richard Tidd and John Brunt. In 1820 a new recruit arrived in the form of George Edwards, a stonemason from Eton, who swiftly impressed them with his radical spirit. On the evening of 22 February, Edwards pointed to a notice in the *New Times* newspaper stating that the Prime Minister, Lord Liverpool, intended to dine with Lord Harrowby in Grosvenor Square, along with his cabinet. Edwards suggested that this represented the ideal opportunity to overthrow the government. A plan was swiftly formed to storm the house, murder every member of the Cabinet, and behead Lord Castlereagh, who was particularly vilified. Castlereagh's head was to be displayed on a spike on Westminster Bridge, and the ultimate aim was to seize the Bank of England and proclaim a provisional government.[24]

The following evening, 23 February, Thistlewood's gang of around twenty-three men assembled in a hayloft in Cato Street off Edgware Road, a short distance away from Grosvenor Square. The gang had stockpiled guns, swords, cutlasses, home-made hand-grenades about the size of oranges and even an improvized explosive device in the form of a 14 lb bomb with an attached fuse. As they made the final preparations, the conspirators had no idea that they were already surrounded. A detachment of the Coldstream Guards was heading towards Cato Street, whilst a squad of twelve Bow Street Runners led by veteran Runner George Ruthven had already surrounded the hayloft. Without waiting for reinforcements, Ruthven started his assault by scrambling up the single ladder to the hayloft. Startled, Thistlewood realized he had been betrayed and responded with a volley of gunfire. Shooting at one Runner, Westcot, he missed his target. Three bullets whistled through Wescot's hat but he was unharmed. Bow Street Runner Richard Smithers was not so fortunate. Thistlewood ran him through with his sword, inflicting fatal injuries, before escaping through a window. When the Coldstream Guards arrived they mounted a full-scale assault on the hayloft, overpowering the conspirators. Thistlewood and three others were arrested later that same night.[25]

When the conspirators went on trial for treason at the Old Bailey on 28 March, George Edwards was revealed as a police spy who had infiltrated the cell on the orders of his brother, a Bow Street Runner, and incited the conspirators to murder.

On Edwards' evidence, the conspirators were convicted. When sentences were passed, five of the conspirators were sentenced to transportation. Thistlewood, Davidson, Ings, Brunt and Tidd received the death sentence for treason, while George Edwards, his cover blown, embarked for Australia and was never heard of again.

The death penalty for treason stated that: 'Your heads shall be severed from your bodies and your bodies divided into four quarters to be disposed of as His Majesty shall think fit.' In previous years, the obvious place for such an execution would have been Tyburn. But now public executions had moved to Newgate Gaol, and it was here, early on the morning of 1 May 1820, that the gallows were erected outside the Debtors' Door, and festooned with black fabric. Barriers went up thirty yards from the gallows, manned by dozens of soldiers and constables. A headsman's block and sawdust sprinkled liberally on the ground signified that the outcome of this execution would be particularly gruesome.[26] A massive crowd had already gathered. Ringside views, from windows overlooking the scaffold, had sold for exorbitant sums. The square tower of St Sepulchre's was packed, and the iron railings collapsed from the pressure and gave way, taking down sixteen people with it. By seven o'clock, magistrates ordered the Riot Act to be read, threatening the onlookers that if they did not behave in an orderly fashion, the army would be sent in. The Home Secretary, Lord Sidmouth, had to dispense with the tradition of drawing the conspirators to the scaffold on hurdles, in case they were seized by the crowd and rioting broke out.[27]

According to John Hobhouse, a government minister who observed the executions, 'the men died like heroes'.[28] Ings turned to Tidd and said gruffly, 'Come on, my old cock, keep up your spirits, it all will soon be over,' and began singing 'Death or Liberty' at the top of his voice. At this point Thistlewood, whose patience was understandably at its limit, turned to Ings and said wearily, 'Be quiet, Ings; we can die without all this noise.' Even Tidd wanted to leave something for posterity. His last words, as the noose was placed around his neck, were: 'Let it be known that I die an enemy to all tyrants!'

The executioner spent a long time tying up the prisoners. During this operation a dead silence prevailed among the crowd, but the moment the trapdoor opened, 'the general feeling was manifested by deep sighs and groans'. Thistlewood, Davidson and Tidd expired without putting up a struggle but Ings died hard, with the executioner's assistants pulling at his legs. So did Brunt, whose horrifyingly contorted face showed that he was suffering 'the most excruciating torture'.[29]

After half an hour the bodies were cut down and placed in coffins, and the executioner informed the sheriff that the time had come to carry out the next part of the sentence, upon which point a grotesque figure wearing a mask and dressed like a sailor sprang up through the trapdoor armed with a butcher's knife. He dragged Thistlewood's body back out of its coffin, up to the block and cut off his head. More deeply moved by the indignity to the dead than the sufferings of the living, the crowd erupted into roars of outrage. The executioner held up the dripping head, crying three times: 'This is the head of Arthur Thistlewood, a traitor!' as the crowd hissed and groaned. The other four bodies were also decapitated and the heads placed in the coffins. The executioner accidentally dropped the last head, Brunt's, and the crowd shrieked. By this stage in the proceedings, there was so much blood on the scaffold that it looked like a slaughterhouse. The quartering of the bodies was, mercifully, omitted.[30]

The skill with which the bodies were decapitated led some of Thistlewood's supporters to suspect that the executioner had been the surgeon Thomas Wakeley. That night, Wakeley's house was set on fire, and the surgeon severely injured. But

The decapitated body of Arthur Thistlewood, ringleader of the Cato Street Conspiracy, executed for treason at Newgate in 1820.

Wakeley survived the experience and went on to become a leading surgeon and the founder of *The Lancet*.

If the Cato Street Conspiracy had not been reason enough to lobby for an organized professional force, then the riots following the funeral of Queen Caroline the following year represented conclusive evidence. Queen Caroline, estranged wife of the Prince Regent, had not always been popular. However, the British public loathed the Prince Regent even more than they disliked Queen Caroline, and the tipping point came when the Prince publically humiliated the Queen by refusing to allow her into Westminster Abbey to attend his coronation in 1820. After the Queen died of peritonitis on 7 August 1821, there was such a public demonstration of grief that it was feared her funeral procession on 18 August might degenerate into a riot.

To prevent this outcome, Lord Liverpool ruled that the funeral procession taking the Queen's body to Harwich for burial in Germany would bypass the capital. But the Queen's loyal subjects had other ideas, determined that the cortège would pass through central London. By six o'clock in the morning a vast crowd had assembled at Hyde Park Corner, desperate to join the procession. By nine-thirty, the cortège arrived at Kensington Palace accompanied by a Guard of Honour, and then turned towards Hyde Park, preparing to travel north, up Park Lane and out of London. When the cortège arrived in Hyde Park at noon, vast numbers of people on foot and on horseback surged forward, intent on blocking the Cumberland Gate leading to Park Lane and forcing the cortège to take a different route. The Guards galloped through Hyde Park in a bid to reach Cumberland Gate before the crowd did, during which stones and mud were thrown at the military. A magistrate who was present sanctioned the use of armed force, and the soldiers fired their pistols into the unarmed crowd. 'Screams of terror were heard in every direction,' as forty or fifty shots rang out, and two people were killed. As the rain fell in torrents, the cortège was eventually forced through the city by the crowds.[31] Following this debacle it became clear to the authorities that an organized professional police force was essential if such scenes were not to be repeated at a later date.

In 1829 the Home Secretary, Sir Robert Peel, finally saw through the Act that created the Metropolitan Police. The new recruits went on parade for the first time on 26 September 1829 in the grounds of the Foundling Hospital in Holborn. The old system of constables and Charlies was replaced with 3,000 constables wearing blue coats, trousers and top hats. They were supervized by two commissioners, Sir Charles Rowan, a former army officer, and Richard Mayne, a barrister, who were both sworn in as Justices of the

Peace. Many of the police officers were former soldiers, but they were not allowed to carry arms. Instead they were equipped with truncheons, and instantly nicknamed 'Bobbies' and 'Peelers' after Sir Robert Peel. The headquarters of this new force was in the very same Whitehall backwater where Sir Thomas De Veil had set up an office back in the 1730s: Scotland Yard, a name that was to become synonymous with the detection and prevention of crime. As the following chapter reveals, the growth of the Victorian underworld over the following decades meant that the 'Old Bill' had their work cut out for them.

8

DARKEST LONDON

The Victorian Underworld

In the year 1850, Henry Mayhew made an intrepid ascent above London in a hot-air balloon. From his vantage point in the creaking basket, buffeted by the wind, the social reformer gazed down upon the monster city, which had grown out of all proportion over the previous decades. A time-traveller from an earlier era would have recognized the tiny outlines of the ancient walled city and the fortress of the Tower, but this square mile formed but the nucleus of the Leviathan metropolis which had sprawled out in all directions, swallowing up parish after parish and clusters of suburban villages and hamlets. Bow, Islington, Hampstead, Paddington, Kensington and Chelsea, and the towns of Westminster and Southwark had all disappeared into its gaping maw until London covered some 261 square miles of ground and contained three million citizens, a larger number of people than were to be found congregated in any other city in the world. Indeed, as one French commentator observed, London by this period was not so much a city as a province, covered by houses.[1]

A dense canopy of smoke lay across the scene, making it almost impossible to tell where the city began and where it ended. The buildings stretched not only to the horizon on either side, but far away into the distance, where, owing to the coming shades of evening and the dense fumes from the million chimneys, the town seemed to blend into the sky, making earth indistinguishable from heaven. Millions of roofs extended like a dingy red sea, rising up one after the other till the eye grew wearied with following them. Here and there appeared little green patches of parks, and the principal squares, and the fog of smoke that overshadowed the giant town was pierced with a thousand steeples and pin-like factory chimneys.[2]

Henry Mayhew had become an authority on the teeming life that filled the massive, vibrant city streets beneath him. In the course of researching his *London Labour and the London Poor*, Mayhew had interviewed scores of costermongers, flower sellers, street sweepers and hawkers, the dust and chaff who just scraped by, earning a crust on the grimy margins of London life. And Mayhew had also encountered the vast contingent of 'those that will not work', an entire alternative society composed of 'the dangerous classes', ranging from debonair gentlemen jewel thieves and beautiful courtesans to desperate mudlarks, children or old women who waded barefoot onto the Thames mudflats at low tide to pick up lumps of coal which they could sell for a halfpenny.

As London had expanded across the map like a blot of Indian ink, so too had its underworld, producing thousands of rogues and reprobates, tramps and beggars, fortune-tellers, dog-stealers, prigs (thieves), area-sneaks (opportunistic burglars), smashers or *shofulmen* (counterfeiters), broadsmen (card-sharps), bug-hunters (robbers of drunks), dragsmen (thieves who stole from carriages), hoisters (shoplifters), maltoolers (pickpockets who worked the omnibuses), *speelers* (gamblers), rampsmen (footpads), bogus wounded soldiers, sham shipwrecked sailors, 'epileptics' who faked fits of convulsions by chewing soap, and an entire cast of idlers, vagabonds and dissolute persons. All human life was here, from the *gonophs* (child thieves) to the swell mob (elite pickpockets), from the portico thieves and cat burglars to the card-sharps and cracksmen (safe-breakers), the aristocrats of the underworld. Every single one of these pursued their shadowy calling under the constant fear of the policeman's hand on the shoulder, followed by arrest and imprisonment. And yet, reared on the legends of Dick Turpin and Jack Sheppard, the dangerous classes preferred 'a short life but a merry one' to dull respectability or the workhouse. In this chapter, we meet the denizens of the Victorian underworld, and also visit 'the underworld of the underworld', the prisons to which so many felons were condemned.

Although the methodology of Henry Mayhew's 'cyclopaedia' is idiosyncratic by the standards of modern social scientists, his interviews with pickpockets and prostitutes provide fascinating insights into his age. Mayhew serves as a useful guide through the dark regions of criminal London. So too does Charles Dickens, for although his plots were outrageously contrived, Dickens' reporter's eye ensured that his details of dress, location and speech rang true. None more so than in *Oliver Twist* (1838), in which his eponymous hero arrives in the big city after being taken up by another young boy known as 'the Dodger'. As they descended from Islington turnpike down into Angel and then past Sadler's Wells theatre and into the slums of Saffron Hill, Oliver concluded that 'a dirtier or more wretched place he had never seen. The street was very narrow and muddy, and the air was impregnated with filthy odours. There were a good many small shops; but the only stock in trade appeared to be heaps of children, who, even at that time of night, were crawling in and out at the doors, or screaming from the inside.'[3] The only places that seemed to prosper were the pubs, which seemed full of brawling Irishmen. In narrow alleyways and yards, drunken men and women were positively wallowing in filth. And from several of the doorways, ugly, hulking men were cautiously emerging, looking as if they were up to no good.

Oliver Twist, a child whose very surname suggested that he was born to hang, soon found himself apprenticed to a life of crime by Fagin, who lived with his gang of youngsters in Field Lane, Holborn. Fagin was a viciously anti-Semitic caricature of Isaac 'Ikey' Solomons (d. 1850), a notorious receiver who was transported in 1831. It is in Fagin's teeming rookery that Oliver acquires the skills that will equip him for a criminal career, many of which have changed little since 'Wotton' set up his school for apprentice pickpockets in the London of 1585. The training session began with Fagin playing the part of a wealthy old gentleman, loaded with bounty, from the snuff-box and wallet in his trousers to the pocket-watch hanging from his waistcoat and the diamond pin stuck into his shirt. As Fagin parades across the room, pretending to stop and look into imaginary shop windows, the Dodger and another boy, Charley Bates, follow him. Whenever Fagin glances around nervously, slapping his pockets to make sure his possessions are still intact, the boys hide, only to re-emerge once Fagin resumes his stately progress. Eventually, in the time-honoured fashion, it is time for the boys to make their move:

At last, the Dodger trod upon his toes, or ran upon his boot accidentally, while Charley Bates stumbled up against him behind; and in that one moment they took from him, with the most extraordinary rapidity, snuff-box, note-case, watch-guard, chain, shirt-pin, pocket-handkerchief, even the spectacle-case. If the old gentleman felt a hand in any one of his pockets, he cried out where it was; and then the game began all over again.[4]

This 'game' was popular all over London, as boys as young as five or six were trained up to be gonophs by a 'kidsman' or thief trainer. The majority of these ragged urchins were the neglected offspring of costermongers or Irish immigrants from the slums of Westminster and Seven Dials. At all times of year, from the summer dusk to the foggy November evening, they were to be seen swarming barefoot across Blackfriars Bridge, London Bridge, Drury Lane, and Bishopsgate, on their way to pick the pocket tails of gentlemen.

Fagin was a benevolent kidsman compared with his real-life counterparts. One police officer, giving evidence against a receiver at Middlesex Sessions in 1850 testified that he had seen apprentice gonophs knocked down and kicked for 'not having exhibited the requisite amount of tact and ingenuity'.[5]

Oliver Twist embarks on his career as a 'gonoph' or child pickpocket.

Children made ideal thieves because they were treated with comparative leniency by the magistrates. The lack of a comprehensive criminal records system allowed many youngsters to provide false names and addresses and claim to be younger than their years. The vision of a small child pitifully protesting his innocence, his head scarcely visible above the dock, was guaranteed to pluck at the heartstrings. But as well as stealing, gonophs were exploited in another, profoundly disturbing fashion. The censorship laws of the day prevented Dickens from spelling out to his readers exactly what he meant, but many of these young boys also worked as child prostitutes. Brothels offering the sexual services of children were a grim fact of life in Victorian London. A resourceful kidsman would see no distinction between sending his lads off to pick pockets or pimping them out to wealthy perverts who could later be blackmailed on account of their peccadilloes.

The gonophs had their counterparts in the 'mudlarks' of the River Thames. Mostly aged between four and fifteen, this unique class of boys and girls confined their attention to stealing from the ships, barges and other vessels moored along the 367 wharfs of the Thames, including Shadwell and Wapping, Bankside and Borough, Waterloo Bridge, and the Temple and St Paul's Wharf. As soon as the tide was out, they appeared, and stayed on the muddy banks of the river until the tide came back in. Lumps of coal and coke that had fallen from the barges were an obvious target, but the most enterprising paired up, with one clambering onto a vessel and throwing down plunder to his companion. The coal was sold on in the street for a few halfpence, and arrests were frequent. After a short sentence of two or three weeks, the children were back. Occasionally, they were joined by robust older women; one in particular was often to be seen picking coal from the mud outside Wapping Police Office, and then parading around the neighbourhood with a bag of coal on her head.[6]

A more audacious breed of mudlarks sailed the Thames in decrepit little boats, boarding empty barges laden with coffee, sugar, rice, and other goods, and stealing anything they could lay their hands on. If pursued by the police, they took to the water like rats, splashing through the mud. Generally expert swimmers, their ages ranged from twelve to sixteen. Many of these strong, healthy boys were orphans, who slept in the barges at night, covering themselves with old sacks and tarpaulins. When one inspector from the Thames Marine Police found two little boys of nine and eleven who had been living in an old barge in Bermondsey for six months he took them before a magistrate to see if they could be provided for. The magistrate sent them to a workhouse for shelter, but they soon ran away, back to the river.[7]

As for the gonophs on dry land, the boldest and most determined rose to the top of their profession. Ten years on from being a ragged little boy, stealing a silk handkerchief from a gentleman's pocket, the skilful thief or 'buzzer' had joined the ranks of the 'swell mob', promenading around the Bank of England or strolling arm-in-arm along Cheapside with his handsome companion.[8] Henry Mayhew spotted just such a pair as he was being shown around Fleet Street one day by a police officer. As Mayhew watched, two tall, 'gentlemanly' men crossed the road outside St Clement Dane's church and entered a restaurant. 'They were wearing suits of superfine black cloth, cut in a fashionable style. They entered an elegant dining room and sat down to a costly meal with wine.' Mayhew was astonished when the police officer told him that these men were pickpockets.[9]

These 'swells' operated across London, in crowded streets, at railway stations, on omnibuses and steamboats, pursuing their trade in the Strand, Fleet Street, Holborn and Whitehall, out on all public occasions looking for plunder.[10] Expensively dressed, so that they could mingle undetected with their wealthy victims, these pickpockets travelled in first-class railway carriages to race meetings at Ascot and Epsom, often luring their fellow passengers into rigged card games during the journey, leaving their victims fleeced and robbed but too embarrassed to report the crime. Women particularly excelled at the new crime of 'portmanteau robbery'; dressed as respectable widows in heavy mourning garments, they hovered in railway station waiting rooms, biding their time until a passenger's attention was distracted, upon which they would pick up his suitcase and silently steal away. The swell mob mixed with the sightseers at Crystal Palace or the Zoological Gardens, and attended the theatre, the opera and other fashionable places of amusement. When 'the female Blondin' tiptoed precariously along the high wire at Cremorne Gardens, the buzzers were there, ready to take advantage as the audience craned their heads back to admire her performance.

Once business was concluded for the day, the swell mob retired to quiet, respectable homes in Islington, Hoxton or Lambeth, where they were careful to avoid drawing attention to themselves, and ready to move at a moment's notice if they were being observed by the police. To relax and unwind, the buzzer and his girl would head to the 'flash houses', the underworld pubs of King's Cross, Stepney and Whitechapel. Dressed up to the nines in flamboyant gowns and expensive (stolen) jewellery, the girls might have passed for ladies until they opened their mouths. The Rose and Crown in Seven Dials was a typical flash house, patronized by all members of the light-fingered gentry. In the tap room you could listen to Black Charlie, the fiddler, with ten or twelve lads and lasses enjoying a dance, and singing and smoking over glasses of gin and water, all seemingly free from care. The cheeks might turn pale when a policeman opened the door and glanced round the room, but when he departed the merriment would be resumed with vigour.[11]

But for all its rewards, buzzing was a young man's game, and by the age of twenty-five most swells had seen better days. As the effects of alcohol and imprisonment took their toll, the smartest swells changed tack and became receivers or kidsmen. Others slipped into destitution, their courage spent and their souls sapped. Henry Mayhew interviewed just such a young man, who I shall refer to as 'Edward'. Edward was 'rather melancholy and crushed in spirit, the result of repeated imprisonments, and the anxiety and suspense connected with his wild criminal life'. Edward's girl was in prison, and he was living in a seedy lodging-house in the West End. Handsome if weary, with a moustache and beard and dark, penetrating eyes, Edward was also intelligent and literate, having read Thomas Paine, Dickens and Bulwer-Lytton amongst others. Edward's story is a familiar one, but Mayhew's narrative renders it compelling.[12]

Like Oliver Twist, Edward was a runaway. A minister's son from Shropshire, he had left home at the age of nine following a bitter quarrel with his father. Edward had soon spent the four pounds he had stolen from his mother's purse and in a matter of weeks he was utterly destitute. Eventually, he 'palled up' with a gang of boys who lived in the arches underneath the Adelphi theatre and stole handkerchiefs for their master, 'Larry'. Handkerchief theft was a specialist trade with its own vocabulary, the handkerchiefs given names as beautiful and evocative as those of butterflies: the blue silk *watersman*, the green and white *randlesman*, and the yellow and white *fancy yellow*. The most sought after was the black silk mourning handkerchief, known as the *black fogle*.[13] The embroidered initials of the original owner were skilfully unpicked, and the handkerchiefs sold on.

Larry took an instant liking to Edward, immediately spotting his potential. Smart and well-spoken, Edward could pass without comment among the gentry, and soon showed outstanding prowess as a gonoph. Larry was so proud of his new acquisition that he invited other receivers to come and watch him in action, with a view to selling him to the highest bidder. But before this could happen, Edward was arrested and spent three months in Westminster Bridewell.

When he emerged, Edward found a reception committee waiting for him in the form of a gang from Whitechapel. Taken in, Edward was washed and fed, and within days had acquired his specialist training as a 'tooler' or a 'fine-wirer', picking the pockets of ladies. Dressed up in the full mourning of a middle-class child, Edward mingled with the crowds in St Paul's churchyard. And despite further sojourns in gaol, Edward flourished. By the age of thirteen he had a mistress and a luxurious lifestyle that more than compensated for the constant risk of being caught.

But as he matured, Edward's distinctive good looks became a burden; readily identifiable, he had lost that anonymity which is vital to the professional thief. It was time to move into a different field, and so he teamed up with a gang of burglars. The plan was to rob a building in the City, on the understanding that it would be empty on the day of the raid. But the gang, badly organized and inept, had been misinformed, and the robbery was already in progress when an irate employee discovered the men and sounded the alarm. As Edward ran for his life, a public-spirited bystander overheard the cries of 'Stop! Thief!' and adroitly tripped him up with his umbrella, sending Edward crashing to the ground. Edward received eighteen months in Holloway – a comparatively light sentence – but the 'silent system', under which he was forbidden to talk to his fellow prisoners, reduced him to a breakdown.

By the time he spoke to Mayhew, Edward had lost his nerve; his reputation had been damaged by the botched robbery, his mental and physical health were in decline and he was reduced to selling broadsheets in the street, the only job he could be trusted with. Edward's one consolation was his girl, and he believed relationships were stronger between thieves than between a law-abiding man and wife. 'It gives a zest to us in our criminal life, that we do not know how long we may be at liberty to enjoy ourselves. This strengthens the attachment between pickpockets and their women, who, I believe, have a stronger liking to each other, in many cases, than married people.'[14]

One reason for Edward's decline was his decision to move from one criminal speciality to another. While buzzers were highly regarded for their manual dexterity, the burglar's craft demanded a combination of stamina, athleticism and brutality, which Edward was quite incapable of. Prepared to resort to violence if necessary, the burglar carried a cosh as well as a jemmy. The character of Bill Sikes, who tried to employ Oliver as a 'snakesman' in an ill-fated robbery, was the stereotypical Victorian burglar – violent and aggressive, with his broad, heavy features, three weeks' growth of beard and black eye. In fact, there were as many different types of burglars as there were types of houses. The 'area sneaks' slipped down the steps into the 'areas' or basements of large houses, rattling door handles or testing windows; 'portico thieves' were more daring, climbing in over balconies and window ledges, often while the family was dining downstairs. Many burglars worked in cahoots with the domestic staff, investing time in chatting up a maidservant who could leave a door unlocked in return for proceeds from the robbery. The most daring dressed and spoke like landed gentry, and rented houses in Mayfair or St John's Wood. Insinuating themselves with their neighbours, they made a note of their movements and when the quality had left town for their country estates, they drove round in a smart carriage, systematically ransacked the house and trotted smartly away, with the swag concealed in a special compartment underneath the seat.

Burglars, like buzzers, generally served an apprenticeship. A promising lad would enter the trade early in life as a snakesman, slipping through the narrowest of windows to steal or unfasten the doors for his masters. Agile young chimney sweeps were particularly favoured, and the most famous 'climbing boy' was a lad called Henry Williams, who managed to escape from the Press Yard of Newgate in 1836 after being sentenced to death for burglary. Although the fifty-foot-high walls, topped with *chevaux de frise* (fearsome curved spikes), made escape well-nigh impossible, Williams, a former chimney sweep, managed to scale the wall behind the water cistern in the corner of the Press Yard. He achieved this extraordinary feat by removing his boots, pressing his back against one wall and bracing his bare feet against the opposite wall, clawing his way up with his hands and toes. Eventually, he was at a level with the water cistern, and managed to clamber on top of it and drag himself along the wall, dangling from the spikes. From there, Williams leapt nine feet onto a nearby rooftop and emerged into an adjacent property, dazed and bleeding. When Williams staggered in, he pleaded with the horrified residents to let him go, and they agreed not to raise the alarm. The tide of public opinion was turning against hanging people for burglary, and Williams disappeared into the streets surrounding the gaol.[15]

The Victorians were great innovators, quick to take advantage of all the latest developments, and Victorian criminals proved no different. The Victorian robber was no longer the flamboyant highwayman, mounted on his 'Black Bess' with a brace of pistols in his belt. Instead of ambushing stagecoaches, he robbed the express trains, despite the fact that these iron horses sped through the countryside at sixty miles an hour. This is how the Great Victorian Train Robbery was accomplished, when £12,000-worth of gold bullion (£809,417 at today's prices) was stolen from a moving train. For sheer planning and audacity, this was one of the crimes of the century.[16]

Around the time of the Crimean War (1853–6), numerous shipments of gold were sent from London to Paris for the British army. This was a regular enough occurrence to catch the attention of criminal gangs, such as the one led by a man called Edward Pierce who had a criminal record and had worked in a betting shop. Pierce teamed up with William Tester, a clerk from the traffic department of South Eastern Railways, and Robert Agar, a skilled safecracker. The gang doubtless had other accomplices who may not have been fully aware of the extent of the plan.

The gold bullion was packed in sealed iron-bound boxes which were placed inside steel safes. They were then loaded onto the passenger train from London to Folkestone. At Folkestone harbour they were transferred to the Boulogne steam packet. The railway officials clearly believed that the heavy modern safes constituted security enough. The consignments travelled in the guard's van along with other luggage, and the guard did not leave the van once the train was moving. The safes had heavy double locks that required two keys to open them; and there were two sets of keys, one held by the traffic superintendent in London, the other at Folkestone.

The robbery took over a year of planning. First, the gang needed an insider, in the form of a guard called Burgess, who sometimes worked on this route. They also needed duplicates of the two sets of keys. This was made more difficult by the fact that the keys were not kept together, and the regulations in the London office were strict. The gang's chance came when the safes were temporarily withdrawn and sent to the manufacturer, Chubb, for a service. Tester, the traffic clerk from South Eastern Railways, managed to get hold of one key for long enough for Agar to take a wax impression.

Meanwhile, Pierce had been keeping the traffic department at Folkestone under surveillance. His opportunity came when the office was briefly empty and he slipped in, found the second key in an unlocked cupboard, stole it, took it to Agar to take an impression and returned it to its rightful place without anybody noticing.

The safes had finely tuned mechanisms, and it was unlikely that they could be opened with crudely copied keys. However, the gang soon found a loophole. Passengers were permitted to travel in the guard's van if they were looking after a valuable item – a painting, perhaps, or an animal. Burgess, the guard who had been bribed to participate in the plot, allowed Agar to accompany him when he was carrying a consignment of bullion. This gave Agar the opportunity to try out his keys on the safes, tinkering with them until they worked perfectly. The time had come.

On 15 May 1855, Agar and Pierce travelled first class to Folkestone, equipped with a number of bags. If these bags seemed particularly heavy when the porters heaved them into the first-class compartment, it was because they were full of small-shot, sewn into the linings. Pierce took a seat but Agar waited until the train was moving and climbed into the guard's van. Burgess was on board, along with three safes. Agar unlocked the first safe, opened a bullion box, removed the gold and substituted lead shot. He refastened the box, locked the safe, and put the gold in his bag. As the train arrived at Redhill station, Tester appeared and collected the bag containing the gold, while Pierce joined Agar in the guard's van. During the rest of the journey, the men plundered the other two safes, removed the contents, substituted the lead and locked the safes. When the train arrived at Folkestone and the safes were being unloaded, they hid at the back of the van. Once the coast was clear, they got off the train and headed for Dover. They had already obtained tickets for the Dover–Ostend crossing and passed themselves off as travellers from the Continent.

The robbery did not come to light until the safes arrived in France. Alerted by a discrepancy in the weight of the safes, the authorities opened the safes and found that they were filled not with gold but with lead. This dramatic discovery made sensational newspaper headlines as the authorities assumed that the robbery had taken place at source, and the men who had packed the gold must be the culprits. It took eighteen months of bungled arrests and fruitless inquiries before the police got a lead, and this was purely by chance, when Agar was arrested for forging a cheque and imprisoned in Newgate. Agar had a child with his mistress, and wanted to give her some of the proceeds of the robbery. Pierce, who was in charge of the gold, was reluctant, either because he wanted to cheat Agar or did not want the woman to know about the money. But Agar's mistress had some knowledge of the robbery and once she found out that Pierce would not let her have the money, she turned Queen's Evidence. Agar, who was awaiting transportation, did the same. Pierce, Tester and Burgess were arrested and sentenced to long prison terms. Despite an almost faultless plan, the robbers had fallen prey to that most unpredictable factor, human nature. Even if Agar's desire to do the decent thing by his mistress and provide for his child had not given the game away, the woman's anger at Pierce's greed had been the final straw.

For those who were apprehended, arrested, tried and convicted, conditions in gaol remained as variable as ever. Wealthy and influential prisoners could still bribe their keepers with a little 'garnish', ensuring soft treatment. When Captain George Chesterton became governor of Cold Bath Fields prison in Islington in 1829, he was appalled to discover that as well as deriving a handsome secondary income from the sale of liquor, tobacco and food, the gaolers also rented out rooms in the attic on weekday afternoons where male and female prisoners could enjoy sexual congress.[17] The sneaking suspicion that conditions in gaol were cushy for many professional criminals is demonstrated in this extract from *Punch* magazine, where 'Toby Cracksman' writes to 'Bill Sikes' from Newgate, reassuring him that the old 'stone-jug' (prison):

> Is still the same snug, free-and-easy old hole,
> Where MACHEATH met his *blowens* [whores] and
>   WYLDE floor'd his bowl.
> In a ward with one's *pals*, not locked up in a cell,
> To an old hand like me it's a *fam'ly-hotel*.

This poem satirically promotes the popular misconception of Newgate as a villains' paradise, where the warders do as they are instructed, and at 'darkmans' (night-time) the prisoners run the place as they please. The poem concludes with a hearty prayer that:

> Long over Newgit their Worships may rule,
> As the *High-toby, mob, crack and screeve* [forgers] model-
>   school;
> For if Guv'ment was here, not the Aldermen's Bench,
> Newgit soon' 'ud be bad as *'the Pent'* or *'the Tench'*.[18]

The 'Pent' and the 'Tench' are references to Pentonville prison (opened 1842) and the Millbank Penitentiary (1816), which were among the first truly modern prisons. As a result of the work of the reformer John Howard, the political philosopher Jeremy Bentham and the philanthropist Elizabeth Fry, the legislature had come to understand that it was no longer acceptable to lock offenders up and throw away the key. Instead, the new wave of prison buildings were designed to provide the opportunity for repentance, sober reflection and the acquisition of a legitimate trade to equip former prisoners for life on the outside. Or such was the intention. Despite the recognition of the need for reform, progress was slow, with the penal system remaining a random hotchpotch of institutions with little coherent policy over the successive decades.

The beginning of an improvement in prison conditions owes much to the pioneering approach of John Howard (1726–90). Appointed High Sheriff of Bedfordshire in 1773, Howard was appalled by the conditions under which prisoners were held at Bedford Assizes, and horrified to discover that gaolers derived their only income from 'garnish'. A frail but determined man, driven by his Calvinist faith and reforming zeal, Howard undertook an inspection of the nation's prisons, at a risk to his own health. During this thankless task, he wrote, the disgusting reek of prison effluvia clung to his clothes. Howard stank so much after one prison visit that he had to abandon travelling by coach, even with the windows down, and took to travelling on horseback instead. [19] The pages of his notebook reeked to such an extent that he could not read them straight away but had to fumigate the book for an hour or two first, by placing it in front of the fire.[20] In 1777, prompted by 'the sorrows of the sufferers, and love of my country', Howard published *The State of the Prisons in England and Wales,* which incited outrage among philanthropists and reformers and marked the beginnings of the penal reform movement with which his name is still associated. Among Howard's most far-sighted recommendations were separate wings for younger prisoners, to prevent them mixing with hardened criminals in an 'academy of crime', separate quarters for female prisoners, an apothecary and a prison infirmary.[21] These improvements were gradually introduced over the following decades, but life in gaol was harsh for the majority, many of whom remained at the mercy of sadistic governors and warders who compelled them to perform strenuous and ultimately pointless tasks designed to crush mind, body and spirit.

When Millbank Prison or the 'National Penitentiary' opened in 1821, it was the biggest prison in England. Initially, Millbank was intended to hold all those prisoners who had been sentenced to transportation as they awaited their passage to the penal colonies of the New World. Built on a marshy site on the north bank of the Thames, Millbank or 'the Tench' was a unique structure, inspired by the theories of the Utilitarian philosopher Jeremy Bentham (1748–1832). Bentham had devised a 'Panopticon' or 'Inspection House' for prisoners in 1791, derived from a concept by his brother, the naval architect Samuel Bentham. The fundamental principle behind the Panopticon was that the prisoner was forever under surveillance but would see nothing of his watcher, or his fellow inmates. The original Panopticon consisted of a circular building, with the prisoners' cells side-by-side all round the circumference. The inspector's lodge was positioned at the centre. The cells were so completely divided from each other that no prisoner could see or communicate with his neighbours. Each cell had a window in its outer wall and in place of a fourth wall was a large iron grille containing a door. The lighting was to be arranged so that the inspector could watch all the prisoners from his lodge, but remain invisible to them.

The 'invisible omniscience' of the warder represented a method of obtaining control over prisoners' minds. Conscious that they were continually being watched, the prisoners had no option but to obey. The sensation of being under observation rendered manacles unnecessary, and any attempt at riot or a gaolbreak became impossible because the prisoners were so isolated. Bentham's theory was essentially the first example of what the French philosopher Michel Foucault later defined as 'social surveillance', the concept that by being watched, or suspecting that they were being watched, prisoners were frightened into compliance, and reluctant to reoffend.[22]

The original Panopticon never left the drawing board. Much to Bentham's disgust, his plans were eventually discarded in favour of a design by Robert Smirke. While Smirke's design was slightly different from Bentham's, taking the form of a six-pointed star with the chapel at its centre and each of its six separate radiating wings being three storeys high, Bentham's central premise remained. Each of the 1,000 cells contained a water closet, a hand basin, a hammock and a loom. On arrival, the prisoners were shut up alone for the first five days to reflect on their situation. Thereafter, they had to spend the first six months of their sentence alone in their cells, where they worked at tasks such as picking oakum. The prisoner was presented with a quantity of old rope cut into lengths, each of which had to be unravelled down to its thinnest strands. At the end of the day, the pile of rope was collected by a warder and weighed; if it did not reach the target weight prescribed by the prison governor, the prisoner was disciplined.[23]

Sundays were devoted to worship and meditation. Disciplinary offences were punished by a spell in a 'refractory cell' or 'solitary' for hours or even days at a time. According to one warder, this was a dreadful experience. 'It's impossible to describe the darkness; it's pitch black; no dungeon was ever so dark.'[24] The environment at Millbank was dreadful in another way, too. Located on the marshy banks of the Thames, it became a breeding ground for regular outbreaks of cholera.

From Millbank, male convicts progressed to Pentonville or the prison ships known as 'the hulks', decommissioned warships moored in the Thames and used as floating prisons. The first hulk was the *Justicia*, anchored in the Thames off Greenwich in 1776. By 1841, there were nine hulks holding 3,500 convicts moored in the Thames and at Plymouth,

Portsmouth, Sheerness, Chatham Bermuda and Gibraltar. Conditions were appalling, with prisoners suffering scurvy, typhus or dysentery and frequent outbreaks of cholera. Writing in 1841, one commentator said that the shirts of the prisoners, hung out on the rigging, were so black with vermin that the linen appeared to have been sprinkled over with pepper.[25]

Convicts went on shore to work at 'hard labour', breaking stones and cleaning sewers. Many convicts worked on the construction of the new London docks.[26] When Pentonville or 'the Pent' opened in 1842, Millbank became an ordinary prison and increased its capacity to about 1,500 prisoners, who shared their cells. Inmates were only held for a few months before their transfer to other prisons, so around 4,000 to 5,000 passed through its gates every year. It became a military prison in 1870 and closed in 1890.

Pentonville, which still operates as a prison, opened on Caledonian Road, Islington, in 1842, and was originally designed to hold convicts prior to transportation. In the course of researching their book on prisons, Henry Mayhew and his colleague John Binny watched a party of prisoners arriving at Pentonville from Millbank in 1862:

> The miserable wretches were chained together by the wrists in lines. Some were habited in the ordinary light, snuff-brown convict suits, and others wore grey jackets, all having Scotch caps and small bundles of Bibles and hymn-books tied in handkerchiefs under their arms. Jackets, trousers, caps and grey stocking were all marked with red stripes.[27]

Pentonville had been designed as a 'convict academy' where specially selected prisoners would undergo a period of moral instruction before transportation; they would also learn a trade that would provide them with a livelihood in exile once

*Exercise yard at Pentonville, 1840. Note the prisoners' hoods and masks,
designed to humiliate and break the spirit.*

they had completed their sentence. The regime was a notoriously harsh one. Anonymity was imposed, and the prisoner was addressed only by the number of his cell, which was displayed on a brass badge pinned to his chest. Whenever he left his cell, he was required to wear a brown cloth cap with a mask that completely covered his face. One visitor to Pentonville remarked on the prisoners' eerie appearance:

> For the eyes glistening through the apertures in the mask give the notion of a spirit peeping out from behind it, so that there is something positively terrible in the idea that these are men whose crimes have caused their features to be hidden from the world.[28]

Mayhew and Binny described the gaol as 'a kind of penal purgatory where men are submitted to the chastisement of separate confinement so as to fit them for the afterstate'.[29]

To enforce discipline and prepare them for manual work in the colonies, prisoners were subjected to a regime of hard labour. In theory, hard labour served to train the flabby and feckless into a useful workforce. In practice, many of the tasks that the prisoners performed were backbreaking and soul-destroying, such as the treadmill, the crank and the shot drill.

The treadmill consisted of a large cylinder with steps on the outside. As prisoners stepped onto it, the treadmill would begin to turn and the prisoner would have to climb onto the next step, then continue climbing in order to remain upright. Sessions lasted three or four hours a day, with over 340 prisoners on the treadmills at one time, and although the treadmills were lined up side by side, prisoners were forbidden to talk to each other. Caroline Fox, a reformer who visited Coldbath Fields in 1842, observed the female prisoners on the treadmills and wrote that 'it was sad to see the poor

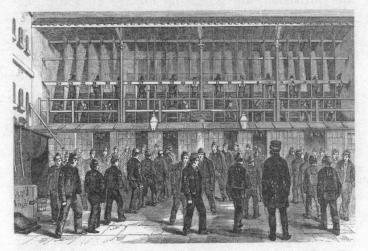

The treadmill at Coldbath Fields, c. 1870. An exercise in futility with prisoners toiling forever upwards, forbidden to speak to each other.

exhausted women ever toiling upward without a chance of progress'.[30]

Another meaningless task consisted of 'the crank', which a prisoner could use alone in his or her cell. This consisted of a narrow drum, placed on legs, with a long handle on one side, which on being turned caused a series of cups or scoops in the interior to revolve. At the lower part of the interior of the machine was a thick layer of sand, which the cups, as they came round, scooped up and carried to the top of the wheel, where they upturned and emptied themselves, along the same principle as a dredging machine. A dial-plate, fixed in front of the iron drum, showed how many revolutions the machine had made. This tedious task was known among inmates as 'grinding the wind'.[31]

Perhaps most soul-destroying of all was shot-drill, compulsory for all male prisoners who were not excused on medical grounds. After watching a session of shot-drill, Henry Mayhew declared that 'it was impossible to imagine anything more ingeniously useless than this form of hard labour'. Shot drill took place in the open, with the prisoners ranged on three sides of the exercise yard with the warder at the centre. At one end of the line of prisoners a number of cannon balls were piled into a pyramid. When the warder gave the command, the three men closest to the pyramid each picked up a cannon ball and placed it on the ground at their feet. On another word of command, they lifted the balls and passed them to the men alongside, who in their turn placed the balls at their own feet. The process was repeated, with the balls passing down the ranks in continuous succession, until they were eventually built up into another pyramid by the men in the last three lines. When all the cannon balls had been stacked in their new position, the operation was reversed and began all over again. The sessions lasted for over an hour every afternoon, and by the end of it the men were visibly distressed.[32]

Despite being subjected to these sadistic regimes, the prisoners continued to defy the silent system and insisted on communicating with one another even while being punished. In 1836, prison inspectors at Coldbath Fields recorded no less than 5,138 punishments for talking and swearing, with prisoners talking even when engaged on the treadmills. Despite the fact that 'turnkeys' or warders were stationed at each treadmill, the prisoners constantly spoke to each other; if reprimanded, they resorted to a form of sign language, indicating with their fingers what crime they had committed, and how long they were in for. Ever resourceful, prisoners succeeded in communicating through the wink of an eye, a cough, or a sneeze.[33] Mayhew and Binny, in the course of their investigations, observed that the silent system was ultimately doomed, since the convicts who had been subjected to the discipline of Millbank and Pentonville were then sent to the hulks, where they were brought into contact with offenders who had undergone no discipline whatsoever. 'All the care which has been taken at Pentonville and at Millbank to prevent the men talking together, and associating with one another, is thrown away.'[34] The silent system was eventually abandoned in 1854.

Toby Cracksman's 'Newgit' continued to occupy its minatory position in London's underworld well into the Victorian era. With its fortress-like appearance, *chevaux de frise* and high walls, Newgate had become London's high-security prison, generally used to hold prisoners awaiting trial at the Old Bailey. Thanks to the reforms led by the Quaker philanthropist Elizabeth Fry (1780–1845), improved conditions meant that prisoners could now expect regular meals, clean cells, and a laundry. Female prisoners in particular benefitted from Fry's innovations, which included education, child welfare and a modest uniform with a cap and apron.

Nevertheless, Newgate could not shake off its vestigial air of melancholy. Mayhew and Binny noted that the women's cells were 'more gloomy and lonely in appearance than [those] in any other prison we have visited – partly caused by the overhanging clouds of smoke which loom over the City, and partly by the sombre lofty surrounding walls of the prison'.[35] The investigators watched a party of felons in the exercise yard, marching around in their own 'miserable, poverty-stricken attire', including one youth in shabby black, who was charged with attempted suicide, and a pale-faced, knock-kneed youth 'with a very sinister look' who was on a fraud charge. Mayhew ends his deliberations by observing that on the whole, 'most of the prisoners were ordinary-looking people, charged with common offences,' a timely reminder of the banal reality of criminal life for the majority of offenders.[36] Stripped of bravado and camaraderie, the bold denizens of the Victorian underworld were more like Edward, the failed burglar, than Bill Sikes.

Unlike his real-life counterparts, Oliver Twist the gonoph did not die upon the gallows. Instead, the foundling was traced by his long-lost aunt and adopted by a kindly old gentleman. Even the Dodger was spared, sentenced to transportation rather than hanging. Fagin, the kidsman, was not so fortunate, and his fate reflected the grim reality of the Victorian penal system. In his most compelling depiction of Newgate, Dickens described the scene when Oliver visited his old master in the condemned cell on the eve of his execution, and Fagin's last night of torment behind the 'dreadful walls of Newgate, which have hidden so much misery and such unspeakable anguish'.[37] The tiny condemned cell itself, just nine by six feet, had changed little since this description by John Howard in 1777:

The doors are four inches thick. The strong stone wall is lined all round each cell with planks studded with broad-headed nails. I was told by those who attended them, that criminals who had an air of boldness during their trial and appeared quite unconcerned at the pronouncing of sentence upon them, were struck with horror and shed tears when brought to these darksome, solitary abodes.

This is certainly the case with Fagin, who has gone out of his mind with despair. After a distressing encounter, Oliver and his guardian left the prison as preparations were being made for the old kidsman's execution. The space before the Debtors' Door had been cleared, and a few strong barriers, painted black, had already been thrown across the road to break the pressure of the expected crowd. There was the sound of men's voices, mingled with the noise of hammering and the throwing down of boards. They were building the scaffold. By the time Oliver and his guardian emerged, shaken, with Fagin's howls of anguish ringing in their ears, it was daybreak. A vast crowd had already assembled. Neighbouring windows were crammed with onlookers, smoking and playing cards to pass the time. The crowd was quarrelling, joking, pushing against the barriers. 'Everything told of life and animation but one dark cluster of objects in the centre of all – the black stage, the cross-beam, the rope, and all the hideous apparatus of death.'[38]

This 'hideous apparatus of death', and its many victims, will be the theme of the following chapter.

THE HIDEOUS
APPARATUS
OF DEATH

*Murder and Execution
in Victorian London*

Over the centuries, Tyburn gallows and Newgate Gaol had become two of the most sinister landmarks in the history of London and crime. With the removal of the gallows from Tyburn to Newgate in 1783, the execution ground and the prison had converged to form a single 'prototype of Hell'. With the Old Bailey standing guard alongside, Newgate reared above the stinking carcasses and filth of Smithfield Market in all its evil glory, striking fear and awe into everyone who saw it.

The smouldering shell of Newgate had been rebuilt in 1780, after the Gordon Riots. Designed in the Palladian style, the new prison cost £50,000 and was intended as a fitting companion to the Old Bailey, also recently rebuilt. Improved conditions included separate accommodation for debtors, male and female wings, a chapel and infirmary. However nothing could disguise the purpose for which this institution had been conceived, and the new prison, with its massive blank walls and entrances decorated with shackles, resembled nothing so much as a giant mausoleum. The old condemned cells had survived the fire, and the architect, George Dance (1741–1825), retained these. A subterranean passageway known as Birdcage Walk or Dead Man's Walk was constructed, through which prisoners were led from the condemned cells to the Press Yard. This dismal thoroughfare had been built over the burial ground, so that prisoners walked to their deaths over the mortal remains of previous inmates, whose corpses had been stripped naked and buried in lime. The walls of Dead Man's Walk told their own story, etched with the initials of former prisoners, the dark history of Newgate carved into the stones.

It was from Dead Man's Walk that the condemned prisoners made their way to the 'New Drop', the trapdoor method of execution first used in 1760 which had now become established as the most efficient way to ensure a quickly broken neck.[1] The gallows measured around eight to ten feet across, depending on the number of prisoners to be hanged, and the trapdoor was held in place by several levers which, when operated by hand, would draw back the bolts. In what was to become a familiar weekly ritual, the portable gallows was rolled out in front of the Debtors' Door of Newgate on Sunday evenings, in preparation for the Monday hanging day. With the scaffold draped in black cloth, and the bells of St Sepulchre's tolling solemnly throughout the execution, the sheriffs intended to create a sober, elegiac mood, a world away from the raucous Bacchanalia of Tyburn.

But, given the sensational nature of public executions, this was not the case. After the very first execution outside Newgate on 3 December 1783, when ten men were hanged, outraged householders were begging the sheriffs to reinstate the gallows at Tyburn. Executions outside their own front doors, in the middle of London, were too close for comfort, evoking the spirit of an earlier, brutal age.

One particular episode lingered in the collective memory: the burning to death of a woman for coining. In 1788, the execution of Phoebe Harris was attended by 'a great concourse of people'.[2] As Phoebe emerged from Newgate, she appeared 'languid and terrified, and trembled greatly as she advanced to the stake'. Phoebe was hanged for half an hour before two cart-loads of faggots were piled around her and lit. The fire was still smouldering four hours afterwards. A year later, Catherine Murphy proved to be the last victim of this barbaric practice, which was abolished in 1790.

As a method of execution, the New Drop was far from foolproof. In 1789, as William Skitch, a burglar, was being hanged, the rope broke and he fell through the trapdoor to the ground. Amid the consternation, Skitch cheekily turned to the crowd and commented: 'Good people, be not hurried. I can wait a little!'[3] Skitch had (quite literally) fallen foul of the prevailing practice, which was to measure the rope in accordance with the prisoner's height, and not his weight. Although Skitch's execution contained an element of black comedy, the fate of many other prisoners was grotesque. Once the noose had been placed around the prisoner's neck, only two inches or so of rope were left to suspend them over a three-foot drop. One development, ushered in by the sheriff, Peter Laurie, consisted of a scaffold beam with adjustable chains. This meant that the prisoner no longer had to go to the gallows with his rope wound around his waist. But even this refinement could not diminish what Laurie referred to as the 'barbarous feelings' of the execution procedure.[4] The combination of a short rope and a short drop meant that most prisoners died of asphyxiation due to the constriction of the windpipe, and were left to kick convulsively. It was not an easy way to die; the majority of prisoners would have been conscious, for a moment or two, that they were hanging, and further humiliation included the involuntary expulsion of urine and faeces, while men often experienced erection and ejaculation.

Relocating the gallows to Newgate did not improve crowd safety. In 1807, over 40,000 people turned out to watch the execution of John Holloway and Owen Haggerty, convicted of a murder which had been committed five years earlier. Their accomplice, Benjamin Hanfield, had turned King's Evidence in return for a pardon. Both men went to the gallows protesting their innocence. A pie stall collapsed and in the ensuing commotion, over thirty people were crushed to death, while around seventy were injured. Fearing for her baby's life, a young woman handed over her baby before being trampled, and the baby was tossed like a ball from hand to hand until it was in a safe position away from the crowd. 'This dreadful scene continued for some time,' declared the Annual Register. 'The shrieks of the dying men, women and children were terrific beyond description, and could only be equalled by the horror of the event.'[5]

Far from being the solemn spectacle that the authorities had intended, executions at Newgate swiftly proved as lurid as anything witnessed at Tyburn. Dr Johnson might have lamented the fact that the crowd had been deprived of a procession, but it could still enjoy the drama of a good hanging, particularly if an attractive young woman was involved. Such was the case of Eliza Fenning.

Eliza Fenning went on trial at the Old Bailey on 5 April 1815, charged with attempted murder.[6] Eliza had only been in service to Robert Turner and his family at 68 Chancery Lane for a few weeks when the incident took place. On the night of Tuesday, 21 March 1815, Robert Turner and his wife

Charlotte were joined for dinner by Mr Haldebart Turner, Robert's father. Upstairs, the family sat down to a dinner of beef stew with dumplings, while down in the kitchen Eliza and the other servants ate the same meal. Almost immediately the entire household, including Eliza, was seized with vomiting and excruciating pain. While the most likely cause was a bout of food poisoning, stemming from a combination of Eliza's inexperience and contaminated meat, Robert Turner had another theory. Claiming that a packet of arsenic, kept to control vermin, had recently disappeared from his desk, he accused Eliza of lacing the dumplings with arsenic in a bid to poison the entire family. This allegation was supported by the surgeon who was called out to the Turners later that night. When the surgeon, Mr John Marshall, gave evidence during Eliza's trial, he maintained that Mr Turner had shown him a dish in which the dumplings had been prepared. When tested, it contained traces of arsenic. This was the extent of the prosecution case.

Few individuals could afford to hire a barrister in those days, and Eliza was forced to conduct her own defence. Naïve and inexperienced, her only recourse was to plead her innocence; if there had been something wrong with the dumplings, she argued, then that fault lay with the ingredients. Eliza had been very happy in service at the Turners' house, and had no motive to kill them. She even provided four glowing character references, testifying to her good reputation. Unfortunately these references were undermined by Mrs Turner, who accused Eliza of having an affair with an apprentice, despite the fact that she was engaged to be married.

At this point, the Recorder, Sir John Silvester, might have intervened. Sir John, or 'Black Jack', was known to be a legendary lecher, who would demonstrate leniency towards pretty young defendants if they responded to his amorous advances.[7] Eliza did not, and when the jury returned a guilty verdict, he sentenced her to hang. Eliza collapsed in a fit of hysteria and had to be carried out screaming.

The following day there was a public outcry at the severity of Eliza's sentence and the demand that it be commutated to transportation. As Eliza languished in the condemned cell at Newgate, she was visited by William Hone (1780–1842), a radical author who was convinced of her innocence.[8] Hone swiftly became obsessed with Eliza and founded a newspaper, *The Traveller,* to campaign for her release. Hone even moved out of the family home into a shabby little room opposite the prison so that he could spend more time with Eliza, and wrote a book about the case that was to become a classic of investigative journalism. Demolishing the prosecution case against Eliza, Hone suggested that Robert Turner, a mentally unstable man who had frequently threatened suicide, had tried to murder his own family and placed the blame on Eliza when the attempt went wrong.

Young, pretty and ostensibly innocent, Eliza swiftly became a *cause célèbre,* her popularity boosted by an engraving of her reading the Bible in Newgate. This image, by Robert Cruickshank, emphasized her attractive face and full breasts, turning her into 'an icon of wronged womanhood'.[9] But it was all in vain. At eight o'clock on the morning of 26 July, Eliza was escorted from her cell and down Dead Man's Walk to the Press Yard, to face a crowd of 45,000 people. She wore the white muslin gown that had been laid aside for her wedding, a white muslin cap bound with a white satin ribbon, and pale lilac boots, laced in front. When the Ordinary, Reverend Cotton, asked if she had anything to say in her last moments, Eliza paused, then said: 'Before the just and Almighty God, and by the faith of the Holy Sacrament I have taken, I am innocent of the offence with which I am charged. My innocence will be manifested in the course of the day.' Maintaining her composure, Eliza mounted the scaffold. A scarf was placed over her face, and she began to pray fervently before Oldfield, the hangman, gave the signal to open the trapdoor. She moved once, and was cut down after an hour.

When Eliza's parents claimed the body, they had to pay her execution bill of 14 shillings and 6 pence.[10] Eliza's body went on display at her parents' home in Eagle Street, Red Lion Square, as was the custom after death. According to witnesses, she lay in her coffin as if in a sweet sleep and her body was not seen to change colour within three days of her execution. As the victim of a miscarriage of justice, Eliza had been elevated to the sainthood.

The process of beatification continued with Eliza's funeral procession on 31 July. With a coffin carried by six female pall-bearers dressed in white, a mounted escort and hundreds of mourners following the coffin, it became one of the most notable funeral processions of the nineteenth century. 'Many thousands accompanied the procession, and the windows, and even the tops of the houses, as it passed were thronged with spectators. The whole proceeded in a regular manner until it reached the burying-ground of St George the Martyr. The number of persons assembled in and about the churchyard was estimated at ten thousand.'[11] Eliza's funeral was followed by riots that night, and several nights after; and an angry mob attacked the Turners' house in Chancery Lane.

Charles Dickens, who was to become a notable campaigner against capital punishment, had his own theory surrounding events at the Turner residence. Dickens argued that the apprentice had poisoned the family, after falling out with Eliza, and that he was 'more convinced of anything in my life' that Eliza was innocent.[12]

The outrage sparked by Eliza Fenning's death marked the beginning of a growing unease with public execution and even with capital punishment itself. Further misgivings emerged after the peculiarly unpleasant hanging of Charles

White outside Newgate in 1823. White, a bookseller, had torched his shop when bankruptcy threatened in order to claim the insurance. As arson constituted a capital offence, he was sentenced to hang. The night before his execution, White made several attempts to kill himself, and on the gallows he lashed out at the executioner, John Foxon, kicking him and struggling to free himself from his ropes. The hood covering White's face became loose and, seeing the chance of freedom, White hurled himself forward as the trapdoor flew open and balanced precariously on the edge. As the crowd roared its approval, White struggled with Foxon until the executioner eventually hurled him through the trapdoor, and two assistants dragged at his legs. White's face as he died would have been visible for all to see, the livid, swollen face with its contorted features and distended tongue, the eyes swollen and popping out of their cavities, the bloody froth or mucus seeping out of the mouth and nostrils.[13]

When John Foxon died in 1829, William Calcraft was appointed Executioner to the City of London at the rate of a guinea a week, plus another guinea for each execution he performed. Calcraft had previously been employed to flog juvenile offenders, but after being required to conduct a hanging at Lincoln in an emergency he had found his vocation, and was also retained at Horsemonger Gaol at the rate of another guinea a week. Described as a 'mild-mannered man of simple tastes, much given to angling in the New River', Calcraft was also fond of breeding rabbits.[14] But he hanged people like dogs and enjoyed entertaining the crowds with his antics, which included leaping onto the back of the prisoner as he fell through the trapdoor or disappearing into the pit beneath the gallows to pull on the prisoner's legs.

In 1831 Calcraft officiated at the hanging of John Bishop and Thomas Head, who went to the gallows after confessing to suffocating an Italian boy, intending to sell his cadaver to the surgeons for anatomy practice. The 'Italian' boy, who actually came from Lincolnshire, was one of three victims; the other two being another boy and an elderly woman. Bishop and Head's technique consisted of rendering their victims unconscious with laudanum and rum and then drowning them in the well behind Bishop's house, by lowering them down head first with a rope tied to their feet. The pair were nicknamed 'the Burkers' after William Burke and William Hare, the notorious murderers who scandalized Scottish society by intoxicating and smothering seventeen victims in Edinburgh in 1827–8, in order to sell the corpses for dissection at the University.

Outraged by 'the Burkers'' crime, a huge and angry crowd turned out to watch these child killers being executed, and despite the efforts of the New Police, barriers were broken down and three people trampled to death as the mob surged forward, intent on tearing Bishop and Head limb from limb.

A shocking murder and a sensational trial were guaranteed to draw a massive crowd outside Newgate. One of the largest ever assembled, numbering over 100,000 people, converged on Newgate for the hanging of James Greenacre on 2 May 1837. The newspapers, which fed a grisly fascination with murder, had dubbed this crime 'the Edgware Road Murder', and the mystery had begun months earlier, on 28 December 1836.

On that cold, blustery morning, George Bond, a bricklayer, had been walking to work when he passed Canterbury Villas, a newly completed terrace just off Edgware Road. Intrigued to see a flagstone propped up against one of the walls with a large bundle tucked away underneath it, Bond rolled away the flagstone to discover that a pool of frozen blood had congealed around the object. Bond called his gaffer and a workmate and together they unwrapped the package, which contained the headless torso of a woman, about fifty years of age. The head had been crudely severed from the trunk, with the neck having been partly sawn through and partly broken off; and the legs had been chopped off in a similar way. An inquest was held on Saturday 31 December, at the White Lion Inn, Edgware Road, when the jury returned a verdict of 'Wilful murder against some person or persons unknown' and the body was buried.

On 6 January 1837, the lock-keeper was summoned to the Ben Jonson Lock on the Regent's Canal in Stepney. One of the lock gates was blocked and would not open properly. The reason soon became evident. The lock gate was blocked by a woman's head. The headless torso was exhumed and Mr Girdwood, the local surgeon, confirmed that the head and the torso were part of the same body. But the corpse had yet to be identified, and there were no clues as to the murderer. Girdwood accordingly preserved the head in medical alcohol and retained it for further examination.

Meanwhile, the mystery surrounding the case grew deeper every day. Police enquiries met with no success until 2 February, when James Page, a labourer, was cutting osiers in Mr Tenpenny's reed bed off Coldharbour Lane, between Camberwell and Brixton. As he stepped over a ditch, Page spotted a large bundle partly immersed in the water. When he picked the bundle up, the toes of a human foot emerged from the end. Shocked, Page shouted for his workmates, and when they opened the package they found it contained a pair of human legs. When the legs were examined by Mr Girdwood, they proved to be part of the same body which had been dis-covered in the Edgware Road. The sack, which had originally belonged to a potato merchant and still had his name on it, was traced to a Mr Greenacre, of Kennington.

On 20 March, a Mr Gay of Goodge Street requested per-mission to view the remains. Mr Gay, a stockbroker, was concerned about the disappearance of his sister, Hannah Brown, who had left home on Christmas Eve and had never been seen again. As soon as he laid eyes on the preserved head, Mr Gay confirmed that it was indeed the head of the unfortunate Miss Brown. Mr Gay told the police that Hannah had announced that she was engaged and left her lodgings near Middlesex Hospital on Christmas Eve, to prepare for her impending nuptials the following Monday. Hannah's 'intended' lived in Camberwell, and his name was James Greenacre.

Marylebone Police Office immediately issued a warrant for Greenacre's arrest, and on 24 March 1837, Inspector Feltham and a police constable from L division raided Greenacre's small house at St Alban's Place, Kennington Road, where they found Greenacre in bed with his common-law wife, Sarah Gale. At first Greenacre denied all knowledge of Hannah Brown but then admitted that he had been planning to marry her, and that she had disappeared the night before the wedding. Once the couple had got dressed, Greenacre commented that the police were lucky to have come that night, since they were sailing for America in the morning. The number of trunks and suitcases, packed and labelled, seemed to bear this out. But an examination of the contents revealed important evidence. Many of the items in the trunks belonged to Hannah Brown; but alongside these, the police discovered the remains of an old cotton dress that exactly matched the pieces of fabric the body had been wrapped in when it was first discovered off Edgware Road.

On 10 April 1837 Greenacre and Gale went on trial at the Old Bailey. The courtroom was packed. Greenacre was charged with wilful murder while Gale was accused of being an accessory after the fact, consorting, aiding and assisting her fellow prisoner. In the course of the proceedings, Greenacre was unmasked as a bigamist who had been married at least four times. His victims had been wealthy older women and he had helped himself to their fortunes, a simple task in the days before the Married Women's Property Act of 1839.

In his desire to absolve Sarah Gale of all blame for the murder, Greenacre claimed that, during a quarrel, Hannah had fallen off her chair and died as a result of hitting her head on the floor. Rather than try to explain her accidental death, Greenacre admitted that he had dismembered the corpse and disposed of the body. Although Greenacre's account of events was sketchy, it appeared that he had travelled by omnibus from Camberwell to Mile End carrying Hannah's head in his lap, wrapped in a cotton handkerchief. Returning home, he took the legs down to the reed bed at five o'clock the following morning, and finally set out to dispose of the torso. It was too heavy to carry, so he placed it on a carrier's cart and walked alongside it until they reached Elephant and Castle. When a passer-by asked what was in the sack, Greenacre became nervous, and completed the journey with his grisly bundle by cab to Edgware Road.

Greenacre's defence that Hannah had died accidentally was smashed to pieces by the prosecution. It was pointed out that Hannah had been killed by a blow to the head with a stick, and that the force of the blow had been so severe that it had put her eye out. Greenacre then admitted that he had accidentally swung round with a silk-weaving roller, which had hit her. It took the jury just fifteen minutes to reach a guilty verdict. Greenacre was sentenced to death, while Sarah Gale was ordered to be transported for the rest of her natural life.[15]

The sensational details of Greenacre's crime guaranteed the massive crowd at Newgate, which gathered the night before his execution. In addition to the usual hanging-fair attractions of pies and prostitutes, rooms with a view of the gallows went on hire for £12 a time. A boy was almost crushed to death, and only survived because he was snatched up and passed over the heads of the crowd.[16]

Greenacre protested his innocence to the end. In a letter to his children, he warned them to profit by his example and never to panic if they were present at fatal accidents, which, it seemed, ran in the family, such as the incident when their uncle had apparently killed their grandmother, and 'shot off your Aunt Mary's hand!' Greenacre brusquely brushed off the Ordinary who wanted to pray with him before he died, but when it came to mounting the scaffold, 'he was totally unmanned'; his bravado had deserted him and, unable to speak, he had to be supported up the steps, otherwise he would have fallen over.[17] As he stumbled towards the gallows, Greenacre's appearance was greeted with a storm of hisses and boos, and cheers that could be heard several streets away as he dropped to his death. The *Weekly Chronicle* for 7 May 1837 described the strange, celebratory spectacle thus:

> As the body hung quivering in mortal agonies, the eyes of the assembled thousands were riveted upon the swaying corpse with a kind of satisfaction . . . the crowd seemed as if they never could satisfy themselves with gazing at the hanging murderer. The women were, if possible, more ruthless than the men.[18]

While the crowds seemed to enjoy such outrageous spectacles as never before, opposition to public executions was growing, fuelled by reformers and polemicists. In 1840, Charles Dickens invited his friend William Thackeray to witness the hanging of François Courvoisier outside Newgate. Dickens was then a journalist, and saw Thackeray, a barrister as well as a fellow writer, as a possible recruit to the abolitionist cause. Courvoisier had been sentenced to death for killing his master, Lord William Russell, motivated apparently by robbery.

The gallows might have been moved from Tyburn to Newgate but the crowd had not changed. Around 600 people crammed into the narrow street between the gaol and St Sepulchre's. Entire families had arrived, with picnic hampers, for a day out, eager to spot the celebrities, the actresses, statesmen and aristocrats who had paid upwards of £10 for a good spot on a balcony or at a window. Among the day-trippers, drunks and prostitutes, Dickens did not see 'one token in all the immense crowd of any one emotion suitable to the occasion; nothing but ribaldry, levity, drunkenness and flaunting vice in fifty other shapes'.[19]

As Courvoisier mounted the gallows, Thackeray observed that the condemned man 'turned his head here and there and looked about him for a while with a wild, imploring look. His mouth was contracted into a sort of pitiful smile.' The writer found himself unable to forget the troubling scene:

> For the last fourteen days, so salutary has the impression of this butchery been upon me, I have had the man's face continually before my eyes; I can see Mr Ketch [William Calcraft] at this moment, with an easy air, taking his rope from his pocket; I feel myself shamed and degraded at the brutal curiosity that took me to that brutal sight ... I have been abetting an act of frightful wickedness and violence and I pray that it may soon be out of the power of any man in England to witness such a hideous and degrading sight.[20]

It was to be another eighteen years before Thackeray's prayers were answered and capital punishment was hidden from the vulgar gaze, locked away behind the walls of Newgate in an execution shed.

Meanwhile, the gallows failed to act as a deterrent to London's criminals. As the capital was shaken by a succession of gruesome murders, it was becoming evident that the police required a dedicated team of professional detectives to run the perpetrators to ground. Whilst surviving members of the Bow

Street Runners had acted in this capacity up until 1839, taking on cases for anyone who would pay their expenses, the 'New Police' had no organized criminal investigation department. The need for such a body of men was thrown starkly into focus by the case of Daniel Good in April 1842.

On 11 April 1842, PC William Gardner was called to investigate the theft of a pair of trousers from a pawnbroker's shop in Wandsworth High Street. The suspect was Daniel Good, who worked as a coachman in Roehampton. PC Gardner went to Good's employer's house, arrested him, and began a thorough search of the premises. When they reached the stables, Good threw himself against the stable door and refused to let anyone inside. A neighbour was summoned to stand guard over Good, while PC Gardner searched the stable. Lifting his lantern, PC Gardner saw what appeared to be a plucked goose stashed behind a bale of hay. And then, with an exclamation of 'My God!' he realized that it was the body of a woman.

Meanwhile, Good seized his opportunity, locking the policeman and the neighbour in the stable and making his escape. It was fifteen minutes before they were released, and the police could do no more than track Good's footprints across the field towards Putney. After this, the trail went cold.

A surgeon's assistant was summoned who confirmed that the body was that of a pregnant woman in her mid-twenties, and that she had been dismembered with a sharp saw. A horrible smell drew them to the tack room, where they found the charred remains of her head and limbs, and an axe and saw stained with blood. Further enquiries revealed that the body was that of Jane Jones, Good's estranged wife. Good had a reputation as a ladies' man who had enjoyed a string of affairs. He was currently engaged to a young woman named Susan Butcher who lived in Woolwich. It was four hours or so before Good's details were circulated.

Over the next few days, nine divisions of the Metropolitan Police became involved in the chase for Daniel Good. In the days before telephones, the Metropolitan Police operated a system of 'route papers' which consisted of officers from neighbouring divisions meeting at pre-arranged points and exchanging messages and papers for other parts of London. Good always seemed to be a day or so ahead of the pursuing police, and this was reported in great detail by a critical press. Good was at large after having been arrested; there was a hue and cry all over the country and the very people who had been vociferous in opposing the establishment of the police were now accusing them of inefficiency. And yet, despite the defective communication system of the time, the police did their best.

D Division, for instance, learnt that Good had a ten-year-old son who lived with his aunt, Molly Good, off Manchester Square, but when they called in the afternoon, their suspect had left an hour or so earlier. A cab driver came forward to say that he had driven Good to Manchester Square and commented on his fare's nervousness and pallor. Good had merely retorted that he was recovering from a heavy drinking session the night before. It later emerged that Good returned to his wife's lodgings, told her landlady that Jane had been offered a job in Roehampton, and sold her mangle and bedding. Some of her clothes, which she had worn on the day of her murder, he gave to his fiancée, Susan Butcher.

Inspector Nicholas Pearce, assisted by Sergeant Stephen Thornton, both of whom were later to be among the original select band of six officers appointed for detective duties, took up the case and followed Good's trail from Spitalfields to Deptford, and then to Bromley where they could find no other clues. Two weeks later, Good was traced to Tonbridge where he was working as a bricklayer's labourer. One of his work mates, Thomas Rose, was a former police officer who recognized him and told the local police. Good was arrested and denied his identity, until it was observed that he had combed his hair over the bald spot which might have helped distinguish him.

Eventually, Good admitted his identity, but then claimed that his estranged wife had killed herself and a friend had recommended that he conceal the body. However, medical evidence quite clearly demonstrated that Jane Good had not cut her own throat. Good protested his innocence to the end, although he did break down in the dock when his own son entered the witness box to testify against him. Good was found guilty of murder and was hanged at Newgate on 23 May 1842, unaware that he had unwittingly contributed to the Metropolitan Police improving their crime-fighting performance by introducing specialist detectives.

A few days after Good's execution it was announced that a Criminal Investigation Department consisting of two inspectors and six sergeants would be attached to Scotland Yard for the investigation of crimes committed in the Metropolitan area. At first, because these officers were not specialists, the CID was not particularly successful. However, as public servants rather than private detectives, the CID team could investigate crimes straight away, rather than waiting for their expenses to be guaranteed.[21] Although slow to gather momentum, the formation of such a team was to be vindicated seven years later in the case of 'the Bermondsey Horror', when new methods secured the arrest and conviction of Frederick and Maria Manning.

Born Maria de Roux in 1821, Maria Manning was a handsome, raven-haired but somewhat plump young woman who arrived in London in 1846, as maid to Lady Blantyre, daughter of the Duchess of Sutherland. Shallow and materialistic, Maria was enraptured by her glamorous new surroundings and swiftly came to feel at home among the trappings of wealth. So much so that soon being a lady's maid was not enough for her. Maria wanted to be a lady herself. For this, she required a rich husband, and at first Patrick O'Connor, a customs officer at London docks, seemed to fit the bill. True, O'Connor was fifty years old and with a weakness for drink, but he also had substantial savings.

However, O'Connor had competition in the form of Frederick Manning, a railway guard on the Great Western. Frederick was poor, but handsome, and he told Maria that he expected to inherit a small fortune. Maria and Frederick were married at St James's, Piccadilly, a fashionable West End church, in May 1847, and the couple moved to a house in Minerva Place, Bermondsey. Within weeks, Maria's dreams of a life of leisure were dashed. The money was running out, and she discovered that Frederick had been lying about his promised inheritance. After an abortive attempt at running a pub in Taunton, the pair returned to London and Maria picked up her relationship with O'Connor, visiting his lodgings in the Mile End Road. Frederick, still smitten with Maria, condoned the affair, as he realized that the wealthy O'Connor represented the solution to all their problems.

On the evening of 7 August 1849, the Mannings invited O'Connor to dine at Minerva Place. O'Connor duly arrived, with some misgivings; he was a hypochondriac and the cholera outbreak in Bermondsey made him reluctant to visit. But Maria plied her lover with brandy, assuring him that the spirit provided great protection against infection. Under the influence of drink, O'Connor was persuaded to sign away a number of railway shares to the couple. The Mannings might have achieved more had it not been for the presence of a Mr Walsh, visiting their lodger. As it was, Frederick Manning escorted O'Connor safely home. Flushed with excitement, Maria realized that the dream was within her grasp. The following day, she invited O'Connor round again, teasing him with the suggestion that they would have dinner *à deux*. On the way home, she purchased some quicklime and a shovel, and dug a grave under the kitchen floor.

That night, when O'Connor arrived at Minerva Place, Maria suggested that he might like to smarten himself up, as the lodger was expecting his sister to call. She led him down to the basement kitchen, and as he bent over the sink, reached up and stretched her arm affectionately around his neck. As O'Connor turned to reciprocate, she shot him in the head with a pistol. But the wound was not fatal. As Frederick Manning came downstairs, he found O'Connor collapsed on the floor, writhing in agony. Manning battered him to death with a ripping chisel, justifying his actions later on with the laconic remark that 'I never really liked him.' The couple buried the body under the kitchen floor and covered it with quicklime.

The following evening, two of O'Connor's friends arrived at the Mannings' home. They knew that he had been invited for dinner there, and had become concerned when he did not arrive at work the following day. Maria told them that although O'Connor had dined with them on 7 August, he had never arrived for dinner the following evening. Rattled by these visitors, who Maria strongly suspected were detectives, the couple argued before agreeing to run away. Next morning, Maria sent Frederick off to find a furniture dealer so that they could sell off their possessions, while she cleaned up the murder scene. As soon as Frederick had left the house, Maria invited a twelve-year-old match seller in from the street and offered him five pennies to wash the kitchen down. The lad readily agreed, and Maria hurried out to O'Connor's lodgings, where she blagged her way into his room, and stole cash, two gold watches and more railway shares. By the time Frederick returned home, Maria was in a cab to King's Cross Station and the match seller had absconded with an egg, a razor, a purse and a pair of Maria's stockings. Frederick took one look at the house, panicked, and fled to Jersey.

By this time, O'Connor's friends had reported him missing, and shared their suspicions about the Mannings. When the police arrived at Minerva Place, one officer noticed that the mortar between two of the flagstones in the kitchen was still damp. The flagstones were raised and O'Connor's battered body was found lying underneath. This was clearly a case for Scotland Yard. Superintendent Hayes launched a manhunt for the couple, and the cabbie who had driven Maria to King's Cross came forward. When Hayes discovered that Maria had bought a ticket for Edinburgh he telegraphed his Scottish colleagues only to be told that Maria had already been arrested. She had been caught trying to sell the railway shares to a firm of stockbrokers, who realized that the shares had been stolen and were suspicious of her French accent. Maria was brought back to London and charged with murder. Frederick was arrested a week later in Jersey, where he had been recognized by an acquaintance who had read about the murder in the papers.

When the Mannings went on trial at the Old Bailey on 25 October 1849, they both attempted to blame each other for the crime. It took the jury just forty-five minutes to pronounce them guilty, at which point Maria lost the icy composure which she had displayed throughout the trial. Picking up the bundles of herbs which were traditionally strewn around the courtroom to ward off gaol fever, she threw them at the judge, screaming, 'You have treated me like a wild beast of the forest!' and continued to rant and rave as the judge sentenced her to death. Maria was placed on suicide watch, with three female warders in her cell at all times. Despite this, she attempted to strangle herself and slashed her windpipe with her own fingernails.[22]

The night before the Mannings' execution, a crowd began

to gather outside Horsemonger Gaol. Charles Dickens arrived at midnight, and his blood ran cold when he heard 'the shrillness of the cries and howls' raised by the boys and girls who had already found good vantage points. As the night went on, there was screeching and laughing, and a parody of a minstrel song in which *'Mrs Manning!'* had been substituted for *'Oh Susannah!'*

By dawn the crowd numbered 50,000, with 1,000 police officers struggling to maintain order. Dickens described the scene as an audience of thieves, prostitutes and vagabonds, delighting in offensive behaviour of every kind, jostling, fighting and whooping with indecent delight when fainting women were dragged out of the crowd by the police with their dresses disordered.

Inside the gaol, Maria struggled to maintain her composure. Taken to the chapel for the final sacraments, she nearly fainted as her arms and legs were being tied up. Maria only revived when Calcraft the hangman offered a slug of his brandy. Holding her nerve, Maria produced a black silk handkerchief for a blindfold, and a black lace veil to cover her face. Leaving the chapel by Dead Man's Walk, she walked over what was to be her own grave, just as she had walked over the grave of her victim. As Maria stepped out boldly towards her doom, Frederick Manning was scarcely capable of tottering to the scaffold.

Calcraft enjoyed his work that morning, with an approach characterized by 'unseemly briskness, jokes, oaths, and brandy'. Frederick Manning was hanged first, and he died instantly. Maria took longer to die; according to Dickens, she kicked and struggled for some minutes. Dickens was haunted, for years afterwards, by the vision of those two dangling forms: 'The man's limp, loose suit of clothes as if the man had gone out of them; the woman's fine shape, so elaborately corseted and artfully dressed, that it was unchanged in its trim appearance as it slowly swung from side to side.'[23] Maria had chosen to wear a gown of black satin, the most fashionable material of the time, for her execution. Inevitably, this fabric was tainted by association, and Maria's epitaph became 'the woman who murdered black satin'.

Dickens immortalized Maria as the murderous French maid Hortense in *Bleak House,* with her 'flashing eyes' and 'tigress mouth'; on a practical level, the author's distaste for the scenes at the Mannings' execution inspired him to write to *The Times* calling for an end to public executions. *The Thunderer* responded with an editorial stating that 'the mystery of private executions would be intolerable', as the public needed to see that murderers really had been hanged. In reply, Dickens suggested that a special 'witness jury' of twenty-four people drawn from all backgrounds should be summoned to attend private executions.[24]

Popular opposition to public hangings was gathering momentum. In 1840 a radical MP, William Ewart, had unsuccessfully attempted to get the death penalty abolished; a secondary campaign to abolish public executions gained widespread support from MPs and writers. A House of Commons Select Committee in 1856 recommended that all executions take place in private, but this motion was thrown out by the House of Lords. However, further support for private executions developed after appalling scenes at the hanging of William Bousfield in 1856.

Facing financial ruin, Bousfield had murdered his wife, two daughters aged six and four and his baby in a fit of despair before giving himself up to the police. The night before his execution, Bousfield had attempted to kill himself by throwing himself in the fire in his cell. Discovered in time, Bousfield had to be carried to the scaffold, wrapped in bandages.[25]

The hangman, William Calcraft, mounted the scaffold nervously. An attractive man during his youth, he had become scowling and surly, with shabby black attire and unruly hair. Over the years Calcraft had developed a reputation for incompetence, having been described in one newspaper as 'the public strangler', and on this occasion he was worse than usual. After hanging several Irish republicans he had received death threats, and was terrified of being shot as he stood on the gallows. Calcraft therefore drew the bolt swiftly to release the trapdoor and rushed back into Newgate before he could be picked off by a sniper's bullet.

Bousfield plunged through the trapdoor immediately – but then, to the utter astonishment of the crowd, drew himself up again and put his feet against the sides of the drop. A warden pushed him off the platform, but once again Bousfield scrambled back up. Eventually, after four attempts, Calcraft reappeared and leapt into the dark pit beneath the scaffold, where he dragged on the prisoner's legs until he died.

Such appalling scenes eventually led credence to the abolition of public executions, and in 1864 a Royal Commission on Capital Punishment recommended that in future all executions should be carried out inside a prison, 'under such regulations as might be considered necessary to prevent abuses, and to satisfy the public that the law has been complied with'.[26] A Bill to abolish public executions received its first reading in March 1866 and became law in the summer of 1868.

The last public execution to take place at Newgate was that of Michael Barrett on 26 May 1868. Barrett was a twenty-seven-year-old Irish Republican or 'Fenian' who had blown up Clerkenwell House of Detention in an effort to free some of his comrades, incarcerated there following an armed robbery. The massive explosion brought down the prison wall and blew up a terrace of houses nearby, killing six people and injuring over fifty, and inciting public outrage against the Irish. Karl Marx, who was living in London at the time, rightly predicted that the London working class, who had previously been sympathetic towards the Irish nationalists, 'will be made wild and driven into the arms of a reactionary government. One cannot expect the London proletarians to allow themselves to be blown up in honour of Fenian emissaries.'[27]

Fuelled by hatred, and intrigued by rumours of the death threats against William Calcraft, a massive crowd turned out to watch Barrett's execution. To the evident satisfaction of the crowd, Michael Barrett 'died hard'. The *Daily Telegraph* and *Daily News* referred to his 'protruding tongue and swollen distorted features discernible under their thin white cotton covering, as if they were part of some hideous masquerading'.[28] When he was taken down from the scaffold his red hair and beard had, it was said, turned black.

The majority would have been unaware that this was the last public execution they would ever see. Following the new legislation, a gallows shed was built in the Press Yard, adjacent to the chapel. Prisoners arrived from the condemned cells through Dead Man's Walk. It was first used on 8 September 1868, when Alexander Mackay, an eighteen-year-old waiter in a coffee house, was hanged for murdering his employer's wife.

Public executions had been a familiar feature of London life for centuries; generations of Londoners had witnessed at least one hanging and learned the sordid details of many more. Yet hanging had failed to act as an effective deterrent. It would remain to be seen whether hiding executions away would increase the mystique of the procedure. In the meantime, London's fascination with brutal murder continued, as the city became the setting for the crime of the century: the Whitechapel Murders, and the mysterious killer commonly referred to as 'Jack the Ripper'.

10

FROM HELL!

A Murder Guide to Victorian London

Murder, the unique crime, exercised a powerful fascination upon the Victorian imagination, from the courtroom to the gallows. The publishing industry responded to the demand at every level, from court reports in *The Times* to the lurid drawings in the *Illustrated Police News*, an early tabloid. The names of certain cases resonate to this day, while others are forgotten. The Whitechapel murders sent a collective shudder throughout the metropolis and across the globe, and yet Harriet Lane and Kate Webster are little more than faded names from yellowed press cuttings. When these sources had been exhausted, thrill-seekers could turn to the 'sensation novels', mystery stories published in serial form, with each episode leaving readers desperate for more. Wilkie Collins (1824–89) was the greatest exponent of this genre. *The Moonstone* (1868), conceived in a fog of opium and brandy, proved such a runaway success that readers were queuing outside the publisher's offices in

Wellington Street for each new instalment. Between episodes, Collins' legions of fans could follow the real-life cases, which I revisit now, in this tour around some of the most notorious murder cases from Victorian London.

The murder of Harriet Lane in 1875 was one of the most lurid cases of the time, remarkable even by Victorian standards for its sheer gruesomeness. By the time it reached the Old Bailey, the case contained many of the key elements of the sensation novel, including a mutilated corpse, a chorus girl and a cigar-chomping villain.

The story began one Saturday night in September 1875, as a young man was spotted chasing a four-wheeler as it bowled along Whitechapel Road. 'Stop! Police!' he was shouting, to anyone who would listen. As his cries fell upon deaf ears, the young man went on running, chasing the cab over London Bridge as it headed towards Southwark. It was only when the vehicle stopped near the Hen and Chickens public house on Borough High Street, that the youth, by the name of Albert Stokes, managed to flag down two police officers. He begged them to search the vehicle. Despite outraged protests from the passengers, a bearded middle-aged man and an attractive young woman, police constables 48 and 290 wrenched open the door of cab number 8505 and promptly turned away vomiting, met by an overwhelming stench.

The cab was ordered to Southwark police station, where it was found to contain two parcels wrapped in canvas. The smallest parcel contained the decomposed trunk of a woman, while the second, which was larger, contained her head, arms and legs. The victim's auburn hair, with a distinctive fringe or 'bang' was partially burnt off and her eyes had decomposed The remains were taken to St Saviour's mortuary, and the male passenger, whose name was Henry Wainwright, was arrested along with his companion, Alice Day, a chorus girl.

Alice Day, who barely knew Henry Wainwright, was released without charge. But Wainwright, a brash East End entrepreneur, aged forty-three, was charged with murder.[1]

Once he had recovered his composure, young Albert Stokes told police that he had been passing through the Whitechapel Road when Alice Day had accosted him and asked him to help her move some parcels from a warehouse in Vine Court, just off Whitechapel Road. Wainwright, Stokes' former employer, had then appeared in a four-wheeler and asked the driver to wait while he went to fetch some luggage. When he went into the warehouse, Stokes was horrified to see two bloodstained bundles standing in the corner. From one of the bundles protruded a mutilated hand. The stench was appalling, and at first Stokes refused to help, but Wainwright offered him an impressive tip, so Stokes helped Wainwright load the bundles into his cab and resolved to chase after it and inform the police.

A post mortem conducted the following day showed that the corpse was that of a woman of about twenty-four, who had been dead for around one year. The body had been buried in a shallow grave, probably under a wall or floor. Although internal decomposition had taken place, the corpse had been preserved by the action of the quicklime that had been liberally sprinkled all over it. The murderer had failed to realize that while dry quicklime will destroy, wet quicklime preserves. The moisture in the soil had formed a chemical reaction with the quicklime that had served to embalm the corpse so that the cause of death was still immediately evident. The victim had been shot in the head, and her throat had been slashed. The corpse had then been disinterred and an attempt had been made to burn it. When this had ended in failure, it had been dismembered, presumably with a view to dumping the remains.

Next day, Chief Inspector James McDonald of H Division

led the search of Wainwright's warehouse. The police found a new spade and a hatchet, alongside a broken silk umbrella and a velvet hair band. Led by the smell of decomposition to a space beneath the floorboards, they discovered a jet button, a kneecap, and a human tooth.[2]

In an effort to identify the corpse, the remains went on display in a glass-topped coffin at the Southwark dead house, and within days a grieving family came forward to claim it. A Mr Lane approached the police saying that he had not seen his daughter Harriet, a milliner, for over a year. Relations had become strained when Harriet had become the mistress of a married man in 1872, and proceeded to bear him two children. When the relationship faltered, Harriet had begun drinking heavily, and complaining that her lover never gave her enough money to feed and clothe the children. Subsequently, Mr Lane received a letter saying that Harriet had married another man, her lover's brother, and fled abroad, and that her father must on no account come looking for her. Desperate to find her, Harriet's family hired a private detective, but Harriet had vanished without a trace.

Now the sensational newspaper coverage of the case had brought them forward, and they endured the horrific ordeal of identifying Harriet's body. When the chief inspector asked Mr Lane the name of Harriet's erstwhile lover, the father of her children, he could have predicted the response. 'Wainwright,' said Mr Lane, bitterly. 'Henry Wainwright.'

When Henry Wainwright went on trial for Harriet's murder at the Old Bailey, it emerged that by 1874 Wainwright had tired of Harriet, having become exasperated by her demands for money. Witnesses testified to the fact that Wainwright was often overheard saying that he wanted rid of Harriet. He even attempted to palm her off on his brother, Thomas, who went on trial alongside him, but this proved unsuccessful. At some point that year, Harriet was murdered and buried in Wainwright's warehouse. After constant complaints from the neighbours about the smell of his drains, Wainwright had scattered chloride of lime over the corpse. But instead of destroying the body, this substance had effectively embalmed it. A year later, Wainwright's business collapsed and he was forced to give up the warehouse and move to cheaper premises across the river in Borough High Street. Harriet's body stank so badly that he had to take her with him.[3]

Sentenced to death, Wainwright showed no remorse. He spent his last night on earth smoking cigars and boasting to the Newgate turnkeys about his sexual exploits. Around 100

The Illustrated Police News *showing the unrepentant Henry Wainwright sneering from the gallows.* 'You curs! Come to see a man die, have you!'

people were invited to witness his execution inside Newgate Gaol, and when he saw them, Wainwright turned on the spectators and sneered: 'You curs! Come to see a man die, have you!'[4] The scene, showing Wainwright unrepentant on the scaffold as the hangman prepared to put the hood over his head, was a front page special in the *Illustrated Police News*.

Lurid as it was, this publication and others like it did much to enhance the reputation of the police. While the traditional distrust for authority lingered in the Londoner's character, the detection and arrest of killers such as Wainwright marked the beginnings of tolerance, and even respect. There was some comfort to be derived from the knowledge that, if one were murdered in one's bed, then certain dour-faced men in bowler hats would almost certainly catch the murderer. The 'men from the Yard' or 'the detective force' as the Criminal Intelligence Department was originally known, had become a source of fascination. As the century progressed, Scotland Yard had developed from a small tract of land behind Whitehall to an ugly but imposing fortress built of granite quarried by the convicts at Dartmoor. The Yard looked like a prison but was the heart of the British police system, 'the centre of a mighty spider's web, which widens in a series of rings that are bound together in an eccentric and (often to the criminal) unexpected fashion, and extend to the utmost limit of the London district' and beyond.[5] Scotland Yard had begun to develop its own mystique.

In fiction, police detectives such as Dickens' Inspector Bucket and Wilkie Collins' Sergeant Cuff were portrayed as intelligent, tenacious men of the highest integrity. Dickens in particular had been highly impressed by the detective squad from Scotland Yard, 'forever on the watch, with their wits stretched to the utmost,' playing their games of chess with live pieces.[6] The world's pre-eminent fictional detective made his debut in 1887, when Arthur Conan Doyle published *A Study in Scarlet*. From his rooms at 221b Baker Street, the formidable investigator solved intricate mysteries and developed into a complex and compelling creation, with his first-class mind, low boredom threshold and recreational drug habit. The success of Sherlock Holmes demonstrated the 'lure of the detective' and the continuing mystique of 'the greatest hunter of all, the hunter of men'.[7] Holmes was, however, a fictional creation, and his cases, with their intriguing titles such as 'The Speckled Band' and 'The Engineer's Thumb', were beautifully constructed intellectual puzzles, far removed from the grim reality of late Victorian London.

Maria Manning, who featured in an earlier chapter, was the most notorious female murderer of the Victorian period, but by no means the only one. Although only 10 to 15 per cent of murders are committed by women, the majority of which constitute self-defence against an abusive partner,[8] Victorian London nevertheless produced some chilling examples of female killers. Three sensational cases of female murderers caught the public imagination during this period. The first took place in the unlikely environs of Park Lane in April 1872, at the residence of Madame Riel, a retired actress and the mistress of Lord Lucan, the general who had ordered the charge of the Light Brigade during the Crimean War. On the morning of 8 April 1872, Madame Riel's body was discovered in the pantry. She had been strangled, and the rope was still around her neck, with a deep indention beneath the ear where the slipknot had been tightened.

Suspicion immediately fell upon the Belgian cook, Marguerite Dixblanc, who been overheard quarrelling with her employer the previous day. Madame Riel had dismissed Dixblanc with just a week's wages and in return it appeared that Dixblanc, a powerfully built veteran of the Paris commune, had rifled the safe and fled to France. Dixblanc was arrested, extradited and sentenced to death, but when her former colleagues testified to Madame Riel's appalling treatment of her, Dixblanc was pardoned and given a custodial sentence. While the crime stoked the fears of the nervous middle classes that docile domestics might become cold-blooded murderers, Dixblanc was exonerated in the curious chauvinism of the times, on the grounds that her victim was also a 'foreigner' and a courtesan at that.[9]

Dixblanc's crime pales into insignificance compared with the exploits of another homicidal servant, Kate Webster. In 1879, Webster was hired by the elderly Julia Thomas, a wealthy widow of 2 Vine Cottages, Park Road, Richmond, but Mrs Thomas soon regretted her decision. On more than one occasion, Mrs Thomas confided to her friends that she found the high and mighty Miss Webster downright frightening, particularly during her drunken rages. Webster, meanwhile, had found an admirer in the form of John Church, the proprietor of the Rising Sun public house. Then the neighbours noted the absence of Mrs Thomas, and, more alarmingly, the sight of Webster, dressed in her mistress's gowns, striding boldly into a local shop and attempting to sell off Mrs Thomas's jewellery.

The following day, Webster invited Church round to Vine Cottages to buy the furniture. He stayed the night. The neighbours went to the police with their suspicions and the next day Vine Cottages was raided. An axe and fragments of charred bones were discovered in the kitchen. The copper, which would normally have been used to wash laundry, contained a scummy ring of fat. Mrs Thomas was nowhere to be seen, but within days a human foot was washed up in Twickenham, and a torso, believed to be that of the employer, was found in a hatbox at Barnes. Kate Webster had ensured her place in the murderers' hall of fame by attacking her mistress with the axe, hacking the corpse to pieces, and boiling down the remains in the copper, removing the bones. Most grisly of all was the fate of the fat. Webster had scooped the fat from the copper and sold it around the neighbourhood as dripping. One street urchin even claimed Webster had offered him a bowl of dripping as an act of charity.

Webster, who had fled home to Ireland, was arrested, tried and hanged by William Marwood, Calcraft's successor, at Wandsworth.[10] In a bizarre footnote, in 2010 Julia Thomas's skull was unearthed in the garden of the broadcaster and naturalist Sir David Attenborough. A team of builders discovered the skull when they were excavating foundations for an extension, at the spot where the Rising Sun once stood. In July 2011, the West London coroner Alison Thompson formally identified the skull as belonging to Julia Thomas and recorded a verdict of unlawful killing.[11]

Kate Webster – the killer servant who murdered her mistress and boiled up the body on the stove.

Horror rather than sympathy attended the conviction of Kate Webster. While the murder served as a terrifying reminder to all potential employers to check the references of domestic staff, the famous waxwork museum Madame Tussaud's was swift to exploit its potential. A disturbing wax effigy of Kate Webster, with minatory eyes, went on display in the 'Chamber of Horrors', which had been a crowd-pleasing feature of the museum since the 1840s.

The third instance of 'woman beware woman' is the most distressing of all. The abiding image of this case consists of one dark, unsettling vignette. It was an autumn night in October 1890, as Mary Pearcey steered a heavy black perambulator through the chilly streets of Camden Town, along Ivor Street, up to Chalk Farm, and then west to Maida Vale. A young woman wheeling a pram should be one of the most familiar and reassuring sights in the world, but something about this picture was unsettling. The big black perambulator with its looming hood was so heavy that she could scarcely push it uphill. The coachwork was collapsing under the weight of its sinister burden.

The perambulator did indeed hold a baby, eight-month-old Phoebe Hogg. But in addition it contained the baby's mother, a woman of thirty-one, also named Phoebe. Both were dead. The mother had been battered with a poker, and her throat cut so violently that the head was almost severed from the neck. The baby had been smothered by her own mother's corpse. Pearcey dumped the mother's body at Crossfield Road, and the baby at Cock and Hoop Field. She left the blood-stained pram at Hamilton Terrace, and went home to Ivor Street, to the house paid for by her lover, Charles Crichton. Although Crichton paid the rent, Pearcey also received visits from another long-time lover, Thomas Hogg, a furniture remover from Haverstock Hill. A year previously Hogg had married Phoebe, but continued to see Pearcey, and even had his own key. This arrangement proved satisfactory at first, but soon Pearcey became resentful, especially once Phoebe had given birth to a daughter and Hogg began paying more attention to his new family. One afternoon in October, Pearcey invited Phoebe and her daughter round to tea, attacked the mother with a poker, slit her throat and piled her into the pram.

A day later, the police came for Pearcey. She did not resist arrest, but instead sat at the piano in her bloodstained clothes, humming to herself and ignoring their questions. Finally, when one officer asked why there were bloodstains all over the walls, Pearcey replied, over and over again, that she had been 'killing mice, killing mice, killing mice!' Pearcey, who suffered from epilepsy and depression, was clearly mentally ill, but public outrage at the murder of baby Phoebe ensured that she was bound for the gallows.

During her custody, Pearcey waited every day for Hogg to visit her, convinced that now Phoebe was gone they could be together. The fact that Hogg would never forgive her for murdering his baby daughter never seemed to occur to her. Three hundred people gathered outside Newgate Gaol when Pearcey was executed on 23 December and cheers went up when the black flag was raised. Pearcey was subsequently demonized, and there was even lurid speculation to the effect that she had been 'Jill the Ripper', perpetrator of the Whitechapel murders.[12]

There have always been unsolved murders in London. The perpetrator of 'the Waterloo Bridge Mystery', when a carpet-bag containing a woman's torso was found floating down the Thames in 1857, escaped detection.[13] The deaths of so many prostitutes went unreported that it was impossible to calculate how many of these unfortunate women had not committed suicide but become the victims of a serial killer. They were nobody's daughter, nobody's wife. But it is the Whitechapel

Murders, perpetrated by a killer referring to himself as 'Jack the Ripper', which remain the greatest series of unsolved murders in London's history. The case contained many of the elements of the sensation novel, including the distinctive locale, the wretched female victims and the perception of the murderer as a sinister foreign gentleman.

When Whitechapel police were called out to a body on the morning of 31 August 1888, they had no conception of the horrors to come. Domestic tragedies and attacks on prostitutes were a sadly familiar part of 'the job', and there was no reason to believe that this case would be any different. The police had been summoned after a driver from Pickford's removals spotted a woman's body lying in Buck's Row, just off Whitechapel Road, yards from the London Hospital. Assuming that she was either dead drunk or dead, the driver and his mate had walked over to investigate, only to discover that the victim's throat had been cut, almost severing the head from the body. At the mortuary, one officer, an Inspector Spratley, casually turned up the victim's clothes and saw that the lower part of her abdomen had been ripped open. The injuries were 'the work of a madman' according to one officer, while the police surgeon, Dr Ralph Llewellyn, had never seen a more horrible case. 'She was ripped open just as you see a dead calf at a butcher's shop. The murder was done by someone very handy with the knife.'[14]

After the victim had been identified as Mary Ann Nicholls, the police were left with no idea as to a motive. With the local division out of its depth, Chief Inspector Frederick Abbeline, who had extensive experience of Whitechapel, was seconded from Scotland Yard to head up the case.

A week later, on 8 September, the corpse of Annie Chapman was found in a passage leading to a lodging house at 29 Hanbury Street, Spitalfields. Annie's body was discovered at six o'clock in the morning by a fellow lodger, John Davies, who lived on the top floor. He called across to some workmen, saying that a woman had clearly been murdered. 'Her clothes were thrown back, but her face was visible,' said James Kent, another eyewitness. 'Her apron seemed to be thrown back over her clothes ... it seemed as if her inside had been pulled from her, and thrown at her. It was lying over her left shoulder.'[15]

At this point, rumours began to circulate to the effect that John Pizer, a local tradesman, was the murderer. This was based on a rumour that a man in a leather apron, carrying a knife, had been seen at both crime scenes, and Pizer fitted this description. As a Jew, Pizer was also a convenient scapegoat for locals eager to pin the killings on a 'foreigner'. Pizer was arrested but released once he had satisfied the police that he had no connection with the killings.

On 27 September 1888, the Central News Agency received a letter that was subsequently forwarded to the Metropolitan Police. 'Dear Boss,' the letter began, 'I am down on whores and I shant quit ripping them till I do get buckled ... ' The letter was signed 'Jack the Ripper'. A day later, the body of Swedish 'Long Liz' Stride was discovered in an alley off Henriques Street. Liz's throat had been cut and she had died of massive blood loss, but there were no mutilations to the abdomen, suggesting that her killer was disturbed during the attack. Three-quarters of an hour later, the body of Catherine Eddowes was found in Mitre Square in the City of London: her throat had been cut and a major part of her uterus, and her left kidney, had been removed.

On 1 October, a postcard was sent to the police written in red ink. In this, the writer referred to himself as 'saucy Jack' and referred to 'the double event' before signing off as Jack the Ripper once more.[16]

The press seized on the gruesome potential of 'Jack the Ripper' and the murders inevitably became a source of public fascination. *Reynold's Weekly Newspaper* ran with a piece of doggerel to the effect that 'Murder is stalking red handed 'mid the homes of the weary poor,' while newsboys ran up and down the streets crying: 'Latest Hawful Horror. A woman cut in pieces! Speshul!'[17]

Meanwhile, Chief Inspector Abbeline, in an early form of criminal profiling, had noted the similarity between the victims: all prostitutes, all of middle years and medium height, all with missing teeth. 'Jack' was murdering the same woman over and over again, but why? As the chief inspector tried to find a motive, vigilantes were taking the law into their own hands and targeting Jewish immigrants, in an updated version of the blood libel, with cries of 'It was a Jew wot did it!' and 'No Englishman did it!' Racist outbursts were further fuelled by a mysterious piece of graffiti that appeared on Goulston Street, Whitechapel, where Eddowes' body had been found. In chalk, it read: 'The Juwes are The men that Will not be Blamed for nothing,' which was either a message from the murderer, an anti-Semitic statement or an enigmatic reference to an item of Freemasons' regalia, the 'juwes'.[18]

The discovery of a female torso in the cellars of the new police building under construction at Whitehall added to the air of horror on 2 October 1888, while a deluge of copycat 'Jack the Ripper' letters overstretched police resources. Then on 16 October 1888, George Lusk, Chairman of the Whitechapel Vigilance Committee, which had been set up to crack down on prostitution in the neighbourhood, received half a human kidney in a cardboard box through the post, accompanied by a letter scrawled in a spidery hand, addressed 'From Hell' and concluding: 'Catch me when you can Mishter Lusk.' The writer claimed to have fried and eaten the other half of the 'kidne' [sic], which was 'very nise'. The shaken Lusk took both kidney and letter to the police. While the police surgeon suggested it was probably a hoax by a medical student, others believed it was part of Eddowes' missing organ.[19]

On Friday 9 November the body of Mary Jane Kelly was discovered in her room at 13 Miller's Court, off Dorset Street, Spitalfields, the same street where Annie Chapman had been murdered four months earlier. Mary Jane had been murdered with such ferocity that it beggared description. Her throat had been severed down to the spine, and her abdomen virtually emptied of its organs. Her heart was missing and she was so horribly mutilated as to be virtually unrecognizable. It was impossible for the police to enter the room without slipping on her blood and flesh. The Ripper's latest atrocity led to the resignation of the Metropolitan Commissioner of Police, Sir Charles Warren.[20]

The Whitechapel murders dominated the newspapers from Europe to the Americas, and there was increasing pressure on the police to make an arrest. An image of the killer had taken shape in the popular imagination, a vision of a genteel man dressed in black and carrying a doctor's bag. In response, the police made a number of arrests ranging from doctors and tradesmen to sailors and tramps, but lacked sufficient evidence to charge. Those questioned included Aaron Kosminski, Montague Druitt, and Dr Francis J. Tumblety.

Kosminski, a poor Polish Jew resident in Whitechapel, was arrested on the orders of Sir Melville Macnaghten, Assistant Commissioner at Scotland Yard. Released for lack of evidence, Kosminski ended his days in Colney Hatch mental asylum.

When Montague Druitt (1857–88) drowned himself in the Thames and the killings stopped, Macnaghten concluded that he had been the perpetrator. A barrister with medical training, Druitt had the knowledge of anatomy to carry out such hideous crimes, and he was also, according to his family, 'sexually insane'. Druitt, a product of Winchester and New College, Oxford, was an amateur cricketer of national standing and a member of the MCC, with good prospects as a barrister. However, after being dismissed from his post as a master at a minor public school, Druitt's body was found floating in the Thames on 31 December 1888. Druitt's dismissal may have resulted from the school's discovery of his homosexuality (then a criminal offence), while a family history of severe depression may have contributed to his taking his own life. Although Druitt's death offered a convenient solution to the riddle of the Ripper, this unfortunate young man appears to have been an unlikely candidate for the role of serial killer.[21]

Francis Tumblety was an American 'quack' aged fifty-six and regarded as a very strong suspect by Detective Chief Inspector John Littlechild, a former head of the Special Branch. Tumblety, who specialized in selling spurious herbal remedies, had been arrested for gross indecency (homosexual activity) in November 1888, and fled the country soon afterwards, having obtained bail at a very high price.[22]

A more compelling suspect was Severin Klosovski, commonly known as George Chapman, who had arrived in England in 1888 and worked as a barber in Whitechapel. Apprenticed to a surgeon, Chapman never took his degree, preferring instead to run a pub. When Chapman was arrested in 1905 and charged with poisoning three of his wives, Inspector Abbeline, now retired, commented to the arresting officer, 'You've caught the Ripper, then?' But this seems unlikely. Chapman poisoned his wives because he became tired of them, rather than butchering prostitutes.[23]

One killer claimed, with his dying breath, that he had indeed been Jack the Ripper, and in many ways he fitted the profile. Dr Thomas Cream (1850–92) was an abortionist, who accidentally killed two patients with overdoses of chloroform, but escaped prosecution for lack of sufficient evidence. Fleeing to America, he had an affair with the wife of a patient, and was imprisoned when her husband died from an overdose of strychnine. As well as having the requisite medical training,

Cream satisfied the criteria in another respect. A sexual sadist, his particular fetish was to hire prostitutes and issue them with 'lucky pills' intended to pep them up, issuing strict instructions that they take these only after he had left. The pills were lethal and the poor women died in agony. Cream enjoyed playing cat and mouse games with the police, writing to them in the guise of a private detective with teasing fragments of 'evidence' but was eventually caught after one of his victims took her pep pill to the police. As he was about to be hanged at Newgate in 1892, Cream boasted that he had indeed been Jack the Ripper. Unfortunately, this proved impossible. Cream had been in gaol in Canada when the Whitechapel murders were committed.[24]

After the Kelly murder, and many more abortive arrests, the panic began to die down. In early 1889 Inspector Abbeline was transferred to other duties and the inquiry was handed over to Inspector Henry Moore. His last extant report on the murders is dated 1896, when another 'Jack the Ripper' letter was received. There were brief flurries of press activity and wild suggestions that the 'Ripper' had returned on the occasions of subsequent murders. The last serious suspect was Tom Sadler, a sailor who was arrested in 1891 for the murder of a prostitute, Frances Coles. When they tracked Sadler down to the Phoenix public house in Smithfield, the police were convinced that they had got their man. Sadler, a violent drunk with a history of assaulting women, fitted their profile. But when Sadler went on trial for murder, the jury remained unconvinced of his guilt and Sadler walked free.[25]

Theories as to the Ripper's true identity circulate to this day. The more bizarre explanations included one from the *British Medical Journal* suggesting that the atrocities might have been committed by a ruthless but enterprising gang of 'Burkers' eager to sell wombs to medical students, another accusing Freemasons of being the perpetrators, or even one suggesting it was the Duke of Clarence, the younger son of Queen Victoria who was rumoured to be insane.[26]

The lack of sexual activity at the crime scene prompted speculation that the killer had been a woman, an abortionist so incompetent that she had mutilated her patients to destroy the evidence of illegal terminations. A similar theory pointed the finger at Amelia Dyer, the baby farmer hanged in 1896 for murdering dozens of illegitimate babies entrusted to her care, suggesting that she had killed the mothers before they could expose her as a child murderer.

What is obvious is the fact that the police were at no stage in a position to prove a case against anyone, and it is highly unlikely a positive case will ever be proved. If the police were in this position between 1888 and 1891, then what hope for the enthusiastic modern investigator?

The enduring fascination of this case has attracted retired and serving police officers, writers and film-makers for over a century. There will never be a conclusive explanation but the case of 'Jack the Ripper' grips the popular imagination to this day, and makes armchair detectives of us all. Meanwhile, reality and art have combined to create a nightmare vision of Victorian London, a city haunted by imaginary sleuths and actual murderers, a fantasy world in which the fictional Sherlock Holmes pursues the real Jack the Ripper through foggy streets and narrow alleyways forever.

This London was already becoming history. In the dying days of the old century, as Queen Victoria's life slipped away with the years, a new age of crime and punishment beckoned from the future. Even those ancient bastions of crime and punishment, Newgate Gaol and the Old Bailey, would not escape unscathed.

CRIMES PASSIONNELS, FEMMES FATALES

Drama at the Old Bailey

On 15 August 1902, at a quarter past three in the afternoon, a piece of stone about the size of a man's foot fell from the wall of Newgate Gaol, just below the statue of Liberty. A hand grasping a chisel emerged and worked away at the hole, as a small crowd gathered to watch the operation. The old pigeons, 'rough and grimy as the prison itself compared with the other flocks in London, fluttered about the statue, evidently talking over the event with much excitement'.[1] But this was no gaol break, no last-minute escape from the gallows. Nor was it the desperate work of rioters, eager to free their comrades. This was the end of Newgate.

After a damning report by Sir Herbert Gladstone's investigative committee in the 1880s, the authorities had reached for the black cap and condemned Newgate to death. The gaol itself was being executed, taken apart, brick by brick. In its place would stand the most famous court in the land, the Old

Bailey, rebuilt at a cost of £392,277 and topped by the formidable bronze statue of Lady Justice, bearing the scales and sword.

Once the demolition work was underway, the governors began to sell off the fixtures and fittings of the old gaol. On 7 February 1903, a sale of relics drew crowds of the curious to gather within Newgate's gloomy precincts. The flagstaff, upon which the black flag used to be flown after an execution, fetched eleven and a half guineas. Equipment from the execution shed went for £5 15s., while souvenir hunters snatched up the death masks of hanged prisoners for £5 each.[2] Piles of official documents, faded and age-worn, were strewn about the rooms. These were records of indictments and sentences and shipments of convicts. They were bought up in their hundreds by second-hand book dealers, aware that there must be something of value in these old accounts of sin and suffering, the endless lists of half-forgotten names recorded in faded copperplate.[3]

Newgate Gaol shortly before demolition in 1904. Many of the massive slab stones went into the rebuilding of the Old Bailey on the same spot.

The demolition work was finally completed in 1904. It had been a laborious task, as the massive stones of the outer wall were several feet thick and weighed around five tons each. Many of these stones were subsequently used in the construction of the new building, an essential replacement for the cramped, ill-ventilated and stuffy courthouse of old. The Old Bailey, which was officially opened by King Edward VII on 27 February 1907, was an iconic monument to justice, a public arena in which some of the most dramatic trials of the twentieth century would be played out. Among these were some of the last examples of the Great English Murder, including that of Dr Crippen, Edith Thompson and Frederick Bywaters and the mysterious Madame Fahmy. Uxoricide and *crimes passionnels* made for dramatic courtroom scenes, filled the public gallery and kept the crime reporters in business.

The major players in these trials were not only the miserable defendants in the dock, but the barristers or King's Counsel who appeared for the prosecution and the defence, and upon whose soaring rhetoric and dazzling charisma their lives depended. The most famous KC of his day, Sir Edward Marshall Hall, was a past master of this art. In 1894, he defended Marie Herrmann, an Austrian prostitute charged with murdering one of her clients. In his closing speech for the defence, he turned to the jury, tears streaming down his face, and declared: 'Women are what men made them. Even this woman was at one time a beautiful and innocent child. Look at her, gentlemen of the jury, look at her! God never gave her a chance. Won't you?'[4] In a satisfactory conclusion to this display of oratory, Marie Herrmann was convicted of manslaughter, and received six years' penal servitude instead of a death sentence. Marshall Hall compared his profession with acting, apart from the fact that he had to write his own lines and conjure up his own *mise en scène*. 'Out of the vivid, living dream of somebody else's life, I have to create an atmosphere; for that is advocacy.'[5]

The public fascination with a nice juicy murder remained undiminished, particularly if those on trial were hitherto 'respectable' men and women who had succumbed to their passion. As George Orwell noted in his perceptive essay on *The Decline of the English Murder,* one of the remarkable factors in these cases is that the perpetrators were from the middle classes, and that the essential motive for killing was to maintain respectability, by obtaining money and marrying their mistress or lover. Another characteristic of a good murder trial was the unmasking of the criminal by some astonishing twist of fate that would have been discarded as outrageous by any crime novelist, such as Dr Crippen fleeing across the Atlantic with his mistress disguised as a boy.[6]

In the modern world of no-contest divorce and serial monogamy, it is impossible to imagine the crushing yoke imposed by 'respectability' a century earlier, and the tensions that led to the domestic murder. London in the 1900s was a city between two worlds, one dying, one struggling to be born. Victorian morality lingered on, in a gas-lit, sepia-tinted world of poverty and narrow horizons. Simultaneously, London existed as a glittering modern metropolis, where intrepid young women took on office jobs, applied to university and even marched for the vote. Many Londoners, confronted with this brave new world, yearned only for 'respectability'. Paradise was a red-brick villa in Camden Town for £50 a year, the respectable surburbia of H. G. Wells' daydreaming clerks or the social-climbing Charles Pooter in *The Diary of a Nobody.* But a few men and women led lives of quiet desperation. This was the world of keeping up appearances while living beyond your means, despising your spouse but relying on their income, biting back the acid reflux of sexual frustration and thwarted ambition and the abiding conviction that you deserved better. This was the world in which divorce spelt scandal and financial suicide, the world where an unhappy marriage was like being handcuffed to a rotting corpse and murderous thoughts flourished behind the Nottingham Lace curtains. This was the world where marriage could be murder. This was the world of Dr Crippen.

Certain names continue to chill the reader years after the event with which they are associated, and Crippen is one of those. Up until the 1940s, 'Crippen!' was a vernacular expression of horror, swearing without the profanity, and therefore safe enough to be common currency. The mild-mannered poisoner from Camden Town had been immortalized in schoolgirl slang. His crime had put him among the immortals, alongside Jack Sheppard, Dick Turpin and Jack the Ripper. The name itself seemed evil, with its nuances of criminal, ripper and *cripes!* Crippen was even celebrated in a second-rate music hall as a 'naughty boy', an illustration of the cognitive dissonance which allows the public to relish the criminal.[7] The Crippen case was notable for another reason, in that it combined the dogged persistence of old-school Scotland Yard sleuthing with developments in forensic science, and it was the first murder case in which a suspect was arrested at sea, following a telegram.

Dr Hawley Harvey Crippen, his full name reflecting the aspirations of his lower-middle-class parents, was an American homeopathic doctor who arrived in London with his second wife, Cora, in 1900. Unqualified to practise in England, Crippen worked in a dentistry practice in New Oxford Street and acted as an agent for Dr Munyon's, a patent medicine firm. The couple rented rooms off Tottenham Court Road before taking a lease on 39 Hilldrop Crescent in September 1905. The house, an imposing villa in a tree-lined street in Camden Town, had a rent of £58 10s. a year. As Crippen only earned a modest £3 per week, some of this cost was borne by Cora.

The Crippens were an odd couple. Photographs show Dr

*Scenes from the trial of Dr Crippen at the Old Bailey,
1910, 'the most sensational trial for many years'.*

Crippen as an unprepossessing figure, just five foot three inches tall, with gold-rimmed spectacles and a sandy moustache. Cora was a vivacious New Yorker, several years his junior. With her dyed auburn hair and expensive jewellery, she cut a striking figure in suburban north London. With a determination that far outstripped her talent, Cora worked the music halls as the singer 'Belle Elmore' and aimed to become a star. Cora also had a series of lovers, including a former boxer who performed as a 'one-man band', while Crippen spent stolen afternoons in cheap hotels with his secretary, Ethel Le Neve.[8]

By December 1909, Cora had told Crippen that she knew about his affair with Ethel, and threatened to leave him, taking their life savings with her. As this sum amounted to around £600 (nearly £600,000 today), she effectively signed her own death warrant when she sent a notice of withdrawal to the bank on 15 December. To keep up appearances, the Crippens spent Christmas together. On 31 January 1910, they entertained the Martinettis, friends of Cora, for an evening of whist. The last guest departed at around one o'clock in the morning, and Cora was never seen again.

Some weeks later, Mrs Martinetti received a note addressed to her colleagues in the Music Hall Ladies Guild. Purporting to be from Cora, it stated that she had returned to America to care for a sick relative, but expected to come back to England before long. The letter was not written in Cora's hand, so Mrs Martinetti called on Crippen and asked after Cora's welfare. Crippen broke the news that Cora had died of influenza while nursing her aunt, and been buried in Los Angeles.

Meanwhile, Le Neve had moved into Hilldrop Crescent and was living openly with Crippen. To the horror of Cora's friends, she was spotted dressed in Cora's clothes and jewellery. Mrs Martinetti's suspicions were dismissed by the police but when another of Cora's friends, John Nash, returned from the United States saying that he could find no trace of her, Chief Inspector Walter Dew interviewed Crippen at his practice and ordered a search of the house. Crippen's status as a doctor and his impressive residence seemed to convince the police that he must be innocent. After a cursory inspection, the police left.[9]

But the visit from Chief Inspector Dew had been enough to rattle Crippen. Panicking, he and Le Neve fled to Belgium, where they boarded the SS *Montrose*, a Canadian Pacific liner bound for Quebec. On hearing that Crippen had disappeared, Chief Inspector Dew authorized another search of Hilldrop

Crescent on 13 July and discovered the rotting remains of a human torso hidden beneath the kitchen floor. Once the search team had revived themselves with the aid of Crippen's brandy, they observed that the corpse was wrapped in a pyjama jacket, and a hair curler with strands of dyed red hair lay nearby. The body had been buried in quicklime, but, as in the case of Henry Wainwright in 1875, the effect of the lime had been to preserve the remains. The head and limbs were never found. The celebrated pathologist Sir Bernard Spilsbury, a pioneer of forensic science, conducted the post mortem and noted an operation scar four inches long on the lower abdomen and 2.7 grains of hyoscine in the bloodstream. Although it was impossible to identify the gender of the body, Spilsbury concluded that the abdominal scar was consistent with an operation Cora had undergone some years earlier, to remove her ovaries.[10]

Meanwhile, the captain of the SS *Montrose*, Captain Henry Kendell, had become intrigued by the curious behaviour of two passengers in the first-class saloon, a middle-aged man and his young son. Captain Kendell noted that the 'boy's' trousers were splitting at the seams and held together with safety pins, and that he had very feminine table manners. Before the Canadian Pacific liner steamed out of range of the land-based transmitters, Captain Kendell sent a wireless telegram to Scotland Yard. It was the first occasion in which a telegram had been used to catch a murderer.

> Have strong suspicions that Crippen London cellar murderer and accomplice are among saloon passengers. Moustache taken off growing beard. Accomplice dressed as boy. Manner and build undoubtedly a girl.[11]

Chief Inspector Dew, who already faced criticism for failing to investigate Cora's disappearance earlier, now faced a race against time. If Crippen succeeded in getting from Canada to his home soil of the United States, an international arrest warrant and extradition procedures would be required to bring him to trial in the United Kingdom. Canada, as a dominion, was still under British legal jurisdiction and so an arrest had to be made as soon as possible. Dew boarded a White Star liner, the SS *Laurentic*, which arrived in Quebec ahead of the SS *Montrose*, and contacted the Canadian police. As the Montrose entered the mouth of the St Lawrence River, Dew boarded the liner disguised as one of the pilots who would guide the liner up the inland waterway. As a courtesy to his first-class passenger, Captain Kendell invited Crippen on deck to meet the pilots. At which point Dew removed his cap with a 'Good morning, Dr Crippen, do you know me? I'm Chief Inspector Dew from Scotland Yard.' A shocked Crippen replied: 'Thank God it's over. The suspense has been too great. I couldn't stand it any longer,' and held out his wrists for the handcuffs. Crippen and Le Neve were arrested and taken back to England on the SS *Megantic*. Jeering crowds awaited the couple when the ship docked at Liverpool, and there was another hostile reception committee when their train arrived at Euston Station.[12]

The lovers went on trial separately at the Old Bailey. Le Neve, an accessory after the fact, was fortunate enough to be acquitted. Crippen, charged with the murder of his wife, claimed that Cora had fled abroad with a lover, Bruce Miller, and that the remains in the cellar must have been buried by a previous resident before the Crippens moved in on 21 September 1905. In his capacity as an expert witness, pathologist Sir Bernard Spilsbury replied that this would have been impossible. In one of the most chilling exhibits to grace the Old Bailey, the sliver of Cora's skin bearing the scar was passed around the jury on a soup plate.

The prosecution then produced a damning piece of

evidence. In January 1910, Crippen had ordered five grains of hyoscine hydrobromide at Lewis and Burrow's chemists in New Oxford Street. This had been such a large quantity that they had to place a special order with the wholesalers, but given Crippen's medical credentials no objection was made to the purchase. Crippen collected the order on 19 January 1910.

Hyoscine had a number of applications. It could be used for pain relief and as a sedative, but proved fatal in large doses. Cora had been described as having a nervous disposition, and Crippen may well have been administering hyoscine to his wife as a herbal tonic. Edward Marshall Hall, who had initially been instructed to represent Crippen, suggested that this was his best defence. Crippen could plead guilty to administering an accidental overdose, and panicking when he realized that he had killed his wife. But Crippen rejected this plea and Marshall Hall rejected the brief.

It took the jury just twenty-seven minutes to find Crippen guilty of murder. He was hanged at Pentonville on 23 November 1910 and buried in the prison grounds. His last request was to be buried with a picture of Ethel Le Neve. On the same day, Ethel emigrated to the United States to start a new life, but she later returned to London, married a clerk and settled down to comfortable obscurity in Croydon, dying in hospital at the age of eighty-four. The house at 39 Hilldrop Crescent was destroyed by enemy action during World War Two, taking its secrets to the grave.[13]

If you were a woman going on trial for murder, good character and the right appearance played a critical part in your defence. In a world where Edwardian standards of female behaviour still prevailed, the dress and deportment of a female defendant carried as much weight as hard evidence. Such was the fate of Edith Thompson, when she went on trial at the Old Bailey in 1922, accused of the murder of her husband.

On 3 October 1922, Edith and Percy Thompson had been making their way home to Ilford after a night 'Up West'. They had been to see *The Dippers* at the Criterion Theatre, Piccadilly.[14] The Thompsons appeared to be a happy couple, rich and successful by Ilford standards. Mr Thompson, at thirty-three, was dull but reliable, while Edith, a former buyer for a fabric importer, was clever and smart, her business trips to Paris reflected in her stylish, chic appearance. As the couple was walking along Belgrave Road, a young man sprang out of the bushes and attacked Mr Thompson. Edith shrieked, '*No! Don't! Don't do it!*' but the young man produced a knife and stabbed her husband to death. When their neighbours ran outside to help, Edith was discovered sobbing over her husband's body, saying again and again, 'Why did he do it? I never wanted him to!' As the police arrived and Edith was led away, she was overheard murmuring darkly, 'They'll blame me for this!'[15]

By the time the police arrived, Percy Thompson was dead, Edith had become hysterical and the killer had fled. Eventually, at the police station, Edith composed herself sufficiently to reveal that she recognized the killer as Frederick Bywaters. It was then that Edith made a fatal mistake. Convinced that she was a witness to the murder, and not an accomplice, Edith confessed that Bywaters had been her lover. The police arrested Bywaters, and when they discovered a box of love letters from Edith, they arrested her too. Despite the fact that Edith had not been actively engaged in the assault, the letters were enough for the prosecution to accuse Edith Thompson and Frederick Bywaters of 'joint enterprise', a term which indicated that if two people wanted a third party dead, and if one of those two people acted, both were equally guilty of murder.

Edith Thompson and Freddy Bywaters went on trial together at the Old Bailey on 6 December 1922. Bywaters had co-operated with the police, surrendering the murder weapon and maintaining that Edith had not been involved. However, when Edith's love letters were produced, the evidence appeared to be damning. In letter after letter, inspired by the romantic novels to which she was hopelessly addicted, Edith described her passionate love for Bywaters and the lengths to which she would go to be rid of Percy. Edith wrote that she had laced his mashed potatoes with ground glass on one occasion, and on another, she had tried to poison him with enough arsenic to kill an elephant, apparently at Bywaters' insistence. But Percy had survived with no obvious ill effects, and so in other letters Edith begged Bywaters to 'do something desperate!'[16]

Edith's counsel, Sir Henry Curtis-Bennett KC, built his case for the defence on his client's physical attractiveness and compelling personality, telling the jury that while writing the letters Edith had believed herself to be bathed in the 'glamorous aura of a great love'. Edith revelled in the attention. Finding herself in the most desperate of circumstances, she was at last where she had always wanted to be: centre stage. But then Edith had to take the greatest risk of all. After her counsel's glowing encomium, Edith had to go into the witness box herself.

It was a disaster. Curtis-Bennett pleaded with Edith not to testify, later telling a journalist:

She spoiled her chances by her evidence and by her demeanour. I had a perfect answer to everything which I am sure would have won an acquittal if she had not been a witness. She was a vain woman and an obstinate one. She had an idea that she could carry the jury. Also she realized the enormous public interest, and decided to play up to it by entering the witness box. Her imagination was highly developed, but it failed to show her the mistake she was making.[17]

If Edith had entered the witness box playing the role of repentant, grieving widow, modestly dressed in mourning black, with a handkerchief to her eyes, she might indeed have carried the jury. Instead, Edith made a dreadful impression. She succeeded in being both maudlin and flirtatious, constantly contradicted herself, and claimed that all the references to poisoning her husband were invented to impress Bywaters. Sir Bernard Spilsbury, the Home Office pathologist, had testified to the effect that he had found no trace of poisoning during Percy Thompson's post mortem. But as if her affair with Bywaters was not enough to damn Edith in the eyes of the jury, her letters also contained graphic references to an abortion, a procedure then both illegal and viewed as morally repugnant. As the prosecution caught Edith out in lie after lie, her arrogance and vanity destroyed any chance of acquittal.

Bywaters maintained that Edith was completely innocent, since he had no intention of murdering Percy Thompson. In Bywaters' version of events, he lay in wait for the couple, intending to challenge Percy Thompson to a fight that went tragically wrong. Bywaters stuck to his story doggedly, claiming that he had never believed Edith would harm her husband but that she had a vivid imagination and her letters saw her acting out a role. Mr Justice Shearman, summing up, described the letters as 'full of the outpourings of a silly but at the same time, a wicked affection',[18] but instructed the jury not to convict Edith Thompson unless they were completely satisfied that both parties agreed that Percy Thompson should be murdered, and that 'she knew that he was going to do it, and directed him to do it, and by arrangement between them he was doing it'.[19]

The jury took just over two hours to find Edith Thompson and Freddy Bywaters guilty of murder. When the verdict was declared, Bywaters shouted out that Edith was innocent, while she succumbed to a fit of hysterics. Both parties lodged appeals but these were dismissed.

Until Edith was sentenced, she had fared badly in the popular press as an adulteress who had undergone an abortion and plotted to kill her husband. Once the death sentence had been imposed, the public attitude swiftly changed. A petition with almost one million signatures went to the Home Secretary, William Bridgeman, pleading for a reprieve. Overnight, Edith had been exonerated as a silly fantasist but nothing more, while there was admiration of Bywaters' protective attitude and enduring loyalty. Edith Thompson also attracted sympathy because the notion of hanging a woman had become distasteful. No woman had been executed in Britain since the double hanging of the baby farmers Amelia Sach and Annie Walters in 1903. Edith believed that it was only a matter of time before she was reprieved. When she was finally given the date for her execution, Edith suffered a complete breakdown and spent her last days crying and screaming, unable to eat or sleep.

On the morning of 9 January 1923, at nine o'clock, the lovers were executed simultaneously just half a mile apart. Edith Thompson died at Holloway, and Bywaters was hanged at Pentonville. Bywaters died bravely, hanged by William Willis, and protesting Edith's innocence to the last. Edith Thompson had become so distressed by the morning of her execution that she had to be heavily sedated. According to Edith's executioner, John Ellis, she had to be carried from the condemned cell by two warders and held upright on the gallows while Ellis completed the formalities.

As the trapdoor sprang open, and Edith Thompson plunged to her death, witnesses were horrified to observe blood gushing out between her legs. Edith, possibly pregnant, had suffered a massive haemorrhage. And yet she had refused to 'plead her belly', to use the archaic phrase, when pregnancy would have brought certain reprieve. Following this particularly horrific execution, several of the prison officers took early retirement. The hangman, John Ellis, retired in 1923 and committed suicide in 1931. As a consequence of Edith Thompson's execution, women condemned to the gallows were obliged to wear reinforced canvas knickers, in an attempt to prevent a repeat of such harrowing scenes.

Edith Thompson was buried within the precincts of Holloway and later reburied at Brookwood Cemetery in 1970, following building work at the prison. Edith was buried alongside the baby farmers Amelia Sach and Annie Walters, and her tombstone bears the epitaph: 'Sleep on beloved. Her death was a legal formality.'[20]

Edith Thompson's KC, Curtis-Bennett, was haunted for the rest of his life by his failure to save her from the gallows. Curtis-Bennett always maintained that Edith had 'paid the extreme penalty for her immorality'.[21] However, one of Curtis-Bennett's last remarks reveals the terrible irony of the entire case. 'Was it not proved that she had *posed* to him [Bywaters] as a woman capable of doing anything – even murder – to keep his love? She had to: Bywaters wanted to get away from her.'[22] Indeed he did. A series of letters between 20 June and 12 September 1922 shows Bywaters trying to break off the relationship. Had Bywaters been sufficiently strong enough to distance himself from Edith, both the lovers might have escaped the noose.

Social status and wealth appear to have been as vital an attribute to a successful court case as good counsel. Compare the fate of Edith Thompson with that of Madame Marguerite Fahmy, accused of shooting her husband, Prince Ali Fahmy Bey, at the Savoy Hotel.

The Savoy was one of the most expensive and exclusive hotels in London. Famous guests included Fred Astaire, and, as befitted the hotel where Oscar Wilde had once entertained his rent-boys, a blind eyed was turned to indiscretion. However, even the urbane patrons of the Savoy were taken aback by events on 10 July 1923. As the night porter was making his rounds at about 2 a.m., he heard three gunshots ring out in quick succession. As he raced into the luxury suite, he witnessed a beautiful, dark-haired woman in an evening gown throwing a gun to the floor, while the body of a young man was slumped against a wall, blood and brains oozing from a wound to his temple. Falling to her knees, the woman whimpered, *'Qu'est-ce que j'ai fait, mon cher?'* ('What have I done, my dear?') over and over again.[23]

The woman was Marguerite Fahmy and her victim was her 23-year-old husband, Prince Ali Fahmy Bey, an Egyptian national. The couple had met in Paris a year earlier, when Fahmy was just twenty-two. Marguerite, ten years older, had been regarded as a gold-digger by Fahmy's family and friends, but they had married in Egypt and Marguerite had even converted to Islam.

The shooting did not come as a surprise to the staff of the Savoy. Ever since they had arrived on 1 July, Marguerite and the prince had been embroiled in a series of bitter public rows. Witnesses testified to seeing the prince with scratches on his face, while Marguerite appeared with a bruised face, the marks inadequately covered with cosmetics. The previous evening, they had returned to the Savoy for supper after a performance of *The Merry Widow* at Daly's Theatre. There had been a terrible quarrel, during which Marguerite seized a wine bottle and threatened to smash it over her husband's head. With the help of the head waiter, the couple eventually settled down, and went off to the ballroom to listen to the band. Refusing to dance with her husband, Marguerite went off to bed.[24]

London had been sweltering under a heat wave for days

and that night the weather broke with a violent thunderstorm. Despite the appalling conditions, and deaf to the protests of his personal secretary, Said Enani, Prince Fahmy had jumped into a cab outside the Savoy and ordered the driver to take him to Piccadilly. When he eventually returned, there was another violent argument, the prince was shot dead and Marguerite was discovered holding a smoking gun.

The case was sensational. The murder of royalty, albeit foreign royalty, in a five-star hotel was enough to guarantee a packed gallery at the Old Bailey. When it emerged that the prince was apparently a sexual pervert who indulged in 'Oriental practices' the public was queuing up outside. Many of these were young women of barely eighteen. Edward Marshall Hall, appearing for the defence, glanced up at the gallery and warned them that if they chose to hear this case, they must take the consequences.[25] Nobody left.

Marshall Hall's strategy consisted of a plea of accidental killing. Marguerite had not intended to kill the prince, he argued. Instead, she had threatened to shoot herself and the gun had gone off accidentally during the ensuing struggle. A cynic might question whether anybody could be the victim of such extremely bad luck. Yet it was difficult to imagine that a woman who had never handled a gun before could blow a man's brains out with almost professional skill.

But Marshall Hall had an additional argument, which consisted of Marguerite's sickening catalogue of abuse at the hands of the prince. This took the form of a prolonged character assassination of the dead man, portraying him as a monster of sexual depravity. The prince had 'abnormal tendencies and he never treated Madame normally', he told the jury. Medical evidence testified to the effect that Marguerite had called the Savoy's doctor and complained of anal injuries caused by 'unnatural intercourse'. The resulting pain was so severe that she needed an operation.[26]

When Marguerite went into the witness box, she described a disturbing scene during which she had been seated 'in a state of undress' when she had noticed a strange noise and pulled aside the hangings to discover one of her husband's manservants spying on her. In response to Marguerite's horrified scream, her husband had just laughed and told her: 'He is nobody. He does not count. But he has the right to come here or anywhere you may go and tell me what you are doing.' Turning to the jury, Marshall Hall commented, 'We in this country put our women on a pedestal: in Egypt they have not the same views.'[27] In a parting shot, Marshall Hall suggested that there had been a homosexual relationship between the prince and his secretary, Said Enani.

'These things are horrible,' observed the judge, in his summing up. 'They are disgusting. How anyone could listen to these things who is not bound to listen to them passes comprehension.' The jury found Marguerite not guilty of murder or manslaughter in less than an hour.[28]

The world's press reported the case with undisguised glee, with headlines such as *Why They Forgave the Princess for Killing Her Husband*, and *Jury Unable to Convict the Unhappy Beauty After Hearing Her Tell How Prince Fahmy Bey's Black Spies Invaded Even the Privacy of Her Bridal Boudoir*.[29] While the French press wondered why English law did not have a defence of *crime passionnel,* the British press enjoyed portraying Marguerite as less than innocent. The prosecution had not been permitted to cross-examine Marguerite. If he had, the jury would have discovered that Marguerite had been a high-class prostitute, and a private detective hired by the prosecution claimed that her husband was not the only one in the marriage to enjoy same-sex relationships.

After the verdict, Marguerite left for Paris, where she found out that she had no claim to her late husband's fortune as he had left no will. After a failed attempt to convince her husband's family that she had given birth to a son, Marguerite became a laughing stock and withdrew from Parisian society. But she owed her life to Marshall Hall. The KC had used every theatrical device at his disposal, even appealing to the jury's latent racism and homophobia to ensure that she was acquitted. It had been a barnstorming performance.[30]

A similar case was heard at the Old Bailey in 1932, in which the socialite Elvira Barney was accused of shooting her lover, Scott Stephen, after a quarrel at her Belgravia home. On the advice of her counsel, Patrick Hastings, Elvira claimed that she had been trying to kill herself and that Stephen had been fatally injured as he tried to wrestle the weapon out of her hands. Hastings argued that the pistol had a hair-trigger, and the gun had gone off accidentally. The defence was successful: Elvira was acquitted.

Following the trials of Marguerite Fahmy and Elvira Barney, it seemed unlikely that any other woman would face execution for murder. Sadly, the fate of Ruth Ellis would subsequently challenge this assumption. In the meantime, let us leave the theatre of the courtroom, the 'little O' of the Old Bailey, and investigate the tide of crime lapping against its walls.

12

EAST END BOYS

The Origins of London's Gangland

The roots of London's 'gangland' have always been a rich source of myth and speculation. Ruled by 'diamond geezers' and 'hard bastards', it has been portrayed as a brutal, dangerous world in which domination was established by violence and neighbourhoods were carved up between rival villains. We have glimpsed the origins of this underworld in previous chapters, emerging like the points of jagged rocks from a stormy sea – the teeming slums of Seven Dials and Saffron Hill, the dangerous thoroughfare of Ratcliffe Highway, the foggy alleys of the East End. Victorian reformers attempted to sweep all this away with a rigorous combination of slum clearance, street lighting and the thin blue line of the Metropolitan Police. The rookeries were torn down and gas lamps glowed in the shadows, but this proved no match for the entrenched lawlessness of London's underworld, as family gangs marked out the city for their own.

By the Edwardian era, the East End was governed by gangs characterized by ethnic and national identity. There were

Irish gangs, Jewish gangs and Italian gangs, confirming the public prejudice that 'dangerous foreigners' were responsible for the majority of crime, as well as home-grown gangs in the form of the Elephant Boys, from Elephant and Castle, and the Titanics from Hoxton. From time to time, rival gangs from other cities would attempt to muscle in, such as Birmingham's Brummagen Boys, led by exiled East Ender Billy Kimber, and the Leeds gang. During this period, London's gangland had the aura of the Wild West about it, with a series of shoot-outs and gun fights. In the glittering gin-palaces mirrors were smashed, hapless thugs were punched across counters and optics were shot out as simmering vendettas erupted into bar-room brawls. But the villains still had their standards. Guns were commonplace but knives were considered unsporting. Top East End 'face' Arthur Harding boasted, 'As an Englishman, I would never use a knife.'[1]

Harding had been born into poverty in 1886, and received his first sentence in 1902, when he was sentenced to twelve months' penal servitude for helping 'One-Eyed Charlie' steal a bale of rags worth eighteen shillings from a cart. After three months in Wormwood Scrubs, Harding went to a Borstal, a specialist prison for young delinquents that had just been introduced that year. This proved the making of him. 'Borstal made me fitter, stronger, taller and when I went back to my old associates I found I was something of a hero.'[2] Harding's biggest rival was Isaac 'Ikey' Bogard, a pimp or *shundicknick*, also known as 'the Coon' on account of his dark complexion. As if to accentuate the frontier town atmosphere of the East End, Bogard affected an American accent, wore a Stetson and leather chaps and carried a gun.

The hostility between Harding and Bogard lasted for years. In 1903 Bogard conspired to have Harding murdered, but the plot failed. The feud culminated at Christmas 1907 in 'the

Vendetta Affair', after a fight over a woman led to a show-down in the Bluecoat Boy in Bishopsgate. Each gang was a dozen strong. Bogard offered Harding a drink. Harding promptly flung it back in his face and then followed it up with the glass. 'The Coon had a face like the map of England,' Harding gloated afterwards.[3] Harding's language, so offensive to the modern reader, did not merely reflect the prejudices of the times. Harding was a racist and subsequently an associate of Oswald Mosley.

Bogard and his gang were up in Old Street Police Court a few days later, and Bogard asked for police protection. He was justified, as Harding and his men attempted to shoot the Bogard gang as they left the court. This had the effect of intimidating any witnesses to the attack in the Bluecoat Boy, and the case collapsed. The landlord was so frightened that he refused to give evidence and retired to Southend, where his pub became a popular retreat for gangland types.

Considering that he had attempted to murder Bogard, Harding received a remarkably light sentence of just three years for affray and possessing a firearm in a court of law. Summing up, Mr Justice Avory commented that it was unacceptable for part of London to be 'infested by a number of criminal ruffians armed with revolvers', and recommended 'remedial legislation' to tackle gangsters. Such legislation was badly needed. Within a month of leaving gaol, Harding was back to his old ways.[4] But 'Ikey' Bogard took a different path. When the First World War came along, he enlisted and emerged with a Military Medal, and ended his days as a book-maker in Wandsworth. By going straight, or reasonably straight, Bogard was something of an anomaly in post-World War I London.

By 1920, the city was in the grip of a crime wave, caused by one of the greatest innovations of the twentieth century, the motor car. Luxury cars left unattended in busy streets were stolen, used to execute a crime and then swiftly abandoned. Impossible to catch, high on excitement, this new breed of armed robbers became increasingly daring. In their stolen vehicles they could cover a considerable distance, with the result that householders in town and country alike were terrorized by masked burglars. Post offices were raided day and night, and female clerks held up at gunpoint. Cashiers, carrying the day's takings to the bank, were knocked down and robbed in broad daylight, while the actual banks were held up at gunpoint. Handbags were ripped from the arms of defenceless women, and West End jewellers were forced to fit metal grilles across the windows to guard against smash and grab. Safe-crackers, meanwhile, found it comparatively easy to transport their heavy oxy-acetylene cutting apparatus by car. Motorists were hijacked and threatened with death if they resisted, and garages pillaged for petrol, oil and cash. The police officers who attempted to intervene were shot with automatic pistols and in some cases murdered. As Detective Inspector Hambrook observed, for all practical purposes, there was no mobile police force at all, 'and criminals snapped their fingers at our impotent efforts to catch them'.[5]

A crime wave of this magnitude deserved a swift response, and it arrived in 1920 in the form of the Flying Squad. The Flying Squad began life as a mobile undercover patrol in 1919. It consisted of a covered wagon, with detectives hidden beneath the tarpaulin in the back, which patrolled the streets on the lookout for known criminals or 'faces'. In 1920, the squad bought two Crossley motor vehicles from the Royal Flying Corps. The Crossleys were unwieldy vehicles compared with the luxury motors favoured by villains. They had thin wheels and tyres, no front brakes and a top speed of 40 m.p.h. One patrolled the streets north of the Thames, and the other south of the river. The *Daily Mail's* crime reporter, G. T.

Crook, is credited with inventing the name 'the Flying Squad', which swiftly passed into Cockney rhyming slang as 'Sweeney Todd' or simply 'the Sweeney'. By 1923, a mobile receiver was fitted to the top of one of the Crossleys, linked to a radio at Scotland Yard. This rudimentary system allowed the Crossleys to receive radio signals while on the move. The heavy wireless antennae looked like bedsteads and made the Crossleys even more difficult to manoeuvre, but the benefits outweighed the disadvantages. According to Flying Squad veteran Inspector 'Nutty' Sharpe: 'What a change that little transmitter wrought in the business of catching crooks. One day the tenders were patrolling blind to what might be happening in the next street. The next, cruise where they might, they were in receipt instantaneously of whatever helpful information found its way into every department of the Metropolitan Police.'[6]

The Flying Squad faced one of its greatest challenges when faced with the formidable team of John 'Ruby' Sparks and Lillian Goldstein. Born in Bermondsey, Sparks was the son of a receiver and a bare-knuckle fighter. Sparks started young, working for a gang of mail robbers who would hide him in a hamper in the guard's van. Once the train was moving, Sparks would leap out and scarper with anything he could lay his hands on. The nickname Ruby derived from the fact that he had once stolen some rubies from a maharaja but had been told they were worthless by an incompetent fence. It was only after he had handed them out like sweeties that one of his acquaintances told him the hoard had been worth thousands of pounds.

Becoming a cat burglar in 1923, Sparks teamed up with Lillian Goldstein, who drove a Mercedes and was believed to have been the brains behind a series of daring country-house robberies. Lillian Goldstein, with her flapper bob and cheeky red beret, had started life as a nice Jewish girl from Wembley, but the rebellious streak had set in early. After a 'wide boy' broke her heart, Lillian abandoned her career as a dressmaker and worked briefly as a prostitute, servicing clients in the back of taxis as they drove round Hyde Park. After a brief gaol sentence Lillian threw in her lot with Sparks and found her true vocation as a getaway driver, keeping the engine running as Sparks slipped into deserted country houses and seized the valuables.

Inspector Nutty Sharpe displayed grudging respect for Lillian. 'She could whiz that great long tourer about with the skill of an artist,' he recalled. 'Her trouble was that she ought to have been a boy.'[7]

This dramatic existence came to an abrupt conclusion in 1927 when the couple was arrested. Sparks received three years in Strangeways, but Lillian was cleared. In 1940, the couple was briefly reunited, when Lillian hid Sparks in her Wembley home after he was on the run from Dartmoor. Lillian got six months for hiding Sparks but only served three weeks, as her willingness to harbour him was interpreted as evidence of her feminine nature. By this time, Lillian had clearly learned her lesson. After leaving prison, when Sparks approached her to take part in another raid which would involve throwing ammonia in a victim's face, she broke up with him for good, telling Sparks, 'I've had enough of this bandit queen lark!'[8] Sparks eventually abandoned the bandit game himself, setting up as a newsagent in Chalk Farm and regretting, in his memoirs, that he had not gone straight years earlier.

Ruby Sparks and Lillian Goldstein operated within the tradition of London crime. The Georgian highwaymen and the swaggering cracksmen of the Victorian era would have recognized the couple's athletic bravado and ruthless ambition, and understood Lillian's pragmatic decision to quit when it all got too much. Sparks and Goldstein emerged as sympathetic figures. 'They're a colourfully rascally lot, these wide 'uns!' as Inspector Nutty Sharpe observed.[9] But it is at this point that a darker element enters the picture. This is the shadowy world of illicit drugs.

In historical terms, legislation regarding the sale of drugs is comparatively recent. Until the Poisons and Pharmacy Act of 1908, 'dangerous' drugs were freely available. Opium, imported from India and China, was a universal sedative. Laudanum, a mixture of alcohol and opium, was a general specific against all ills, from teething to cramps and melancholia. Cannabis constituted a vital ingredient in cough syrup, while cocaine was valued for its uplifting properties. Ernest Shackleton took 'Forced March' cocaine tablets to Antarctica in 1909, as did Captain Scott a year later on his ill-fated journey to the South Pole.[10] Until the Defence of the Realm Act was imposed in 1916, chemists were still selling sheets impregnated with cocaine and opium to send to 'friends at the Front'.

The first stirrings of modern anxiety about drug abuse resulted in the International Opium Convention 1912 (the Hague Convention), which recommended limiting the manufacture, trade and use of opiates to medical purposes, closing opium dens, penalizing unauthorized possession of opiates and prohibiting their sale to unauthorized persons. When this was implemented in the Dangerous Drugs Act 1920, with subsequent legislation in 1925, drugs which had been a common feature of daily life became controlled substances and, with a few strokes of the pen, recreational drug use was criminalized. The impact of this legislation reverberated through London's underworld, from the flappers of Mayfair to the Chinese immigrants of the East End, and created a new breed of criminal: the drug dealer. It also created a new class of victims, the celebrity drug addict or 'dope fiend'. The first of these was Billie Carleton, an attractive young actress. On the night of 28 November 1918, Billie Carleton had a starring role in the Victory Ball at the Albert Hall, appearing in an 'extraordinary and daring costume which consisted almost entirely of transparent black georgette'.[11]

Billie's performance was a triumph, but the following morning she was found dead in bed at the Savoy Hotel. She was only twenty-two years old. A small gold box containing cocaine stood on her bedside table and at the inquest it was suggested that she had died of 'cocaine poisoning', although this is extremely rare and it is more likely that she choked. As the sordid details of Billie's brief life emerged, it was revealed that she was a heavy user of opium and cocaine, and had three 'protectors'. There were two older men who supported her financially and paid for her permanent suite at the Savoy and a third gentleman, a dress designer named Reggie de Veulle, who supplied her with the drugs he purchased from Lau Ping You, a Chinese man from Limehouse, and his Scottish wife Ada.

De Veulle's past as a drug dealer emerged when he went on trial at the Old Bailey charged with manslaughter and conspiracy to supply cocaine. In court, it was revealed that de Veulle had been involved in a previous homosexual blackmail case and with a headline that read *An Opium Circle – Chinaman's Wife Sent to Prison – High Priestess of Unholy Rites*, *The Times* reported that both de Veulle and Carleton had been at an all-night 'orgy' in a Mayfair flat where the women wore flimsy négligées and the men dressed in silk pyjamas while smoking opium.

Billie emerged from the case as a tragic victim, and was described by the *Daily Sketch* newspaper on 14 January 1919 as an innocent girl possessed of 'a certain frail beauty of that perishable, moth-like substance that does not last long in the wear and tear of this rough-and-ready world'. Ada was sentenced to five months' hard labour, her husband escaped with just a ten-pound fine while, despite the judge's direction, the jury acquitted Carleton's friend Reggie de Veulle of her manslaughter. He admitted, however, to supplying Carleton cocaine and was imprisoned for eight months.

A media frenzy followed, with the *Daily Express* warning readers that 'You will find the woman dope fiend in Chelsea, in Mayfair and Maida Vale. An obscure traffic is pursued in certain doubtful teashops,' while the *Daily Mail* asserted that 'Men do not as a rule take to drugs, unless there is a hereditary influence, but women are more temperamentally attracted.' Questions in the House of Commons called for drug dealers to be flogged and all Chinese to be deported, while the press insisted that there was a strong relationship between drug use and the so-called 'white slave trade' in which white women were lured into prostitution after becoming hooked on drugs.[12]

Opium dens had been a fixture of East End life for decades. Opium smoking had been introduced by Chinese immigrants and was popular with Lascars (East India Company sailors), prostitutes and drifters as well as appealing to aristocrats and bohemians. Until the Defence of the Realm Act, the practice was regarded as the Chinese prerogative. One policeman commented, 'They don't care for no drink, and seem to live without eating so far as I know. It's their opium at night they likes; and you'll find half-a-dozen on 'em in one bed at Yahee's, a-smoking and sleeping away like so many lime-kilns and dormice!'[13]

There were relatively low numbers of Chinese people in London during the early twentieth century but they had become associated with the popular myths of the evil genius Fu Man Chu and there was general prejudice against the Chinese. When, four years after the death of Billie Carleton, Freda Kempton died after an overdose of cocaine, the Chinese were again held responsible.

Freda was a 'dance instructress' – her task being to dance with any man who paid. She worked at Dalton's in Leicester Square, owned by the 'Queen of Clubs', Kate Meyrick, a resilient Irishwoman who had turned to club management to pay the school fees after Mr Meyrick had deserted her and their six children. Frequently raided by the police for infringing licensing laws, Dalton's had a secret exit enabling peers of the realm and high court judges to make a swift exit when the Old Bill arrived.[14]

At Freda's inquest, it emerged that on the night of her death she had been dancing with 'Brilliant Chang', a Chinese restaurateur. Brilliant Chang was a small, elegant man, handsome in a lean, ascetic way, who dressed in fur-collared coats and suede shoes. Women found him extraordinarily attractive, but his

Brilliant Chang, London's first celebrity
drug dealer, in 1924. Chang's Chinese restaurant
was condemned as 'a den of iniquity'.

good looks were turned against him by a Fleet Street determined to demonize him as a corrupter of women. According to the *World Pictorial News* he 'dispensed Chinese delicacies and the drugs and vices of the Orient' from his restaurant and his obsession with women required him to be paid 'in kind'. When women agreed to sleep with him, then apparently, 'The flame of evil passion burned more brightly within and he hugged himself with unholy glee!'[15]

At Freda's inquest, Brilliant Chang denied all knowledge of the cocaine. The coroner accepted this, but the press and police were determined to portray Chang as a villain and a series of raids forced him to close his restaurant and move to premises in Limehouse Causeway. In 1924, the police raided his flat and discovered a wrap of cocaine beneath a floorboard. This was all the evidence they needed to arrest the man behind 40 per cent of London's cocaine trade.

During Chang's trial, the press had a field day. The *World Pictorial News* told of girls visiting the 'den of iniquity' above the restaurant, where half a dozen women joined him for 'drug-fuelled orgies'. If drug-taking itself was not sufficient grounds for vilification, the notion that white women were being corrupted by a 'dangerous foreigner' appealed to popular bigotry.

Chang was gaoled for eighteen months in 1924 and then deported. Scores of women turned up at the Royal Albert Dock to see his ship sail. His subsequent life was the subject of wild speculation with some reports claiming he had become a successful drug dealer in Switzerland, and others maintaining he had died in penury. The *Daily Telegraph*'s Stanley Firmin insisted that Chang had gone blind and ended his days working in a kitchen garden. It was left to that keen student of human nature, Inspector Nutty Sharpe, to provide a decent epitaph. Believing that Chang had been framed, Sharpe concluded, 'The Chinaman is a pretty honourable fellow.'[16]

Another police officer, the legendary 'Fabian of the Yard',

Robert Fabian, had plenty to say about London's drug dealers. In his memoirs, he described the first time he set eyes on Eddie Manning. It was his first week in uniform, and he was in the 'mixed-up backyard of Soho', escorted by an old-timer who was due for retirement. Manning was 'a tall slim negro, superbly well dressed in a tightly tailored black overcoat with velvet collar and homburg hat, and cigar in his big teeth'. As Fabian described it:

> 'That's "Eddie the Villain",' says the old timer. 'If you get an urge to talk to him, don't. If he wants to give you a cigarette, refuse it. Never take a drink with him; never go to his place if you want information. Scrub him out of your life – he's the worst man in London ... Some well-known men and women have died at his place under drugs or some other diabolical practice.'[17]

Eddie Manning certainly had form. In 1920 he had shot three men in Cambridge Circus after they had insulted his girlfriend, and was gaoled for sixteen months. In 1922 an ex-serviceman called Eric Goodwin died of a heroin overdose at Manning's house. Manning was arrested in Primrose Hill, carrying a silver-topped cane with a secret compartment for stashing drugs. According to Robert Fabian, Manning held 'dope-parties' all over London, offering injections of cocaine at ten shillings a time. He had a strong-arm gang of black and white henchmen and a sideline as a pimp. After being gaoled for drugs offences, which prompted predictably racist headlines about the 'evil negro', Manning turned to receiving stolen goods. He was arrested again after receiving luggage worth £1,500 stolen from Lady Diana Cooper and died in Parkhurst in 1931.[18]

While the drug trade was lucrative, it would be decades before it dominated the London underworld as it does today. By far the most profitable area of crime in the early twentieth century was gambling, either the off-street variety in clubs or *spielers,* or racecourse betting with bookmakers or 'turf accountants', who took bets from punters on the 'runners'. Bookies' activities were controlled by the Jockey Club, under a strict code of conduct. (High-street betting shops would not come into being until 1963, after a change in legislation.) According to the East End criminal Arthur Harding, 'The racecourse business was a profitable one. When a gang went to a racecourse like Brighton they could clear £4,000 or £5,000 easy. At Epsom, on Derby Day, it could be £15,000 or £20,000.'[19]

Bookies, with their massive quantities of cash, were vulnerable and racetrack gangs operated by offering bookies protection from other gangs in return for a cut of the proceeds. Bookies were charged for the chalk they used on their blackboards, showing the odds, the stools they stood on, and even the sponging down of their boards between races. They were also expected to keep the punters talking so that the pickpockets could set to work, the 'dips' described by DS Charles Vanstone as 'feral, shifty little men' who darted about all over the place. Bookies were also expected to contribute to funds for the distressed wives of gangsters who had recently been gaoled. Young lads started in the business sponging down the boards for the bookies. It was the first job for an eight-year-old lad called Frankie Fraser, better known subsequently as 'Mad' Frankie Fraser.[20]

From 1910, Billy Kimber and his Brummagen Boys controlled the racetracks at Newbury, Epsom, Alexandra Park, Earls Park and Kempton Park. Kimber's rivals were the Italian gangs, the Sabinis and the Cortesis, the Titanics from the East End, the Elephant Boys from south London, and the Leeds gang. Hammers, hatchets, guns and coshes were common weapons, but racetrack gangs particularly favoured razors, which were silent but deadly and could be concealed in a lapel of a jacket or the peak of a cap. Slashings were commonplace and one bookie was killed at Sandown Park. There were also several mass brawls, such as the Battle of Epsom in 1921 when the Brummagen Boys and the Leeds mob decided to take on the Italian gangs. But the Brummagen Boys ambushed the Leeds mob by mistake and there was a pitched battle lasting ten minutes before it became obvious that they were attacking the wrong opponents. In the subsequent court case, twenty-three men were convicted.

'The Italians' consisted of two powerful families, the Sabinis, who boasted that they were descended from the Sabine tribe, and the Cortesis. The Sabinis lived in Saffron Hill, which had become known as 'Little Italy', as an Italian community had been there since the 1840s. The Sabini gang consisted of Charles 'Darby' Sabini, Joe, Fred, George and Harry Boy Sabini. Darby took on the role of Mafia Godfather, dispensing justice, resolving internal conflicts and protecting the honour of young women, such as a barmaid whose dress had been pulled off her by a local yob. The Sabinis possessed a daunting reputation; they would stand side-on at racetracks so that the bookmakers could see the hammers in their pockets.

The Sabinis' biggest rivals were the Cortesi gang, and matters came to a head in November 1922, in an incident remembered as the Battle of the Frattelanza Club. According to Louisa Doralli, daughter of the club's manager, the Cortesi gang, comprising Gus, Paul and George Cortesi, Harry 'Frenchie' and Alexander Tomaso Cortesi, a.k.a. Sandy Rice, had arrived at the club intending to attack the Sabinis. When Frenchie pulled a gun, Louisa grabbed him, assuming that he would not shoot a woman, but Frenchie wrenched the gun out of her grasp and all hell broke loose. Gus Cortesi hit Darby Sabini with a lemonade bottle and fired at him, but the bullet went out of the window.

Frenchie went on the run and the *Daily Express* circulated a description of him: 'He walks with a Charlie Chaplin step, the result of a combination of flat feet and knock knees but he is able to disguise not only his walk but his features.'[21] George, Paul and Tomaso Cortesi were cleared but Gus and Frenchie were gaoled for three years. The incident provoked a great deal of anti-Italian feeling. At the trial Mr Justice Darling warned the Sabinis and the Cortesis that if there were further trouble in the 'Italian colony', those responsible would be deported.

Darby Sabini moved to Brighton and took up permanent residence at the Grand Hotel, where, by corrupting police officers and intimidating witnesses, he assured the success of his next venture. He imported over 300 henchmen from Sicily as enforcers. Then, teaming up with the London gang known as the Yiddishers, and a Jewish bookmaker called Alf Solomons, Darby Sabini decided to challenge Billy Kimber's supremacy of the racetrack syndicate, by launching their Bookmakers and Backers Racehorse Protection Society. The end result was a bloody confrontation later known as the Battle of Lewes in 1936, when Alf Solomons and his clerk, Mark Frater, were attacked by a gang of around thirty anti-Sabini Londoners, mainly from Hoxton and Hackney. Frater was hit with a hatchet by gang member James 'Spinky' Spink, but his bowler hat deflected the impact of the blow. Sixteen of the men involved in the fight were later gaoled, and 'Spinky' became the inspiration for the gangster Pinky Brown in Graham Greene's *Brighton Rock*.

But Darby Sabini was losing control. He sued a newspaper for libel after an unflattering profile, and was then declared bankrupt. With the declaration of war in 1939, many Italians, including several of Darby's brothers, were interned as enemy aliens. The final straw came when Darby's beloved son was killed on active service with the RAF. Immortalized as the gangster Colleoni in *Brighton Rock,* Darby Sabini died in 1950, a broken man.

Rounding up the Italian gangsters was just one consequence of a war that was to change London, and its underworld, forever. As the Luftwaffe bombers wreaked destruction on the East End, the villains grew tougher than ever. It was a classic case of Nietzsche's maxim that whatever doesn't kill you, makes you stronger. The 'hard bastards' called up for military service returned leaner and fitter, equipped with professional weapons training and skills that would prove indispensable in the age of armed robbery, while the 'diamond geezers' took over the black market and traded in everything from ration books to silk stockings. Meanwhile the Metropolitan Police, numbers depleted by the call-up, struggled to maintain law and order. London became an 'unreal city', gripped by a climate of fear.

13

LONDON MONSTERS

Killers in the Smoke

Wartime London was known as 'the Smoke' and no name could have been more appropriate for this sinister shadowland. Coal dust and gas and the fumes of millions of cigarettes hovered over London in a permanent fog. It was easy to become disorientated in a city where familiar landmarks had been blotted out, road signs had been painted out to confuse the enemy and residential streets had been reduced to blackened bombsites. This twilight world of shifting allegiances and smudged identities proved the ideal climate for identity crime. In the Smoke, a conman with forged papers might masquerade as a military hero, while a bachelor with twinkling eyes could prise his victims from their fortunes. In this twilight realm, a sexual predator roamed free, his despicable crimes hidden behind an alias. The Smoke was a psychopath's playground, where appearances were deceptive, and nothing was what it seemed.

This was the backdrop against which a handsome US serviceman stepped into the Black and White Cafe,

Hammersmith, on the afternoon of 3 October 1944. When his eyes met those of a beautiful blonde girl, he introduced himself, in his rich American drawl, as Captain Ricky Rafeld. The girl's name was Georgina Grayson and she told Rafeld that she worked as an exotic dancer at the Panama Club, in Knightsbridge. Eager to impress, Captain Rafeld confided that he was really a Chicago gangster and he produced a Colt 45 revolver to prove it. Thrilled, Georgina arranged to meet him again that night, and Rafeld picked her up in an army truck. Fascinated by her potential role as a gangster's moll, Georgina declared, 'Let's do something exciting!' The resulting chain of events resembled a lurid Hollywood movie as 'the gangster' and 'the showgirl' rampaged through wartime London.[1]

Rafeld and Georgina spotted their first victim, Violet Hodge, dragging a heavy suitcase towards Paddington Station. Violet was on her way home to Bristol, so Rafeld offered her a lift. They drove as far as Egham in Surrey, then Rafeld stopped the truck, knocked Violet unconscious and tried to strangle her. When this failed, he threw her into the river and drove off. Meanwhile, Georgina went through Violet's belongings and stole her ration book and cash.[2]

Next day, Rafeld and Georgina tried to hold up a car. This ended in disaster when the driver turned out to be an American officer and pulled his gun on them. The same evening, driving around London, Rafeld knocked a female cyclist off her bicycle. As she staggered to her feet, the couple approached her as if coming to her aid. Instead of helping, they stole her handbag and threw her bicycle over a hedge. By this point, Violet Hodge had gone to the police. Far from drowning, she had been revived by the cold water and was ready to press charges.

Meanwhile, Georgina and Rafeld had embarked on their next adventure. Rafeld flagged down a taxi cab in

Hammersmith, within walking distance of Georgina's flat. But by this time, Georgina knew better than to question his actions. The cab, a grey Ford V8 saloon, was driven by George Heath from Ewell in Surrey. Heath, aged thirty-three, had one distinctive feature, a cleft chin. The taxi drove off down the Great West Road, and near Staines, Rafeld ordered the driver to stop. He did so, turning round to open the door for Georgina. As she emerged from the cab, she heard a click. 'Then I heard a shot. There was a flash. I was deafened,' Georgina later told the court at her trial.[3] Rafeld was standing at the door of the cab with his gun in his hand. He told Georgina to go through the driver's pockets, and when she refused, picked up the revolver. 'You heard what I said. I'll do the same to you if you don't go through his pockets.' Heath was still alive as she took £8 in change, a watch and a fountain pen from his pockets. Rafeld drove the cab to Knowle Green, a stretch of common near Staines, dragged the body from the car and rolled it into a ditch. As Georgina handed over the driver's handkerchief so that Rafeld could wipe the blood off his hands, she said: 'He's dead, isn't he? This is cold-blooded murder. Why did you do it?' Rafeld replied, 'People in my profession are used to things like that.' Georgina shook her head. After all, Captain Rafeld was a Chicago gangster, wasn't he?[4]

Rafeld drove the taxi back to Hammersmith and parked in Lurgan Avenue W6, near Georgina's flat. The following day, the couple spent Heath's £8 dog racing, then went 'Up West' to get Georgina a fur coat. This would not be obtained by the conventional method of entering a shop. Instead, Rafeld tried to steal a woman's coat at gunpoint as she was leaving the Berkeley Hotel. When her shrieks of terror brought a hotel doorman to her rescue, Rafeld and Georgina scarpered.[5]

By this time, Heath's body had been discovered, and was quickly identified by his cleft chin. Then the stolen taxi was found in Lurgan Avenue. When Rafeld got into the taxi at nine o'clock that night, he was arrested. Meanwhile, Georgina got drunk and started dropping hints to an old boyfriend that she had done something terrible. Since this ex-boyfriend, Henry Kimberley, was a special constable, he went straight to his superiors and Georgina was quickly arrested.

Once the gangster and the showgirl were in custody, their extraordinary facade of lies was revealed. Handsome 'Captain Rafeld' was really Karl Hulten, a 22-year-old private, who had stolen the captain's identity, along with an army truck, when he went AWOL. Far from being a Chicago gangster, he was a grocery shop assistant from Boston. As for glamorous Georgina Grayson, she was really eighteen-year-old Betty Jones from Neath, the widow of an English paratrooper. Between the two of them, Karl and Betty had created a fantasy world, with terrible consequences for their victim, George Heath.

The US courts waived their rights to court martial Hulten and he went on trial in Britain. Inevitably, each blamed the other for Heath's murder, Hulten maintaining that the gun had gone off accidentally and there had been no intention to kill. Jones was defended by Mrs Ethel Lloyd Lane, the first female barrister to appear for the defence of a prisoner charged with murder. The trial lasted six days and both were sentenced to death. Hulten was hanged on 8 March 1945 but Jones was reprieved, provoking widespread indignation and streams of telegrams to the Home Secretary. 'SHE SHOULD HANG!' was chalked on the walls of Neath, her native town, beside pictures of a figure dangling from a gallows.[6] Among those calling for Jones' execution was the playwright George Bernard Shaw, who declared that Jones was unfit to live in a civilized community.[7] George Orwell, whose essay on *The Decline of the English Murder* was inspired by this case, had a more thoughtful response. Orwell regarded the couple's *folie à deux* as a product of its times, influenced by the false consciousness of American gangster films. 'The whole meaningless story, with its atmosphere of dance-halls, movie-palaces, cheap perfume, false names and stolen cars, provided distraction amid the doodle-bugs and the anxieties of the Battle of France,' he observed. 'Jones and Hulten committed their murder to the tune of V1, and were convicted to the tune of V2.'[8] Betty Jones went to prison for nine years, and was released on licence in 1954.

Jones had a lucky escape. Young and impetuous, she had been transfixed by the glamour of crime and plunged into a fantasy world. Despite public protests, she was spared the gallows. Jones was also spared the grim fate of another regular at the Panama Club, a young woman named Margery Gardner.

On 21 June 1946, Superintendent Reginald Spooner, of the CID F Division was called to Room Four of the Pembridge Court Hotel, Pembridge Gardens, Notting Hill, where he found the body of a woman lying on the bed. With her long legs and luxuriant red hair, she must have been attractive in life. But in death, she was hideously mutilated. Her wrists and ankles had been bound, her face had been whipped with a riding crop, which had left distinctive diamond-shaped marks, one nipple had been bitten off and a poker had been thrust into her vagina, causing a fatal haemorrhage. Home Office pathologist Keith Simpson commented on the marks from the whip, and told the police, 'Find that whip and you've got your man.'[9]

When the crime reporter Duncan Webb heard about the case from a police contact, he guessed the victim's identity at once. Her name was Margery Gardner, and she was a regular at the Nag's Head in Kinnerton Street, a Knightsbridge pub frequented by ex-servicemen, debutantes and would-be bohemians. According to the landlord, Len Cole, Margery was a spirited woman in her thirties who had abandoned her husband and daughter in Sheffield and run away to London to be an artist. While she waited for that dream to come true, Margery worked as a film extra. Recently, Margery had taken up with a man who referred to himself as Lieutenant Colonel Bill Armstrong, a regular at the Nag's Head. With his unforgettable personality and blond good looks, Armstrong was a distinctive figure in the West End, towering over his fellow drinkers and regaling them with tales of his wartime exploits in the South African air force. The previous evening, Armstrong had left the Nag's Head for the Panama Club, where he had been seen drinking with Margery Gardner.[10]

Armstrong was swiftly identified as Neville Heath. Far from being a war hero, Heath was a cashiered RAF officer with a string of convictions for fraud. Dishonourably discharged from the Royal Army Service Corps in 1940, he had eventually joined the South African Air Force and risen to the rank of captain before being court martialled for wearing medals to which he was not entitled. Heath's photograph was circulated in the *Police Gazette* and every station in the country from Inverness to Worthing. There was a systematic hunt of Heath's haunts and, since he held a pilot's licence, a special watch mounted on all airfields. At this point, a woman came forward and told police that she had gone to a hotel room with Heath months earlier. The woman, who did not wish to be identified, had been the victim of a violent attack and owed her life to the hotel detective who burst into the room when he heard her screaming.[11]

Heath had fled to Worthing, and the family home of his fiancée, Miss Yvonne Symmonds. Yvonne's parents had been very impressed with the valiant ex-serviceman until his name appeared in the Sunday papers in connection with the Margery Gardner murder. Despite Yvonne's tearful protests, her parents threw him out.[12] Heath travelled to Bournemouth, where he took a room at the Tollard Royal Hotel under the poetic alias of Group Captain Rupert Brook. On 8 July Armstrong picked up a former WREN, Doreen Marshall, who was staying at the Norfolk Hotel, and they spent a day together.

The following morning, when Doreen had not returned to the Norfolk Hotel, the manager reported her missing, and told police that she had last been seen with Group Captain Brook. The police interviewed Heath, who claimed he had walked Doreen back to her hotel the previous evening. When the police searched his room, they found a horse-whip that corresponded exactly with the whip that had been used on Margery Gardner. At this point, when it became evident that 'Group Captain Brook' was in fact the wanted Neville Heath, Heath was arrested and taken back to London, where he was charged with her murder. During Heath's interview, the corpse of Doreen Marshall had been recovered from Branksome Chine, Bournemouth. Heath's last victim had been tied up, stabbed and horribly mutilated, while she was still alive.[13]

Neville Heath went on trial for the murder of Margery Gardner on 24 September 1946. His counsel, J. D. Casswell KC, told Heath to plead guilty on the grounds of insanity. However, this defence was destroyed by the prosecution who called two doctors to testify that – although Heath was a sexual psychopath – he was not insane and he was well aware of the consequences of his actions when he killed Margery Gardner.[14] Heath was found guilty and sentenced to death. Just before his execution at Pentonville on 16 October 1946, he was offered a glass of whisky. 'Considering the circumstances,' he quipped, 'better make it a double.'[15]

The hangman Albert Pierrepoint later recorded that Heath was the most handsome man he had ever hanged.[16] Pierrepoint also noted in his diary that he had used a special strap of pale calf leather to bind Heath's hands. Pierrepoint used this special strap on only a dozen or so occasions, when he wanted to indicate, he said, 'more than a formal interest in this particular execution'.[17]

When the crime reporter Duncan Webb interviewed Margery Gardner's husband, he encountered a pathetic little man who, far from being heartbroken, was preparing to mount an exhibition of his murdered wife's paintings at a Blackpool fun fair. Webb also traced the final, wretched months of Margery's life as, destitute and homeless, she drifted around Kensington and Chelsea, staying at over thirty different addresses. Eventually, Webb found a room in Earl's Court where Margery had once lived. The walls were covered with her murals, boxes and cupboards overflowed with paintings and sketches, and, most poignant of all, there was an unfinished manuscript. Having given up acting, and art, Margery had turned to writing. The night before she was murdered by Neville Heath, Margery had written, 'She had girl friends, although she got on better with men. She was bold and reckless in those days, finding her feet and her own values – and her mistakes.' She never had the chance to finish writing that novel.[18]

In the chaotic world of post-war London, people lived wherever they could. While the poor camped out in rented rooms, the wealthy took refuge in seedy residential hotels, the stucco mansions that had seen better days and now sheltered a floating population of distressed gentlewomen, choleric colonels, bogus ex-army officers and elderly widows. Such was the scene at the Onslow Court Hotel, just off Old Brompton Road, in 1949. Residents became familiar over the months, as acquaintance deepened into friendship across the separate tables. The older ladies, who sat playing bridge and patience in the lounge, had a particular favourite in Mr John George Haigh, a dapper, well-dressed chap with a neat moustache who referred to himself as an entrepreneur. Haigh got on particularly well with Mrs Olive Durand-Deacon, a colonel's widow of sixty-nine, who had sat next to him at dinner for over three years. Mrs Durand-Deacon had been intrigued by Haigh's proposal to develop an artificial fingernail business, and he invited her to visit his factory in Crawley. On 18 February 1949 Mrs Durand-Deacon left the Onslow Court Hotel to travel to Crawley. She was never seen again.

A day or two later Mrs Durand-Deacon's friend, Mrs Constance Lane, arrived at Chelsea Police Station to report Mrs Durand-Deacon missing. Mrs Lane, who was accompanied by Haigh, said she feared for her friend's safety. Haigh, with his air of polite concern, seemed eager to help, but Woman Police Sergeant Alexandra Lambourne found him deeply suspect. Lambourne reported her misgivings to Chief Inspector Shelley Symes, who sent a request to Scotland Yard. The CID responded with a file on one John George Haigh who had served a prison sentence for fraud. The photograph confirmed that this was the same man who had called at Chelsea Police Station with Mrs Long.[19]

During the course of the investigation it became clear that Mrs Durand-Deacon had travelled to Crawley with Haigh. A fur coat similar to her Persian lamb had been recently pawned in Horsham. At other pawnbrokers' they found pieces of Mrs Durand-Deacon's jewellery. When Haigh was arrested on 1 March 1949, his response was extraordinary. After asking the police what his chances were of escaping from Broadmoor, he agreed to talk, warning them, 'If I tell you the truth, you would not believe it. It sounds too fantastic.'[20]

Then Haigh made his bizarre confession. He told the police that he had taken Mrs Durand-Deacon into his factory and shot her in the back of the head before putting her body in a tank, and filling the tank with sulphuric acid by means of a stirrup-pump. Leaving the acid to do its work, he had popped out to the Ancient Priors tearoom. Before he put the body in the tank, Haigh drained off a glassful of the victim's blood and drank it.

Three days later, there was nothing left of Mrs Durand-Deacon. Her body had been completely destroyed by the sulphuric acid. Only her plastic handbag, a couple of gall-stones and parts of her false teeth had survived. It took several hours to get a full statement out of Haigh. Quite nonchalantly, he told CI Symes that a pile of ration books and other documents discovered in his hotel room 'were concerned with other jobs'. When the details of these 'other jobs' were revealed, they were enough to send case-hardened police officers heading for the pub, in need of a stiff drink. Chatting away, Haigh blithely confessed to the murder of William McSwann in 1944 in the basement of 79 Gloucester Road, SW7. After luring McSwann to his house, Haigh had coshed McSwann and drunk a glass of his blood before disposing of the body in an acid bath. He sold McSwann's valuables, then approached his parents, telling them that McSwann had gone underground to avoid being called up for military service. After befriending the McSwanns, Haigh killed them and disposed of the bodies in the same manner, before passing himself off as William McSwann and gaining control of their assets, worth £4,000. 'The sludge' as Haigh described the remains of this unfortunate family, was disposed of down a manhole in the basement.[21]

Another couple, a Mr and Mrs Henderson, met the same fate after placing an advertisement for their property at 22 Ladbroke Square. Haigh did not buy the house but remained in touch with the couple when they moved to 16 Dawes Road, Fulham. Subsequently, Haigh travelled to Brighton with the pair where they stayed at the Metropole Hotel. He then took Mr Henderson to Crawley and disposed of him there, and subsequently brought Mrs Henderson down to the factory, on the pretext that her husband was ill. 'I shot her in the storeroom and put her in another tank and disposed of her with acid. In each of the last cases I have had my glass of blood as before.'[22] Haigh then obtained the Hendersons' property by forgery. The statement took hours and ran to thousands of words, and Haigh seemed to take a great deal of pleasure in the proceedings, smiling as he told his macabre tale.

Once the press got hold of the story, London was engulfed by a wave of terror. Soon one newspaper was describing Haigh as 'the human vampire', prowling the streets and attacking unsuspecting women, sucking their blood and leaving them to die in the gutters.[23] Female travellers ran the distance home from the Tube and prostitutes became more wary than usual. Meanwhile, Haigh sat in his cell and dreamed of Broadmoor, building up his case for not guilty on the grounds of insanity by drinking his own urine. But Haigh's cunning defence foundered when the prosecution claimed that Haigh was sane and had acted with malice aforethought. Haigh was found guilty within minutes at Lewes Assizes, and hanged by Albert Pierrepoint at Wandsworth prison on 10 August 1949. As he had done with Heath, Pierrepoint used his special leather strap to bind Haigh's wrists.[24]

As Londoners reeled from news stories about these extraordinary pathological killers, there was mounting anxiety about more conventional forms of crime. Far from being smashed by the Blitz, London's gangland flourished. In 1945, the *Daily Express* warned readers:

Crime is on the march in Britain today, boldly and violently. It is double what it was in 1939 and the evil grows by 10,000 cases each month ... within shouting distance of a spot where Eros may soon stand again [Piccadilly Circus], I have seen men pull out fistfuls of pound notes. Guns, revolvers and Tommy guns sold well over the weekend.

There are more guns at the moment than there is ammunition to fit them.[25]

Two years later, in 1947, 10,300 boys in London aged between
fourteen and twenty were convicted members of criminal
gangs.[26] Regular outbursts of moral panic in the popular press
reached a crescendo with the de Antiquis case of 1947.

Just before 2 p.m. on Monday 28 April 1947, three masked
gunmen, Charles Jenkins, 23, Christopher Geraghty, 20, and
Terence Rolt, 17, burst into L. S. Jay's jewellers in Charlotte
Street. In the ensuing confusion, the assistant manager set off
the alarm and a shot was fired, although the staff were
unhurt. The raiders fled empty-handed, jumped into the getaway car then found it had been blocked by a lorry. As they
scattered across Charlotte Street and into Tottenham Street,
a passing motor mechanic, Alec de Antiquis, swung his
motorcycle round and blocked their path, whereupon Chris
Geraghty shot de Antiquis in the head. As de Antiquis lay
dying in the gutter, he said: 'I'm all right. Stop them. I did
my best.' By sheer chance, the executioner Albert Pierrepoint
was walking along Charlotte Street soon afterwards and
glimpsed the crowd that had gathered around de Antiquis'
body.

The robbers were tracked down within less than three
weeks, thanks to diligent policing on the part of the legendary Fabian of the Yard and DCI Bob Higgins. A
Macintosh raincoat, discarded at the scene of the crime, provided a vital clue. The manufacturer's label enabled the
police to trace it to a consignment sold in Deptford High
Street, and ultimately to Charles Jenkins. Soon afterwards,
the gun that had killed de Antiquis was recovered from the
river at Wapping, while a second gun, a fifty-year-old .455
Bulldog revolver, was found near the Thames in
Bermondsey, close by Jenkins' wife's family home. The

Murder in Soho – the scene at Charlotte Street in April 1947 where Alec de Antiquis was gunned down attempting to foil an armed robbery.

remaining bullets in this gun matched the one that had been fired in Jay's.[27]

Although Geraghty had fired the shot that killed de Antiquis, both men were found guilty of murder by joint enterprise. Jenkins and Geraghty were hanged at Pentonville on 19 September 1947. Albert Pierrepoint, who had witnessed the aftermath of the shooting, was chief executioner. Rolt, who was only seventeen, was given a prison sentence and released from gaol in 1956. The de Antiquis case prompted a national outcry about the threat of gun crime and even inspired the film *The Blue Lamp* (1950), in which Dirk Bogarde, as panicky young villain Tom Riley, shoots dead veteran police officer George Dixon. Dixon's character proved so sympathetic that he was resurrected as lead of the much-loved television series *Dixon of Dock Green*.

The de Antiquis case propelled the debate about capital

punishment back into the newspaper headlines. As supporters of the death penalty argued that the execution of Jenkins and Geraghty was justified since it had led to the successful break-up of their gang, the anti-hanging lobby maintained that a hefty prison sentence represented an equally valid deterrent. The anti-hanging contingent had another argument on their side: that of miscarriages of justice. As had been noted as early as 1386, in the judicial error noted by the *Chronicle of the Grey Friars*, the most appalling outcome of the death penalty was the execution of an innocent man. The tragic consequences of such miscarriages are the subject of the following chapter, the first of which concerns the macabre aftermath of one London's most horrific crimes.

WHO BREAKS
A BUTTERFLY
UPON A WHEEL?

*Miscarriages of Justice and the
Abolition of the Death Penalty*

This chapter tells the extraordinary story of three men and one woman whose executions provoked intense public debate about the implications of capital punishment. The executions of Derek Bentley, Ruth Ellis and James Hanratty sent shockwaves throughout Britain, while the case of Timothy Evans changed the public attitude towards capital punishment forever.

Timothy Evans, hanged in 1950 for the murder of his wife and baby daughter, had lived in a shabby terrace in Notting Hill. At the time, this district was not the fashionable quarter that it has become today. Notting Hill consisted of street after street of dilapidated houses, rented to West Indian immigrants by racketeer landlords. Number 10 Rillington Place, its bricks stained black with soot, was a typical example. Three years after Evans was hanged by Albert Pierrepoint, police were once again summoned to Rillington Place after a tenant made a grim discovery.

On the morning of 24 March 1953 an existing tenant, Beresford Brown, went downstairs to clean up the basement flat. He had been offered the basement after a previous incumbent had disappeared without a forwarding address. Determined to investigate the cause of an offensive smell, Brown had discovered what appeared to be two female bodies hidden behind a wall.[1] When Chief Superintendent Peter Beveridge and Chief Inspector Percy Law arrived from Scotland Yard, along with the coroner and a pathologist, the subsequent discoveries were sickening even to hardened officers. The bodies of three naked women, all strangled, were recovered from the kitchen. Following a search, a fourth corpse was discovered beneath the floorboards in the parlour, and two female skeletons were recovered from the garden. A human femur had been used to prop up the fence. More bones were found in flowerbeds and some blackened skull bones with teeth and pieces of a dress turned up in a dustbin. Bones were also found beneath an orange blossom bush, along with a newspaper fragment dated 19 July 1943.[2]

The first three bodies were identified as Hectorina McLennan, 26, Kathleen Maloney, also 26, and Rita Nelson, 25. Rita had been six months pregnant. All three women had worked as prostitutes, and all three had been suffocated with gas diverted from the fire with a rubber tube, and then strangled. Once unconscious, they had been raped and the sexual assaults had continued after death. The fourth body was that of an older woman, Ethel Christie, who had lived in the house since 1938. Ethel had not been sexually assaulted, but she had been strangled in the same fashion. The two bodies in the garden were identified by dental records as Ruth Fuerst, 21, an Austrian refugee who had disappeared in 1943, and Muriel Eady, 32, a factory worker. Ethel's husband, John Christie, was nowhere to be seen.[3]

The discovery of six female murder victims in one house was sensational enough. What intrigued the police more was the fact that at this very same house, four years earlier in 1949, the bodies of Mrs Beryl Evans and her eighteen-month-old baby daughter Geraldine had been found hidden in the wash-house. They had been strangled and wrapped in cloth. Timothy Evans had been charged with the murder of his wife and daughter, although he had gone to the gallows protesting his innocence, and claiming that the killer was in fact John Christie.

The police launched a manhunt and Christie was captured a week later, after an officer spotted a thin bespectacled man with a toothbrush moustache loitering near Putney Bridge. When the policeman asked the man to take off his hat, he did so, to reveal his distinctive domed forehead. It was Christie.[4]

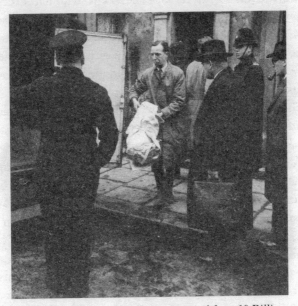

A grisly scene as human remains are removed from 10 Rillington Place, home of the serial killer John Reginald Christie, in 1953.

In custody, Christie confessed to murdering the three women found in the kitchen, the two women buried in the back garden, and Beryl Evans, but he remained adamant that he had not killed baby Geraldine. He claimed that he had gassed the other women accidentally while trying to have sex with them, and that when Ethel had suffered a seizure he had panicked and hidden the body before going on the run. Derek Curtis-Bennett QC, given the impossible job of defending Christie, pleaded diminished responsibility on the grounds of insanity, and argued that Christie had been showing signs of hysteria since developing shell shock in 1918.[5] The murder of his wife, argued Curtis-Bennett, was the final evidence that Christie was 'as mad as a March hare'.[6] After an hour and a half the jury promptly rejected this defence and found Christie guilty. Christie was executed by Albert Pierrepoint at Pentonville on 15 July 1953. Pierrepoint, who had executed over 600 people in the course of his career, later recalled Christie's appalled expression as he stumbled towards the drop. 'It was more than terror,' he wrote. 'At that moment I knew Christie would have given anything in his power to postpone his own death.'[7]

The outcome of Christie's trial immediately led to considerable doubt regarding the conviction of Timothy Evans. The chances of Evans having murdered Beryl and Geraldine when they lived in the same house as a serial killer appeared remote in the extreme. When this argument was combined with the fact that Evans was illiterate and had an IQ of seventy, his execution begins to look like a miscarriage of justice. In the aftermath an appeal committee was formed to clear Evans' name. Influential figures including Sir David Aston, the editor of the *Observer,* and the broadcaster Ludovic Kennedy all campaigned for a posthumous pardon, which was finally granted in October 1966. In 2003, the independent assessor for the Home Office, Lord Brennan QC, accepted that 'the conviction and execution of Timothy Evans for the murder of his child was wrongful and a miscarriage of justice'. In addition, there was no evidence to implicate Evans for the murder of his wife and she was most probably murdered by Christie.[8]

Evans' wrongful conviction was just one of many cases that put miscarriages of justice and capital punishment at the top of the news agenda. An equally controversial case had erupted in November 1952 following a disastrous armed robbery in south London. On 2 November 1952, two young men from Norbury, south-west London, decided to burgle a warehouse. The putative robbers, nineteen-year-old Derek Bentley and sixteen-year-old Christopher Craig, were carrying out an act of bravado, inspired by American gangster movies. Dressed in drape suits and trilby hats, which made them appear older than their years, both carried the weapons that were so easy to come by in post-war London. During a one-day amnesty, the Metropolitan Police had collected 18,500 revolvers, more than 250 machine-guns and over a quarter of a million rounds of ammunition.[9]

Bentley already had a criminal record, and his respectable working-class family were trying to keep him on the straight and narrow, and away from Christopher Craig, an aspiring mobster three years his junior. But Bentley, an epileptic with learning difficulties, was easily led. By 9.15 p.m. on the night of 2 November he was shinning up a drainpipe onto the roof of the Barlow and Parker Confectionary Company, Croydon. Bentley was equipped with a sheath knife and a knuckleduster, while Craig carried a Colt service revolver with the barrel sawn down to fit in the pocket of his drape suit, and several rounds of ammunition, some of which were of the wrong calibre for the weapon, and had to be adjusted to fit into the Colt.

Just as the pair were scrambling up the drainpipe, they were spotted by a nine-year-old girl in a house across the road. The girl quickly informed her father, who telephoned for the police. When the police arrived, Craig and Bentley hid behind the lift-housing, and Craig taunted the police. One of the police officers, Detective Sergeant Frederick Fairfax, climbed the drainpipe onto the roof and grabbed hold of Bentley. Bentley broke free of Fairfax's grasp. What happened then has been a matter of conjecture ever since. According to the police witnesses, Bentley shouted, 'Let him have it, Chris!' to Craig, and Craig fired at DS Fairfax and wounded him in the shoulder. Despite his injury, Fairfax was again able to restrain Bentley. Bentley told Fairfax that Craig was armed with a revolver and had further ammunition for the gun. Bentley had not used either of the weapons that he had in his pockets.[10]

A group of uniformed police officers arrived and was sent onto the roof. The first to reach the roof was PC Sidney Miles, who was immediately killed by a shot to the head. After exhausting his ammunition and being cornered, Craig jumped off the roof and plunged thirty feet onto a greenhouse, fracturing his spine and left wrist.

Bentley and Craig went on trial for murder at the Old Bailey on 9 December 1952. Under the Children and Young Persons Act 1933, sixteen-year-old Craig would be spared the death penalty if found guilty. But Derek Bentley, at nineteen, faced capital punishment. There was no possibility of pleading manslaughter, since the pair were accused of joint enterprise, and 'malicious intent' in attempting to carry out an armed robbery. Bentley's defence was that he had effectively been arrested by DS Fairfax when PC Miles was killed.[11]

The defence claimed there was ambiguity as to how many shots were fired and by whom. A ballistics expert questioned whether Craig could have hit Miles if he had shot at him deliberately. The fatal bullet was never recovered. Craig had used bullets of different under-sized calibres and the sawn-off barrel made it inaccurate to a degree of six feet at the range from which he fired.

Then there was controversy surrounding Bentley's alleged direction: 'Let him have it, Chris!' Craig and Bentley flatly denied that Bentley had said the words, while the police officers maintained that he did say them. Bentley's counsel argued that even if he had said 'Let him have it', it could not be proven that Bentley had intended the words to mean 'Shoot him, Chris,' rather than the literal meaning of 'Give him the gun, Chris.'

The defence's third argument was that Bentley was unfit to stand trial. Dr Hill, a psychiatrist at the Maudsley Hospital, had examined Bentley and reported that he was illiterate, with an IQ of eighty-seven and a mental age of eleven. However, the principal medical officer, Dr Matheson, argued that Bentley was not a 'feeble-minded person' under the Mental Deficiency Acts and was fit to plead and stand trial. The jury took seventy-five minutes to find both Craig and Bentley guilty of PC Miles's murder. Bentley was sentenced to death with a plea for mercy, while Craig was jailed for ten years.

Despite pleas for clemency from the trial jury, 200 Members of Parliament and, most notably of all, Mrs Miles, the widow of the murdered police officer, the Home Secretary David Maxwell Fyfe refused to request a royal pardon. Parliament was not allowed to debate Bentley's death sentence until it had been carried out, and Dr Hill of the Maudsley Hospital was forbidden to publish his report.[12]

Bentley was convinced that he would be reprieved right up until the last minute. But on 28 January 1953, he was hanged at Wandsworth Prison by Albert Pierrepoint. A large crowd gathered outside the prison from early that morning, and some sang the hymn 'Abide With Me' and the Twenty-third Psalm. When it was announced that the execution had been carried out, there were protests and two people were arrested and later fined for damage to property.[13]

Following the execution there was a public sense of unease about the decision and Maxwell Fyfe was criticized for letting the execution go ahead. Convinced that Bentley was innocent, his sister Iris began a long campaign to secure a posthumous pardon for him. In July 1993, Bentley was granted a royal pardon in respect of the sentence of death passed upon him. On 30 July 1998, the Court of Appeal quashed Bentley's conviction for murder on the grounds that the original trial judge was biased against the defendants and misdirected the jury on points of law. Scientific evidence also emerged which proved that the three police officers who testified about Bentley shouting 'Let him have it' had lied under oath. Craig welcomed Bentley's pardon. He has led a law-abiding life ever since the events of 2 November 1952. Tragically, Mr and Mrs Bentley and Derek's sister, Iris, never lived to see the day that Derek Bentley received his posthumous pardon.[14]

Two years after the scenes which had greeted Bentley's hanging at Wandsworth Prison, another angry crowd assembled to protest against an execution. This time, the prison was Holloway, and the demonstrations had been provoked by the decision to hang Ruth Ellis, a nightclub hostess who had been sentenced to death for shooting her lover. On 12 July 1955 the governor of Holloway was forced to call for police reinforcements as 500 people massed outside the prison gates, singing and chanting for hours. Thousands had signed petitions asking for the death penalty to be lifted in this case, including thirty-five members of London County Council who delivered their plea to the House of Commons that night. On the following morning, 13 July, a silent crowd, including women with prams, collected around the prison, waiting for the execution at nine o'clock. Eighteen minutes later, notice of Ellis' death was posted outside and the crowd surged forwards, blocking the road and stopping traffic.[15]

Ruth Ellis had the unenviable distinction of being the last woman to be hanged, a self-destructive butterfly broken upon the wheel of an outdated legal system. To Ellis' supporters, it seemed extraordinary that she should be convicted, thirty years after Madame Fahmy had walked free for killing her abusive husband. But Ellis' story is one of those cases within living memory where details emerge from a fog of speculation and investigation produces more questions than answers.

Ruth Ellis had not always been a victim. Indeed, she appears to have been something of a survivor and, after an abusive childhood and giving birth to a son at seventeen, she had become a hostess at the Little Club in Mayfair. The Little Club, typical of the drinking establishments which had sprung up after the war, was popular with everybody, including King Hussein of Jordan, the film stars Douglas Fairbanks Junior and Burt Lancaster, and Dr Stephen Ward, the society osteopath.[16] Ruth Ellis, with her glittering ash-blonde hair and, in the words of crime reporter Duncan Webb, her 'tinsel-like beauty', was the club's greatest attraction, a good sport, happy to pose nude for the Camera Club when there was no film in the cameras.[17]

In 1950, she had married George Ellis, a wealthy dentist, and moved to the suburbs, but when George Ellis turned out to be a violent alcoholic, Ruth fled back to London with their daughter, Georgina. Leaving both her children with her mother, Ruth returned to work and began a determined course of self-improvement, taking elocution lessons and deportment classes. Impressed by Ruth's ambition, her boss Maurie Conley promoted her to manager of another club, Carroll's. It was here that Ruth first met David Blakely, a tall, handsome young racing driver, and became hopelessly infatuated.[18]

Within weeks Blakely had moved into Ruth's flat above the club and she was bankrolling him. Blakely swiftly proved to be another violent alcoholic, unfaithful to Ruth with women and

Ruth Ellis with her lover, David Blakely, in 1955. After shooting Blakely dead in cold blood, Ruth Ellis was the last woman to be hanged.

men, but Ruth allowed him to run up a tab while Blakely pursued his racing career and returned to his respectable family and his fiancée at weekends. Fuelled by alcohol, the affair was tempestuous, punctuated by terrible rows and violent assaults. On one occasion, Ruth ended up in the Middlesex Hospital with a sprained ankle and a black eye. On another, Blakely assaulted her so severely that she suffered a miscarriage.

It was at such times that Ruth turned to another lover, Desmond Cussens, for comfort. Steady-going, middle-aged Cussens had flown Lancaster bombers during the war and represented stability. Ruth vacillated between both men but events came to a climax at Easter 1955. When Blakely failed to telephone on the evening of Good Friday, Ruth promptly went round to the home of his good friend and mechanic, Seaton Findlater, at Tanza Road, Hampstead. The Findlaters refused to let her in, but she could hear Blakely in the background, laughing with the nanny. Later that evening, the police had to be called. Ruth had smashed all the windows of Blakely's Standard Vanguard car.[19]

There was another doomed expedition the following day, when Cussens had driven Ruth back to Tanza Road to speak to Blakely. Again, the Findlaters refused to let her in. Cussens tried to calm Ruth down with Pernod and tranquilisers, but all she could say was, 'I'd shoot the swine if I had a gun.'[20]

Sunday evening saw the third and final visit to Tanza Road. Driven to the Findlaters' residence by Cussens, Ruth waited in the shadows as Blakely emerged from the house with his friend Clive Gunnell, a car salesman. They drove to the Magdala public house in South Hill Park, and Ruth followed them. The pub was pretty full, with everyone in a bank holiday mood, and Blakely was laughing and drinking along with them. Outside, Ruth watched and waited, taking consolation from the cold steel of the gun between her fingers.[21]

Gunnell left the pub first, and then Blakely followed. He was about to open the car door when Ruth pulled the .38 Smith & Wesson revolver out of her handbag. Blakely glanced round, saw her, and then ignored her. Then Ruth fired at point-blank range. As Blakely fell to the ground she emptied the gun into him. One stray bullet caught a pedestrian, Gladys Yule, wounding her in the hand. Ruth stood motionless and when the gun was empty she said, calmly, 'Call the police.'[22]

When Ruth Ellis appeared before Mr Justice Havers at Number 1 Court of the Old Bailey on 20 June 1955, the crime writer Duncan Webb and his colleagues anticipated a 'long and colourful trial', during which Ruth's defence counsel would put forward all kinds of elaborate pleas 'to justify or mitigate the circumstances'.[23] The public gallery was packed with an enthralled crowd, ranging from East End characters to West End socialites, all agog to see a woman go on trial for shooting her lover.

There was a collective gasp as Ruth entered the witness box. Against the advice of her counsel, Ruth appeared in court wearing an elegant black suit with astrakhan fur lapels and a white silk blouse. As she moved her head, the light glinted on her immaculate ash-blonde coiffure. The governor of Holloway had permitted a hairdresser to visit Ruth in prison, in preparation for her day in court. Far from being the repentant prisoner at the bar, Ruth looked as if she were about to open up Carroll's club for business. The next shock came when Ruth's barrister, Aubrey Melford Stevenson, opened the case for the defence by saying: 'Let me make this abundantly plain: there is no question here but this woman shot this man ... You will not hear one word from me – or from the lady herself – questioning that.'[24]

As the court took in this astonishing approach, the defence pleaded manslaughter and absence of malice. Melford Stevenson's argument was that Ruth had suffered constant and brutal abuse at the hands of David Blakely, 'a most unpleasant person', but had been unable to get away from him, trapped 'in something like an emotional prison guarded by this young man, from which there seemed to be no escape'.[25] A similar defence had been offered for Madame Fahmy. Would a sympathetic jury take the same attitude towards Ruth Ellis, the victim of abuse who had finally turned on her vicious lover?

The prosecution had only one question for Ruth. As the tall, angular figure of Mr Christmas Humphreys, prosecuting, loomed over her, the jury and spectators could have heard a pin drop. Then Humphreys asked his question: 'When you fired that revolver at close range, into the body of David Blakely, what did you intend to do?'[26]

Ruth cast her eyes down to the floor. She pursed her lips. There was a deep hush in court, as if everyone was resisting the impulse to cry out, 'Don't do it! Watch what you say! Be careful!'

'It is obvious,' Ruth replied, in a calm, audible voice. 'When I shot him, I intended to kill him.'

And with that reply Ruth Ellis coolly placed the noose around her own neck.[27] The jury took just fourteen minutes to find Ruth Ellis guilty of murder and she was sentenced to death. The sentence provoked outrage in the press, with the popular columnist 'Cassandra' (William Connor) opining in the *Daily Mirror*, 'The one thing that brings stature and dignity to mankind and raises us above the beasts will have been denied her – pity and the hope of ultimate redemption.'[28] A petition signed by 50,000 people, calling for a reprieve, was rejected by the Home Secretary, while a French reporter, surprised at the lack of a defence of *crime passionnel* in the English legal system reflected that: 'Passion in England, except for cricket and betting, is always regarded as shameful disease.[29] The crime writer, Raymond Chandler, that expert on *femmes fatales*, described Ruth's sentence as 'the mediaeval savagery of the law' in a letter to the *Evening Standard*, while the judge Cecil Havers filed a personal request for a reprieve.[30] It was ignored.

Two days before she went to the gallows, Ruth Ellis gave a statement to her solicitor, Victor Mischon, and his clerk, Leon Simmons. In it, Ruth stated that Desmond Cussens had given her the gun, got her drunk on Pernod and driven her to Tanza Road. By this action, Cussens had effectively signed her death warrant. Mischon and Simmons took this statement to the Home Office, but it was ignored.[31]

On 13 July 1955, Ruth wrote to Blakely's parents, concluding, 'I have always loved your son, and I will die still loving him.' Then she put her diamante spectacles down on the table, saying, 'I won't need these any more,' and went to her death.[32] Ruth was hanged by Albert Pierrepoint who later said, 'She died as brave as any man and she never spoke a single word.'[33]

A rumour still circulates among the legal profession that this hanging was not one of the highlights of Pierrepoint's career, although the autopsy report gives no indication that anything was amiss. But according to grisly anecdote, Pierrepoint miscalculated the weight of Ruth's petite frame and allocated too much rope to the drop. As a result, when the trapdoor opened beneath her feet, Ruth's head was torn off. Following execution, Ruth was buried within the grounds of Holloway but when the prison was modernized in the 1970s, her remains were reinterred in a private grave in Amersham.

The events of 10 April 1955 continue to inspire speculation to this day, not least the involvement of Desmond Cussens, who appears to have manipulated Ruth into the shooting. Cussens' motivation remains unclear. If Cussens had regarded Blakely as a rival, and wanted him eliminated, he must have been aware that by doing so he stood to lose Ruth to prison, if not the gallows. Another theory, advanced by Ruth's sister, Monica Weller, was that Ruth had close links to Stephen Ward and his shadowy world of blackmail and espionage. In *Ruth Ellis: My Sister's Secret Life,* Monica Weller suggested that, as one of 'Stephen's girls', Ruth had been framed by the security services because she possessed compromising details of respected establishment figures.[34]

In conclusion, my own opinion is that Ruth effectively killed herself when she squeezed the trigger of that Smith & Wesson. By shooting David Blakely, Ruth killed both of them. In the ultimate act of self-destruction, Ruth went bravely to her own death, unable to live with Blakely but unable to live without him. And as with every murder, this case left a painful legacy. In the immediate aftermath, Ruth's estranged husband, George Ellis, hanged himself and their daughter Georgina was adopted. Ruth's son, Andy, had a troubled life. Sir Cecil Havers, the trial judge, sent money every year towards his upkeep. But, in 1982, after smashing up his mother's gravestone, Andy killed himself. Mr Christmas Humphreys paid for his funeral. Georgina died of cancer in 2000. In 2003, the case was referred back to the Court of Appeal by the Criminal Cases Review Commission, but was rejected. Ruth's family continue to campaign for her posthumous pardon.

Although the protests against Ruth Ellis's execution were to no avail, the uproar helped strengthen political support for the end of the death penalty. In March 1956 the Death Penalty (Abolition) Bill was passed by Parliament on its second reading, but subsequently overturned by the House of Lords. The following year, in March 1957, as a half-measure, the Homicide Act was passed. This limited the death sentence to five categories of murder that constituted capital murder. Capital murder was defined as murder committed in the course or furtherance of theft, murder by shooting or explosion, murder whilst resisting arrest or escaping, murder of a police officer or prison officer and two murders committed on different occasions. The defence of diminished responsibility was also incorporated into English law by this Act. Of course these changes came too late for Timothy Evans, Derek Bentley and Ruth Ellis, but it might have spared all three from the gallows – Evans and Bentley on the grounds of mental impairment and Ruth Ellis due to the sustained catalogue of emotional and physical abuse she had suffered at David Blakely's hands.

The grim fates of Timothy Evans, Derek Bentley and Ruth Ellis undermined the case for the death penalty and led to increasing demands for mercy and leniency. But it would take another major trial before the death knell tolled for capital punishment. At the heart of this trial was the vexed question of mistaken identity and the possibility that a man went to the gallows for a terrible crime that he did not commit. The name of that man was James Hanratty, and the case became known as the 'A6 Murder'.

On the evening of 22 August 1961, Michael Gregsten and his girlfriend Valerie Storie were sitting in his car at the edge of a cornfield. This spot, near Dorney Reach, Buckinghamshire, was their regular hideaway, since 36-year-old Gregsten was a married man. The couple had met at the government Road Research Laboratory, where Gregsten was a research scientist and Valerie his laboratory assistant. The affair had endured for months despite departmental reprimands and Mrs Gregsten's attempts to wreck the relationship. As they sat in Gregsten's grey Morris Minor that night, planning their part in a motor rally and discussing their future, the mood was more positive. 'The car seemed so snug and reassuring,' Valerie later wrote, 'a private world.'[35] That world was about to be invaded in the most horrific and terrifying manner.

Darkness had fallen when the couple were startled by a sharp tap on the window. Gregsten wound the driver's window down and found himself staring down the barrel of a gun. Before they could stop him, the smartly suited stranger climbed into the back seat and ordered Gregsten to drive. Over the following six hours, Gregsten drove at gunpoint through Slough and across north-west London. The Morris Minor finally came to a halt off the A6 near Bedford, at a spot called Deadman's Hill. When Gregsten created a diversion by throwing a bag at him, the gunman shot him in the head, killing him instantly. As Valerie screamed in horror, the gunman shouted: 'Be quiet, will you? I'm finking.' Worse was to come. The gunman ordered Valerie to help him drag Gregsten's body out of the Morris Minor. Then he raped her over Gregsten's body, before emptying his gun into her and driving away erratically, with a crashing of gears.[36]

At 6.45 the following morning, the couple were discovered by Sidney Burton, a farm labourer on his way to work. Valerie was taken to Bedford Hospital, where she was found to be *compos mentis* and able to provide a statement to the police.

Valerie had escaped with her life, but she was permanently paralysed as a result of her injuries.[37]

When Valerie described her ordeal to the police, she told them that she had only once seen the gunman clearly, in the lights of a passing car, and admitted that she might not be able to pick him out of an identity parade. The police persevered, however, with the aid of the new technology of the Identikit portrait, and Valerie and another witness, who had seen the driver of the Morris Minor, produced two images. The gunman was described as about five feet eight inches tall, with deep-set brown eyes and a strong East End accent. Two days later, on 24 August, the murder weapon was recovered from under a seat on the top deck of a 36A London bus, fully loaded and wiped clean of prints. It was wrapped in a handkerchief, which was to provide DNA evidence at a later date.[38]

Meanwhile, the police lacked a suspect, let alone a motive, for this appalling crime. It was at this point that Mrs Janet Gregsten entered the drama. On 31 August 1961, eight days after her husband's murder, Mrs Gregsten was standing in the antiques shop in Swiss Cottage owned by her brother, William Ewer. Glancing out of the window, Janet Gregsten caught sight of a young man with black hair walking into a dry cleaner's across the other side of the arcade. Letting out a scream, Janet Gregsten grabbed her brother's arm and said: 'That's him! He fits the description. I have an overpowering feeling that it's him!' Janet Gregsten recognized the killer on account of his 'icy-blue saucer-like eyes'. This was despite the fact that Valerie had described her assailant as brown-eyed.[39]

While William Ewer pursued the mysterious young man in Swiss Cottage, the police were interviewing Peter Alphon, an eccentric loner who eked out a living selling almanacks door to door. Alphon provided an alibi for the night of the murder, saying he had taken a room at the Vienna Hotel in Maida Vale. This was confirmed by the manager, William Nudds. In the meantime, William Ewer had traced the young man from the dry cleaner's. His name was James Ryan, and he was a familiar face in the north London antiques trade. But Ewer claimed that his information was dismissed by the police.[40]

On 11 September William Nudds found two cartridges in the basement room of the Vienna Hotel where Alphon had stayed the night. According to Nudds, another guest had also hired that room on 22 August. (This was not unusual, as the Vienna Hotel was a seedy lodging house where rooms were rented by the hour.) This second man had left the Vienna asking for directions to the number 36 bus, and his name was James Ryan. After Nudds made a second statement implicating Alphon on 21 September, the police announced that Alphon was the suspect and launched a manhunt. That same day, Mrs Gregsten visited Valerie Storie at Guy's Hospital, where she had been transferred for specialist treatment. According to the *Daily Mail*, Valerie had asked Janet to visit, and told her what had happened on that terrible night. The murderer had been in his thirties and respectably dressed, with a Cockney accent and 'blue, staring eyes'.[41]

The same night, Peter Alphon gave himself up at Cannon Row police station, and on 24 September he took part in an identity parade. After Valerie Storie did not identify him as her attacker, he was released without charge. At this point it emerged that James Ryan, the other resident of the basement room at the Vienna Hotel where the cartridges were discovered, was in fact James Hanratty. A professional car thief already wanted in connection with two robberies, Hanratty went on the run and was eventually arrested in Blackpool on 11 October. On 14 October, Valerie Storie attended an identity parade, during which she asked each suspect to repeat the sentence spoken by the killer: 'Be quiet, will you? I'm thinking.' Like the murderer, Hanratty pronounced 'thinking' as 'finking'. Unlike the identikit picture, James Hanratty had bright red hair. But Valerie picked Hanratty out of the parade and he was duly charged with the A6 murder.[42]

Hanratty went on trial at the Bedford Assizes on 22 January 1962 charged with the murder of Michael Gregsten. The trial had originally been scheduled for the Old Bailey, but was changed at the last moment to Bedford, where there was understandable hostility towards the accused. Hanratty's defence rested on the fact that he had no apparent motive. Why would an urban car thief stalk a couple in the middle of the countryside and carry out a random killing? Hanratty had no previous convictions for violence or sexual assault. In addition, as a professional car thief, he was an experienced driver, while the killer had struggled to get the Morris Minor into gear and drive away. While the forensic evidence taken at the scene did show the same blood group as Hanratty, it was a blood group he shared with half the population. Hanratty also had the A6 Defence Committee on his side, a group of witnesses, campaigners and experts assembled by his father, James Hanratty, to prove his innocence. But, given the vicious nature of the crime, popular opinion was against Hanratty and all the sympathy lay with the victim, who appeared in court on a stretcher. Hanratty also lost credibility by changing his alibi halfway through. After claiming that he had spent the night in question with friends in Liverpool, he then changed the alibi and said that he had been in Rhyl, north Wales, instead.

Fuelled by popular outrage, the prosecution steamrollered over Hanratty's defence. Arguing that Hanratty had escalated to violent crime and had been practising 'stick-ups' with a gun at the Vienna Hotel, prosecuting counsel convinced the jury that Hanratty had hijacked Michael Gregsten's car and then raped Valerie after being overcome by lust. A fellow prisoner, Roy Langdale, was produced to give evidence that Hanratty had confessed the crime to him while on remand.[43] Charles France, a small-time crook and a friend of Hanratty's, told the jury that Hanratty had informed him that the back of a bus was a good place to conceal a weapon. France's testimony must have come as a shock to Hanratty. Hitherto, Hanratty had been on good terms with France and had dated France's daughter, Carol. But it was Valerie Storie's identification of Hanratty that convinced the jury. On 17 February, after nine and a half hours, the jury delivered the verdict of guilty and Hanratty was convicted and sentenced to death. Despite a petition signed by more than 90,000 people, an appeal was turned down on 13 March. Three days later, perhaps overcome with remorse, Charles France committed suicide.

On 2 April R. A. Butler, the Home Secretary, refused to issue a reprieve, but Hanratty still maintained his innocence. The day before he was due to be executed he wrote to his family from his cell at Bedford Gaol, saying, 'I'm dying tomorrow but I'm innocent. Clear my name.' On the following morning, 4 April, Hanratty still believed that he might receive a last-minute reprieve. But it was not to be and, with shock and incredulity, he went to the gallows. A month later, Carol France, Charles France's daughter and Hanratty's sometime girlfriend, attempted to take her own life with a drug overdose.

Meanwhile, as if the Hanrattys had not suffered enough, Peter Alphon called at the family home and attempted to offer them 'compensation' for the death of their son. Understandably, the family refused to speak to him. This gesture was just the beginning of an extraordinary sequence of actions by Alphon. In *Queen* magazine in September 1966 Alphon claimed that he was the A6 killer, but then denied his guilt a year later in a *Panorama* television programme. And then, in May 1967, Alphon called a press conference in Paris and confessed to the murder, claiming that someone close to Gregsten had given him £5,000 to 'frighten' the couple. Alphon retracted this confession the following September, and insisted that Hanratty was guilty and had been hired by Mrs Gregsten to break up the relationship.

The investigative journalist Paul Foot took up the Hanratty family's cause, and created a compelling argument for Hanratty's innocence in his outstanding book *Who Killed Hanratty?* (1973). When Foot interviewed Mrs Gregsten shortly before her death in 1995, Mrs Gregsten angrily denied any involvement in the murder of her husband, but no longer seemed convinced of Hanratty's guilt and pointed the finger at Alphon. Alphon lived on, an increasingly frail and eccentric figure. In Bob Woffinden's excellent 1992 television documentary about the case, Alphon makes a final appearance, a spectral, ghoulish figure wearing a flapping raincoat in a windswept underground station. Alphon continued to boast of his involvement in the murder until his death in 2009.

After three Home Office inquiries into the case, the surviving exhibits from the trial were discovered in 1991. Hanratty's relatives donated DNA for forensic testing, hoping that this would exonerate him, but the results from testing in June 1999 were said to be equivocal. On 19 March 1997, the Home Office referred the case to the new Criminal Cases Review Commission. In 2001, Hanratty's body was exhumed in order to extract DNA. This was compared with DNA on the handkerchief wrapped round the gun, and with semen on Valerie's underwear. Although no forensic evidence from the crime scene had been linked to Hanratty previously, DNA samples from both sources matched Hanratty's DNA. At the subsequent appeal hearing, Michael Mansfield QC, acting for the Hanratty family, admitted that if contamination could be excluded the DNA evidence demonstrated that Hanratty had committed the murder and rape. But he added that the evidence may have been contaminated because of lax handling procedures. However, neither sample yielded DNA from any second male source, as would presumably have been expected if another male had committed the crimes and the samples had subsequently been contaminated. The argument for contamination was dismissed as 'fanciful' by the judges, who concluded that 'The DNA evidence, standing alone, is certain proof of guilt.' Hanratty's family and their supporters have continued to contest this conclusion.[44] Paul Foot maintained his belief in Hanratty's innocence until his own death in 2004, despite the results of the DNA tests.[45]

Hanratty was one of the last people to be hanged in the United Kingdom. The last two were Peter Allen and Gwynne Evans, hanged simultaneously on 13 August 1964. In 1965, Sydney Silverman MP introduced a private member's bill to suspend the death penalty. The Murder (Abolition of Death Penalty) Act 1965 suspended the death penalty for five years and substituted it with a mandatory life imprisonment. In 1969, the Act was made permanent. This humane and merciful piece of legislation brought an end to centuries of judicial murder and ensured that never again would an innocent man or woman suffer the ultimate punishment for a crime which they did not commit.

In his memoirs the chief hangman, Albert Pierrepoint, reflected on his own attitude towards capital punishment. 'I have come to the conclusion that executions solve nothing,' he wrote, 'and are only an antiquated relic of a primitive desire for revenge which takes the easy way and hands over the responsibility for revenge to other people. The trouble with the death penalty has always been that nobody wanted it for everybody, but everybody differed about who should get off.'[46]

Latterly, attempts to re-introduce the death penalty have not proved successful. When it was last debated in Parliament in 1998, during the passage of the Human Rights Act, it was rejected by 158 votes.[47]

But in London there remained one pair of men for whom the abolition of the death penalty and indeed the law in general had no relevance. These were hard men who made their own rules and took the law into their own hands. Their names were Ronnie and Reggie Kray.

15

HARD BASTARDS AND DIAMOND GEEZERS

How the Firm Ruled London

By the 1950s, London's gangland had become a dark and almost mythical realm. Like the subterranean River Tyburn, the underworld rolled on beneath London, populated by legendary 'old faces' such as Billy Hill and Jack 'Spot' Comer, the terrifying Messina family, and intimidating newcomers such as the Kray twins and their 'Firm'. Billy Hill (1911–84) had been the first to build a new empire of crime among the sooty rubble of post-war London. A self-proclaimed hard bastard, he literally carved out his territory, inflicting vicious knife wounds upon the faces of those who offended him, often in the shape of a 'V' for Victory. Hill insisted that 'chivving', as he referred to it, was only used as a last resort. After someone glassed him in a pub, he pulled the glass out of his face with one hand and set about chivving his assailant with the other, wounding with surgical precision. 'I was always careful to draw my knife down on the face, never across or upwards, so that if the knife slips you don't cut an artery. Chivving is chivving, but cutting an artery is usually murder. Only mugs do murder.'[1]

Hill had teamed up with Jack 'Spot' Comer, a Jewish race-course racketeer noted for his flamboyant dress sense and big cigars. Comer was also a self-appointed enforcer to the Jewish community. In 1936 Comer had taken on Oswald Mosley's Blackshirts during the Battle of Cable Street. Together Hill and Comer had set about seizing the Sabini empire from another gangster, Harry White. After the Italian Sabini gang had been interred as enemy aliens during the outset of the Second World War, Harry White had taken over their realm of nightclubs, *spielers* and brothels. Hill and Comer wrested it off him in a showdown forever after known as the Battle of the Stork Club.[2]

In July 1947 Harry White was drinking in the Stork Club in Piccadilly with a racehorse trainer, Tim O'Sullivan, and another man when Comer walked in with ten heavies. Comer accused White of anti-Semitism, and smashed a bottle over his head. As White collapsed in a pool of blood, Comer's men attacked O'Sullivan and the third man. O'Sullivan was beaten unconscious and pushed into an open fire. The third man was slashed with razors and stabbed. According to Comer, White scarpered as soon as he was able. 'You couldn't see the seat of his trousers for dust.' Afterwards Billy Hill crowned himself the 'Bandit King' of London, with Comer in the role of trusted courtier, and masterminded a series of breathtakingly audacious armed robberies.

The first of these was the Eastcastle Street robbery in May 1952, when a team of masked men held up a Royal Mail van just off Oxford Street and escaped with £287,000 (£6,150,000 today). This was a real 'project crime', planned and executed with military precision. The robbers used two cars to sand-wich the van. The first car emerged slowly from a side street causing the van to slow down, the second car then pulled up alongside. The driver and two attendants were dragged out and coshed and the van was stolen. It was later found abandoned near Regents Park. The Prime Minister, Winston Churchill, demanded daily updates, and yet despite the involvement of over 1,000 police officers, nobody was ever caught. Two years later, Hill was behind a £40,000 bullion heist. Again, despite constant suspicion and allegations that Hill was behind the robberies, no one was ever brought to justice.[3]

Meanwhile, Jack Comer, tired of playing second fiddle, was making his own bid for power. Fearing a coup, Hill had Comer and his wife Rita ambushed outside their Hyde Park Mansions flat by 'Mad' Frankie Fraser and his gang of thugs. Rita was knocked to the ground, fortunately unhurt, but Comer was slashed with razors and required seventy-eight stitches and a blood transfusion. Scarred for life, Comer refused to name his attackers, but Rita had no such reservations and Fraser went down for seven years. Comer had learned his lesson, and retired to Ireland. 'I ain't afraid of anyone,' he said, 'but I want a quiet life now.'[4]

While Billy Hill was organizing textbook armed robberies, a sinister family known as the Messinas had seized control of the vice racket. The Messina brothers, Sicilian by way of Alexandria, had arrived in Britain in the 1930s and operated by importing foreign girls, usually from France and Italy, on forged passports, marrying them off to compliant men and setting them to walk the streets of the West End. Anyone who dared stand up to the Messinas was ruthlessly eliminated. Duncan Webb memorably described the 'men and women left lying in pools of blood on the pavements of London'. Hefty backhanders to corrupt Vice Squad officers ensured the gang's immunity from prosecution. Even the Home Secretary, Mr Chuter Ede, confessed in the House of Commons that

*Marthe Watts with husband Gino Messina and his brother
Carmelo in 1947. The notorious Messina brothers dominated the
London vice trade in the 1940s.*

nothing could be done about the gang, leading Attilio Messina
to boast: 'We are more powerful than the British government.
We can do as we like in England.' Gino Messina's wife,
Marthe Watts, recalled Gino sitting in one of his opulent
Mayfair flats like a spider in a web of vice. He invested in
property, drove a yellow Rolls-Royce, dressed like a film star
and seemed invulnerable. 'London belongs to me!' he bragged
to Marthe.[5]

Despite the public outcry, the police did not interfere in
these turf wars, which is when Duncan Webb of the *Sunday
People* became involved. In true crusading journalistic style,
Webb went undercover to investigate the brothers. Posing as
a punter, he interviewed dozens of Messina girls on their beats
in Shepherd's Market and Bond Street, and was threatened
and beaten up for his trouble.

The main barrier to convicting the Messinas was their anonymity. Although Gino was a distinctive figure, with his Jermyn Street suits and handmade shoes, he and his brothers posed as antiques dealers and used a number of English aliases such as 'Charles Maitland' and 'Edward Marshall' to evade detection. The Messinas had a word-of-mouth reputation as a hydra-headed phantom army of villains, who terrorized the London streets with thuggery, violence and corruption. They controlled an army of mythical women, not one of whom could be positively identified, and operated from scores of different addresses. They had corrupt police officers on their side, and excellent lawyers. It proved almost impossible to get a contact to talk. At the mention of the name 'Messina' most interviewees would gulp down their drink and leave. The word carried an atmosphere of fear and horror to the average crook, whispered with hallowed awe and dubious respect.[6]

Despite continual threats of violence, Webb persevered with his investigation. On 3 January 1950, Webb published his exposé of the Messina gang and their empire of vice in the *Sunday People*.[7] Scotland Yard followed up his enquiries and Alfredo Messina went on trial, after a doomed attempt to bribe the arresting officers. The remaining brothers escaped to Europe, where they continued to run a vice racket before being arrested and gaoled. Gino's wife Marthe Watts loyally followed Gino to Belgium, but after a lifetime of hardship she succumbed to a collapsed lung and a nervous breakdown. Marthe left Gino and published her memoirs, *The Men in My Life*, in 1954.[8]

As the underworld ebbed and flowed, old faces were lost to prison and death. Fresh contenders stepped forward, eager to seize power. The most formidable of these was an up-and-coming pair of twins, former boxers who exuded an aura of menace. Their names were Ronnie and Reggie Kray.

Like Bentley and Craig and dozens of other wannabe gangsters before them, the young Krays had been inspired by Hollywood. The first time Ronnie Kray's nemesis, Inspector 'Nipper' Read, clapped eyes on him, in 1964, Ronnie Kray was arriving outside the Grave Maurice pub in Whitechapel like a member of the royal family. Stepping out of a big American car, dressed like a Chicago gangster in a long cashmere coat, with his hair greased and parted, 'he looked like Al Capone without his fedora'.[9]

The Krays' reign of terror was unique. Their gang, known as 'the Firm', gained exceptional domination over London's underworld. Attempts by Scotland Yard to 'collate' or gather evidence against them were met with a wall of silence. Witnesses were intimidated and threatened with death if they talked to the police. Enemies were blatantly murdered. The Kray twins made a profession of violence.

Born on 23 October 1933, the twins initially showed some promise in the boxing ring, but a dishonourable discharge from their National Service and a spell in military prison meant that they could not obtain the licences they needed to turn professional. Instead, the Krays bought the run-down Regal Billiard Club on the Mile End Road. It was here that they established 'the Firm', an impressive organization composed of the twins, their older brother Charlie, Leslie 'Payne the Brain', who acted as a financial advisor, and Freddie 'the Mean Machine' Foreman. Ronnie, openly homosexual despite the dangers of prosecution, had a constant supply of rent boys who doubled as his spies. Enforcement came in the form of violence, through a beating, or murder, but sometimes it took no more than an intimidating stare from 'the Colonel', as Ronnie liked to call himself, to convince a miscreant of the error of his ways.

By the end of the 1950s the twins had made the East End

their empire, thanks to an extensive variety of protection rackets, hijacking, armed robbery and arson. 'If they drove down Commercial Road, everybody waved to them,' recalled Inspector Nipper Read. 'If somebody had a drink with them, it was like having tea with Princess Margaret.'[10]

In February 1960, Peter Rachman, the violent racketeer landlord, offered Ronnie a nightclub called Esmeralda's Barn in Knightsbridge. The Krays were obsessed with show business, and only too delighted to open their own West End club in which they could play host to such luminaries as Barbara Windsor, Diana Dors (the British Marilyn Monroe), Frank Sinatra and Judy Garland.

By the mid 1960s, the Krays controlled half the illegal gambling clubs in London and had friends in high places, including the Tory peer Lord Boothby, and the homosexual Labour MP Tom Driberg, who attended parties given by Ronnie where rent boys were offered round like so many canapés.[11] When the *Sunday Mirror* published allegations of an affair between 'a prominent peer and a West End thug', Boothby sued for libel and accepted damages of £40,000. The police were ordered to drop their enquiries into the case and the newspapers effectively silenced. 'They were the best years of our lives,' Ronnie recollected. 'The Beatles and the Rolling Stones were rulers of pop music, Carnaby Street ruled the fashion world and me and my brother ruled London. We were fucking untouchable.'[12]

While the Krays enjoyed their reign over London, the British public were briefly diverted by the Great Train Robbery, the crime of the century, during which £2,500,000 was stolen from the Royal Mail night train from Glasgow to London. For sheer planning and execution, this job knocked Eastcastle Street and the bullion heist into a cocked hat. With one major difference – Billy Hill's gang never got caught.

Nine months in preparation, the robbery had been devised in London by Bruce Reynolds, an antiques dealer who enjoyed the good life, driving an Aston Martin and staying at the Ritz. Reynolds had selected his men carefully, for brain, brawn and inside knowledge. There were heavies, like Gordon Goody and Jimmy White, a former paratrooper; a train expert, Roger Cordrey; Buster Edwards, a club-owner; Roy James, a racing driver; and Ronnie Biggs, whose critical asset was his friend, a retired train driver, who would play an essential role in the robbery. The plan was to hijack the train with a false signal, steal the mailbags, lie low at Leatherslade Farm, and quietly launder the money.

At 3.03 a.m. on 8 August 1963, Jack Mills was driving the night mail train along the West Coast Main Line towards Euston Station when a red light signal appeared at Sear's Crossing, between Leighton Buzzard and Cheddington. The fireman, David Whitby, climbed out of the cab and went to the telephone at the trackside to find out what had caused the delay. He was seized by Buster Edwards, dragged down the bank and told to keep quiet. When Jack Mills stuck his head out of the cab and asked what was wrong, he was coshed. As the crime reporter Duncan Campbell has noted, this single act of violence marred the robbery in the eyes of many. Subsequently, nobody could ever agree who hit Mills. Biggs' friend, Stan Agate, proved unable to drive the train as he was only familiar with Southern region trains, so the gang patched Mills up, and offered him a cigarette and a share of the takings, which he refused. However he did agree to shunt the train into position at Bridego Bridge so that the robbery could be completed. Mills and Whitby were handcuffed together and told not to move for half an hour while the robbers completed their raid.

Despite the fact that the train was carrying almost £3 million, there were no security guards. The 121 mailbags were removed via a human chain in twenty-five minutes, and the robbers made their getaway to Leatherslade Farm. But the robbers, hitherto so meticulous, had already made a fatal error. In telling Mills and Whitby not to move for half an hour, they had revealed the fact that they had a base nearby. The deserted farmhouse was quickly revealed as their hiding place. Tiny forensic details gave them away. Roy James had fed the farm cats and his prints were all over a bowl. Buster Edwards had left palm prints on a money wrapper. Within five weeks five members of the gang had been arrested, and thirteen men eventually went on trial in 1964 at Aylesbury, chosen because there was less threat of witness intimidation than at the Old Bailey.

While the British public might have been tickled pink by the gang's audacity, the judiciary took a darker view. The judge, Mr Justice Edmund Davies, handed down twenty-five- and thirty-year sentences that sent out a clear message that armed robbery would not be tolerated, and described the robbery as 'a crime of sordid violence inspired by vast greed'.[13]

This represented a tough new approach on the part of the judiciary. The following years would see the Krays and their greatest rival, the scrap metal dealer Charlie Richardson, boss of the Richardson gang, sent down for unprecedented terms.[14]

Like the Krays, the Richardsons had used violence to control their empire, which operated out of Camberwell, south-east London. The Richardson gang was also known as 'the Torture Gang' on account of the tough tactics used on gang members accused of disloyalty. Following a mock trial, gang members were punished with a range of penalties from cigarette burns to whipping and having their teeth pulled out with pliers, the latter being a speciality of 'Mad' Frankie Fraser. When the 'Torture Trial' opened at the Old Bailey in April 1967, witnesses who had turned Queen's Evidence spoke of having toes removed with bolt cutters, being nailed to the floor and urinated upon or punished with the 'black box', an old field telephone with a hand-operated generator which was used to administer electric shocks. Terminals were applied to the nipples and genitalia, and the victim was sometimes immersed in a bath to increase the shock. Richardson, who denied that the black box had ever existed, was sentenced to twenty-five years for grievous bodily harm, with the judge concluding, 'It must be made clear to all those who set themselves up as gang leaders that they will be struck down by the law as you will be struck down.'[15]

While the Krays must have been relieved to have their rival, Charlie Richardson, safely behind bars, they were beginning to lose control. Ronnie's psychopathic outbursts were intensifying, inspired by prodigious quantities of alcohol. He was already taking credit for the shooting of George Cornell in the Blind Beggar pub, and, fuelled by gin and hubris, had forgotten Billy Hill's warning that 'murder is for mugs'. Then there had been the lapse of judgement that had led the twins to help Frank 'the Mad Axeman' Mitchell escape from Dartmoor Prison in December 1966, only to discover that the burly loudmouth with the low IQ was an embarrassment. Mitchell refused to lie low in his safe house and wrote endless letters to the Home Secretary, petitioning for a pardon. According to Albert Donoghue, a Kray heavy, Mitchell was discreetly bundled into a van and shot. Freddie Foreman claimed that the body was disposed of at sea, while other sources state that he was buried in the foundations of a flyover.[16]

Personal tragedy was also taking its toll. Reggie's wife, Frances, died of an overdose in 1967, aged just twenty-three, and in his grief-stricken state Reggie made a final lapse of judgement that was to bring the Krays down once and for all. He accepted Ronnie's request to kill Jack 'the Hat' McVitie, a minor member of the Kray gang who had failed to kill Leslie 'Payne the Brain', despite being paid £1,500 to do so.

A 'Jeckyll and Hyde character', Jack the Hat (it covered his bald spot) was another liability. Constantly drunk and high on amphetamines, McVitie once committed the sartorial outrage of appearing in Bermuda shorts, waving a machete. In Ronnie's immortal phrase, he would 'have to go'.[17]

In October 1967, Tony Lambrianou, one of the Krays' top men, drove McVitie to 'Blonde Carol's' flat in Stoke Newington, promising a 'party, birds and booze'. But when McVitie walked into the basement flat there was no party, just Ronnie and Reggie, waiting for him. Reggie attempted to shoot McVitie in the head, but the gun failed to go off. When McVitie smashed a window, Ronnie brought out the carving knife. Ronnie held McVitie down and Reggie stabbed him in the face and stomach so severely that, according to Lambrianou, McVitie's liver popped out and had to be flushed down the toilet.

Lambrianou, who was convicted of McVitie's murder along with his brother, Chris, had no regrets about McVitie's death, saying that he was a violent man who had once thrown a woman out of a car.[18] McVitie's body was never recovered, but Ronnie enhanced his personal myth by circulating stories that it had been fed to the pigs in Suffolk, burned in the furnaces of Bankside Power Station or buried beneath an office block in the City. John Pearson, the Krays' biographer, met Reggie shortly after this incident and noticed that his hand was bandaged. When Pearson asked what had caused the wound, Reggie commented laconically, 'Gardenin'.'[19]

Despite the wall of silence that made gathering evidence about the Krays well nigh impossible, time was running out for the twins. Chief Inspector Nipper Read contacted Leslie Payne, who had distanced himself from the Krays after they had taken a contract out on him. Payne gave the police a 146-page statement at considerable risk to his life. After his family had been threatened by the Krays, Albert Donoghue agreed to turn Queen's Evidence, as did an American criminal, Alan Cooper.

The Krays and fifteen other members of 'the Firm' were arrested on 9 May 1968, and once they were in custody, witnesses developed the confidence to come forward and give evidence. The trial at the Old Bailey lasted for thirty-nine days, and the twins were sentenced to life imprisonment with a non-parole period of thirty years for the murders of Cornell and McVitie, the longest sentences for murder ever passed at the Old Bailey. Charlie Kray was gaoled for ten years for his part in the murders. Ronnie Kray died in 1995, aged sixty-one, his passing commemorated by a lavish East End funeral. Reggie was released on compassionate grounds in August 2000, suffering from inoperable cancer. He died in his sleep on 22 September 2000 and was buried alongside his twin in Chingford cemetery.

Half a century later, the Kray mythology endures. Even today, East Enders reminisce sentimentally about 'the good old days' when the Krays represented an alternative method of law enforcement, and neighbours could leave their doors unlocked. Defenders of the Krays will tell you that they were devoted to their mother, and they 'only killed their own', as if that somehow justified the brutal gangland executions. The Krays have inspired industrial quantities of books, ranging from lurid memoirs to criminological dissertations, and dozens of movies, novels and television programmes. Ronnie, so hooked on celebrity, must have been deeply gratified when he and Reggie were portrayed by the handsome Kemp brothers, Gary and Martin, in the 1990 film *The Krays*. Cinematic immortality at last, reminiscent of Jimmy Cagney on the roof of the burning warehouse in the closing moments of *White Heat*: 'Made it, Ma! Top of the world!'

Forty years later, the Krays retain their aura as London's most dangerous family. Occasionally other names emerge from the shadows to claim the crown, but their exploits seem a pale imitation of 'the Firm' at the height of its powers. In 1991 the Arif family hit the headlines after a decade of police surveillance. One brother, Dogan, had already been gaoled for an £8.5 million cannabis smuggling plot and the family enjoyed a flamboyant lifestyle, thinking nothing of a £30,000 wedding celebration at the Savoy Hotel with guests including the families of Frankie Fraser and Harry White, plus the notorious north London Adams family.[20] But it was not until an armed robbery went wrong that the police got their men. In November 1990 a gang of armed robbers descended on a Securicor van in Reigate, Surrey. Hoping for an £800,000 haul, the robbers were disguised in Ronald Reagan masks and carrying enough ammunition to start a small war. But armed police were lying in wait and one robber, Kenny Baker, was shot dead. Dennis and Mehmet Arif were gaoled in 1991 for twenty-two and eighteen years respectively, along with their brother-in-law, Tony Downer, who also received eighteen years.[21]

The closing decades of the twentieth century saw two other audacious armed robberies, both of which would have impressed Billy Hill with their daring. On 26 November 1983, six robbers broke into the Brink's-MAT warehouse at Heathrow Airport, intent on stealing £3 million in cash. Brian Robinson had planned the raid with the help of his brother-in-law, Anthony Black, who worked as a security guard at Heathrow. When they arrived, the robbers actually found three tonnes of gold bullion worth £26 million. The gang was swiftly arrested after police discovered the family connection, and Robinson was sentenced to twenty-five years while Black received six. In the meantime, the gold had been disposed of by Kenneth Noye, an associate of the gang, who melted it down and recast it for sale. Noye's involvement was revealed after the Treasury noted large quantities of money moving through his bank account, and Noye was put under surveillance. In 1985, Noye killed a police officer in his garden but was found not guilty on the grounds of self-defence. In 1986, Noye was found guilty of handling the Brink's-MAT gold and sentenced to fourteen years in prison. Most of the gold has never been recovered, and four other men involved in the robbery have never been convicted. According to the BBC, anyone wearing gold jewellery purchased in the United Kingdom after 1983 is probably wearing Brink's-MAT.[22]

The Millennium Dome raid was an equally bold enterprise, one which might have brought a smile to the face of the old highwayman Claude du Vall himself. On 7 November 2000, a gang attempted to steal the flawless Millennium Star diamond, worth over £200 million, from an exhibition at the Millennium Dome. Armed with smoke bombs, ammonia, a sledgehammer and a nail gun, the gang rammed a JCB excavator into the Dome and smashed their way through to the vault. The plan was to snatch the diamond and escape down the Thames on a speedboat. The robbers had no idea they were surrounded and that the diamond had been replaced with a worthless fake the night before. In an operation codenamed 'Operation Magician', 200 police officers, including forty from the specialist firearms unit C019, were in position at the Dome, disguised as cleaners and employees. A further sixty armed Flying Squad officers were stationed around the Thames, with twenty on the river itself. Five of the robbers were caught and received sentences ranging from four to eighteen years.[23]

The failure of the Millenium Diamond heist, foiled by police intelligence work, may account for the fact that armed robbery has been superseded by other modes of crime over the past decade. There is no need for a gang of men in stocking masks to jump out of a Transit van with sawn-off shooters when an individual can empty a bank account at a keystroke. Criminals have always been early adopters and today technology has brought new possibilities in the form of cyber-crime, online fraud and identity theft. The most lucrative form of crime now is drug trafficking or 'narcotics', which has escalated from scare stories of reefer madness and white slavery in the 1920s to an organized, multi-million-dollar industry defying border controls, with links to international criminal gangs including the Italian Mafia and its American and Russian cousins.

The East End underworld has changed, too, under the impact of immigration from the former Eastern Bloc countries. London has always had an Eastern European immigrant community, notably the Ashkenazi Jewish refugees of the Victorian era. A century later, as law and order collapsed in the former Soviet Union, London became a hub for money laundering, drug dealing and gun-running, with weapons from the former Yugoslavia and Afghanistan circulating freely. The old accusations of anarchy and crime once hurled at the Jewish community were now levelled against Albanian, Ukrainian and Polish immigrants in the popular press. When it comes to modern vice, London can claim to be one of the most cosmopolitan crime capitals of the world.

Not all London crime is international and sophisticated, of course. Throughout its long, grim history, London's underworld has always had its local, street-based gangs, from Elizabethan cutpurses to the child pickpockets swarming barefoot through the Victorian capital at twilight. Towards the end of the nineteenth century, the concept of safety in numbers resulted in gangs based on ethnicity, such as the Yiddishers, the Italian and the Irish gangs. And with the rise of organized crime in the post-war years, the family-based gangs – such as the Krays and the Richardsons – combined a lifelong knowledge of their local neighbourhood and its denizens with a formidable code of enforcement that operated as the alternative local police force.

When the Jamaican or 'Yardie' gangs arrived on the scene in the 1980s, their *modus operandi* was recognizably similar. The Yardies (roughly translated as 'from our own back yard') were Jamaican-born gangsters operating in Britain. Like the Yiddishers and the Italians before them, they were bonded by shared ethnicity and family ties. Over the subsequent decade, black-on-black violence in London escalated, with killings worn as a badge of honour in a series of deadly turf wars and impulsive indiscriminate shootings in which innocent bystanders were fatally injured. In 1993, Yardies were blamed for the cold-blooded murder of PC Patrick Dunne, who was on patrol in Clapham when he stumbled across a shooting incident. In 1999, Yardie involvement was suggested in five black-on-black murders in London in just six weeks. In one particularly appalling incident in May 1999, Laverne Forbes, 28, and her partner Patrick Smith, 31, were shot dead in front of their seven-year-old daughter.[24]

A generation later, the term 'Yardie' has dropped from the headlines to be replaced by the phenomenon of home-grown 'postcode' gangs, and an all-pervasive gang culture that is as widespread as it is disturbing. This impossible-to-ignore phenomenon is the stuff of newspaper headlines, television programmes and public outrage. It can be summed up in a few stark words: stabbings, gun crime, turf wars and riots. Gun and knife crime have become commonplace, and every year dozens of young men are killed in what seem to the outsider to be meaningless feuds over 'respect'.

The common perception is that gang culture is associated with the Afro-Caribbean community. In fact, there are as many types of gangs as there are communities, including all-white gangs, African gangs, and Turkish Cypriot, Pakistani and Indian gangs. The so-called 'postcode gangs' of London and other major cities are characterized by the members' fierce attachment to their immediate neighbourhood and hostility to any perceived rivals crossing their turf. In practical terms, this territorial imperative means that youths have to walk a mile out of their way to get to school, and arrive late, or face being attacked.

While gang culture has become more aggressive over the past decade, the most disturbing factor is that the gangsters themselves have become increasingly younger. Just as Fagin groomed his young pickpockets in Dickensian London, today's 'Elders' force or entice their 'Youngers' into a life of crime. Working as a 'shotter' delivering drugs is attractive compared to a life on benefits, and peer pressure is over-whelming. Even children from stable homes find themselves compelled to join a gang just to survive. Much has been said of the perceived glamour of gang culture, but at a more instinc-tive level, it's all about belonging. And the consequences for not belonging can be lethal. While Fagin's gonophs operated in the shadow of the noose, today's child criminals are desen-sitized, brutalized children killing other children, armed with guns and knives. One of the most shocking murders occurred on Valentine's Day 2007, when Billy Cox was shot dead at his home in Clapham, after a dispute about a small amount of cannabis. Popular, 'girly', much-loved Billy had drifted into gang culture and minor crime, but had recently enrolled on a training course in a bid to go legitimate. He was just fifteen years old.[25]

The news that yet another schoolboy has been murdered in gang-related violence has become depressingly familiar. By July 2011, nine young men had already been killed in this way in London. On 26 December 2011 a young man was stabbed to death on Oxford Street during the Boxing Day sales. Eighteen-year-old Seydou Diarrassouba was killed with a single stab wound to the heart in the Foot Locker sports shop, near Bond Street Tube station. His death led to chaotic scenes as officers tried to restrain the crowd that had gathered outside. At the time of writing, a man of twenty has been charged with murder and is awaiting trial.[26]

But there are occasional glimpses of hope. In September 2011, the *Evening Standard* reported the story of Tony Massiah, a young man from Tottenham who has become a pupil barrister after escaping from a life of crime. Massiah, who had been swept up in gang violence as a teenager, re-evaluated his life after being narrowly missed by a bullet during a brawl. After completing his law degree and starting in chambers, Mr Massiah told the newspaper, 'If anyone says that it is impossible, I am proof that it is not. I sympathize with kids drawn into gangs but if I could say anything to them it would be that they are not your real friends if they are asking you to do a crime.' According to the *Standard,* the Bar Council later commented that 'everyone has a right to turn their life around'.[27]

16

LONDON BABYLON

From the Old Bailey to Tyburn

To stand outside the Old Bailey now is to stand in one of the most notable spots in the history of London's underworld. In this place, thousands of prisoners, known and unknown, famous and infamous, pleaded for their lives. In this place, the brigand Blueskin lunged at the thief-taker Jonathan Wild and cut his throat, and it is here that Dr Crippen, Edith Thompson and Ruth Ellis looked on as the judge reached for his black cap and condemned them to death. In this place, old Newgate Gaol was burnt to the ground, rebuilt in its last, grim incarnation and then demolished forever. And in this place the condemned prisoners filed through Dead Man's Walk, across the buried bodies of the former inmates, on their way to the gallows. For those who believe in such things, the Old Bailey must be one of the most haunted places in London, with the legendary Black Dog of Newgate revealing itself to those who are about to die, slithering out of the shadows and draping itself across the walls in a scene of compelling horror.

Turning away from the Old Bailey, the old road to Tyburn

winds its way through Fleet Street. On hanging days, these streets were black with onlookers, crowded onto rooftops, peering out through windows, shouting and chanting their messages of support or derision for the condemned men and women. Before embarking on the last stages of this journey, I will take a detour through St Paul's. In the days of the first Queen Elizabeth, the precincts of St Paul's had become a den of vice, lined with tobacco sellers, pickpockets, conmen and crooks of every variety. In October 2011, the cathedral became host to the Occupy movement, a gathering of young people protesting peacefully against corporate greed and the collapse of the global economy. The fact that London has become more enlightened over the past 200 years was demonstrated by the fact that when the protestors were evicted following a High Court Injunction from the City of London on 28 February 2012, the majority dispersed peacefully, having made their point. Although it was a sad sight to see the peace camp broken up, there were only twenty arrests and at least the event was not marked by a cavalry charge scything through the crowd, as would have been the case two centuries ago.[1]

That is not to say that London has not witnessed disturbing scenes of crowd violence in modern times. London was hit by another, more aggressive form of protest in August 2011 when a series of riots broke out following the shooting of 29-year-old Mark Duggan by police officers in Tottenham. The riots spread to Enfield, Walthamstow and Brixton and resulted in over 100 arrests on the first night. Over the following four nights, rioting continued elsewhere in London and in other major cities, and led to widespread looting and vandalism. While the original riots were sparked by a genuine grievance at the shooting of Mark Duggan, resentment at police 'stop and search' procedures which disproportionately target young black men, and high levels of youth unemployment and social deprivation, there was also an element of greedy opportunism.[2]

While some looters were children in their early teens, guilty of little more than a youthful foolishness, it emerged that 75 per cent of those arrested had previous convictions.[3]

Magistrates sat through the night, just as the Fielding brothers had done two centuries earlier, and were criticized for handing down stiff sentences. But this should be viewed in perspective. The reader will have some idea of how far the English criminal justice system has travelled when they consider that a fine or even a brief custodial sentence for stealing a pair of trainers is merciful compared with the fate of the young Gordon Rioters, around thirty of whom were publically hanged around the city of London.

This is the last stage of the journey, following in the footsteps of so many, up through Fleet Street, past the Royal Courts of Justice, down Oxford Street and so finally into Tyburn. This last trip through London allows me to reflect on the barbaric history of capital punishment and the extraordinary stories I have encountered along the way, some of which stand out so starkly in the memory: Eliza Fenning, accused of poisoning her employer and his family; the dashing highwaymen Plunkett and MacLaine; Maria Manning, the woman who murdered black satin; and the diabolical Wainwright who rounded upon the spectators at his execution with a cry of 'You curs! Come to see a man die, have you!'

To review these old cases, to enquire as to the guilt of one person or the innocence of another, is to engage with the spirit of London's underworld. It is as if the many ghosts encountered during the long journey of this book still crowd around, and retain the power to haunt. In the words of Ford Madox Ford, 'certain corners of certain streets, certain angles of buildings' bring them back again, conjured up with the glamour of memory, the romance of the old days, the recollection of those griefs and those terrors.[4] The shadows of these crimes and their protagonists and victims linger on 'in the wavering reflections of the rain-washed streets'.[5] Now London's underworld is the stuff of tourist trails, with travellers conducted around the back-streets of Whitechapel where Jack the Ripper blazed his trail of terror, or taken for a drink at the Blind Beggar pub where Ronnie Kray shot George Cornell. Crime, in its literary form, has become yet another of London's most famous exports.

Finally, I have come full circle and stand at Tyburn, outside the Roman Catholic oratory that marks the spot where so many martyrs died. Tyburn's historian Alfred Marks urged his readers to remember the thousands of other 'martyrs' who died at this spot and elsewhere, the victims of 'ferocious laws, the innocent, the martyrs to cruel injustice and iniquitous social conditions' who had the life choked out of them.[6]

It seems fitting to pause here for a moment and honour their memory in the knowledge that the barbaric practice of capital punishment has disappeared from Britain forever, and that its victims here at Tyburn and elsewhere did not die in vain.

In memoriam: the plaque that marks the spot where Tyburn's triple tree once stood.

Bibliography

Babington, Anthony, *A House in Bow Street*, Macdonald, London, 1969

Babington, Anthony, *The English Bastille*, Macdonald, London, 1971

Berresford Ellis, Peter, *A History of the Irish Working Class,* Pluto Press, London 1996

Brandon, David, and Brooke, Alan, *London: The Executioner's City*, Sutton, Stroud, 2007

Brooke, Alan, and Brandon, David, *Tyburn: London's Fatal Tree*, The History Press, Stroud, 2004

Bulwer-Lytton, Edward, *Paul Clifford*, George Routledge & Sons, London, 1877

Burford, E. J., *A Short History of the Clink Prison*, The Clink Prison, London, 1989

Campbell, Duncan, *The Underworld*, BBC Books, 1994

Chesney, Kellow, *The Victorian Underworld*, Temple Smith, London, 1970

Cruikshank, Dan, *The Secret History of Georgian London: How the Wages of Sin Shaped the Capital*, Random House, London, 2009

Defoe, Daniel, *Moll Flanders*, Penguin Classics, Harmondsworth, 1989

De Quincey, Thomas, ed. by Morrison, Robert, *On Murder*, Oxford University Press, Oxford, 2006

Dickens, Charles, *Barnaby Rudge: A Tale of the Riots of Eighty*, Vols 1 & 2, Chapman and Hall, London, 1897

Dickens, Charles, *The Adventures of Oliver Twist*, Chapman & Hall, London, 1897

Fabian, Robert, *London After Dark: An Intimate Record of Night Life in London*, The Naldrett Press, London, 1954

Faller, Lincoln B., *Turned to Account: The Forms and Functions of Criminal Biography in Late Seventeenth- and Early Eighteenth-Century England*, Cambridge University Press, Cambridge, 1987

Fido, Martin, *Murder Guide to London*, Orion Books, London, 1986

Foot, Paul, *Who Killed Hanratty?*, Penguin Books, London, 1988

Foucault, Michel, *Discipline and Punish: The Birth of the Prison*, Penguin, Harmondsworth, 1991

Gatrell, V. A. C., *The Hanging Tree: Execution and the English People 1770–1868*, Oxford University Press, Oxford, 1994

Griffith, Tom (ed.), *The Newgate Calendar*, Wordsworth Editions, Ware, 1997

Grovier, Kelly, *The Gaol: The Story of Newgate, London's Most Notorious Prison*, John Murray, London, 2009

Halliday, Stephen, *Newgate: London's Prototype of Hell*, History Press, Stroud, 2009

Harrison, Brian A., *The Tower of London Prisoner Book: A Complete Chronology of the Persons Known to Have Been Detained*, Royal Armouries, Leeds, 2004

Harrison Ainsworth, William, *The Tower of London*, George Routledge & Sons, London, 1897

Heale, John, *One Blood: Inside Britain's New Street Gangs*, Simon & Schuster, 2008

Herber, Mark D., *Legal London: A Pictorial History*, Phillimore, London, 1999

Hiney, Tom, *Raymond Chandler: A Biography*, Chatto & Windus, London, 1997

Hitchcock, Tim, and Shoemaker, Bob, *Tales from the Hanging*

Court, Bloomsbury, London, 2007

Hodge, James H. (ed.), *Famous Trials 5*, Penguin, 1955

Honeycombe, Gordon, *Murders of the Black Museum*, John Blake, London, 2009

Hooper, W. Eden, *History of Newgate and the Old Bailey*, Underwood Press, London, 1935

Impey, Edward, and Parnell, Geoffrey, *The Tower of London: The Official Illustrated History*, Merrell Publishers Ltd, London, 2000

James, P. D., and Critchley, T. A., *The Maul and the Pear Tree*, Sphere Books, London, 1971

Jonson, Ben, *The Alchemist*, *The Alchemist and Other Plays*, Oxford World's Classics, Oxford University Press, Oxford, 2008

Jonson, Ben, *Bartholomew Fair, The Alchemist and Other Plays*, Oxford World's Classics, Oxford University Press, Oxford, 2008

Kinney, Arthur F., *Rogues, Vagabonds and Sturdy Beggars: A New Gallery of Tudor and Early Stuart Rogue Literature*, University of Massachusetts Press, Massachusetts, 1990

Leeson, B., *Lost London: The Memoirs of an East End Detective*, Stanley Paul & Co Ltd, London, 1934

Linebaugh, Peter, *The London Hanged: Crime and Civil Society in the Eighteenth Century*, Penguin, London, 1993

Linnane, Fergus, *The Encyclopaedia of London Crime and Vice*, Sutton, Stroud, 2005

Darbyshire, Neil, and Hilliard, Brian, *The Flying Squad*, Headline, London, 1993

Madox Ford, Ford, *The Soul of London: A Survey of a Modern City*, Alston Rivers, London, 1905

Majoribanks, Edward, *For the Defence: The Life of Sir Edward Marshall Hall*, Macmillan, London, 1929

Marks, Alfred, *Tyburn Tree: Its History and Annals*, Brown Langham & Co., London, 1908

Mayhew, Henry, *London Labour and the London Poor*; Cassell, London, 1967

Mayhew, Henry (ed.) by Quennell, Peter, *London's Underworld*, Spring Books, London, 1966

Pearsall, Ronald, *The Worm in the Bud: The World of Victorian Sexuality*, Sutton, Stroud, 2003

Pearson, John, *The Profession of Violence*, Harper Collins, London, 1995

Picard, Liza, *Elizabeth's London: Everyday Life in Elizabethan London*, Orion, London, 2004

Pierrepoint, Albert, *Executioner: Pierrepoint*, Harrap, London, 1974

Rivlin, Geoffrey, *Understanding the Law*, Oxford University Press, Oxford, 2009

Salgado, Gamini, *The Elizabethan Underworld*, Sutton, Stroud, 1992

Scott, Sir George Gilbert, *Gleanings from Westminster Abbey*, Parker, Oxford, 1861

Shakespeare, *The Complete Works*, ed. Peter Alexander Collins, London, 1978

Spraggs, Gillian, *Outlaws and Highwaymen*, Pimlico, London, 2001

Stanley, Arthur Penrhyn, *Historical Monuments of Westminster Abbey*, unknown publisher, London, 1868

Stow, John, *A Survey of London Written in the Year 1598*, The History Press, Stroud, 2005

Thomas, Donald Serrell, *The Victorian Underworld*, John Murray, London, 1998

Thompson, Sir Basil, *The Story of Scotland Yard*, The Literary Guild, New York, 1936

Trevelyan, Raleigh, *Sir Walter Raleigh*, Faber and Faber, London, 2010

Watts, Marthe, *The Men in My Life*, Christopher Johnson, London, 1960

Webb, Duncan, *Crime Is My Business*, Frederick Muller Ltd, London, 1953

Webb, Duncan, *Line-up for Crime*, Frederick Muller Ltd, London, 1956

Webster, John, *The White Devil*, ed. F. L. Lucas, Chatto and Windus, London, 1958

Wheen, Francis, *The Sixties*, Ebury, London, 1982

Whitfield, Peter, *London: A Life in Maps*, British Library, London, 2006

Wild, Roland, and Curtis-Bennett, Derek, *'Curtis': The Life of Sir Henry Curtis-Bennett*, Cassell, London, 1937

Wilson, Derek, *The Tower: The Tumultuous History of the Tower of London from 1078*, Scribner, New York, 1979

Yallop, David A., *To Encourage the Others*, W. H. Allen, London, 1971

Young, Filson (ed.), *Trial of Frederick Bywaters and Edith Thompson*, Notable British Trials series, William Hodge, London, 1951

SELECTED WEBSITES

http://eastlondonhistory.com
http://news.bbc.co.uk/onthisday
http://utilitarianism.com
http://www.bailii.org
http://www.british-history.ac.uk
http://www.capitalpunishmentuk.org
http://www.exclassics.com
http://www.lawgazette.co.uk
http://www.met.police.uk/history
http://www.murderpedia.org
http://www.murderuk.com
http://www.nickelinthemachine.com
http://www.oldbaileyonline.org

http://www.outlawsandhighwaymen.com
http://www.thamespolicemuseum.org.uk
http://www.thekrays.co.uk
http://www.trutv.com
http://www.victorianlondon.org

SELECTED NEWSPAPERS AND JOURNALS

Bell's Life in London and Sporting Chronicle
Daily Express
Daily Mail
Daily Telegraph
Evening Standard
Guardian
Independent
Illustrated London News
London Journal
Mist's Weekly Journal
Punch
The Times

Notes

CHAPTER ONE

1 See Webster, *The White Devil*, Act V, Scene 2, line 6
2 See Wilson, *The Tower*, p. 15
3 See Marks, *Tyburn Tree*, p. 62
4 Ibid., p. 28
5 Ibid., p. 80
6 See Stow, *A Survey of London*, p. 35
7 See Marks, op. cit., p. 80
8 Ibid.
9 Ibid., p. 6
10 See http://www.guardian.co.uk/commentisfree/belief/2011/aug/19/church-of-england-capital-punishment
11 See Babington, *The English Bastille*, p. 26
12 See Marks, op. cit., p. 7
13 Ibid., pp. 6–7
14 See Wilson, op. cit., p. 11
15 Ibid.
16 See Marks, op. cit., p. 80
17 Ibid.
18 Ibid., p. 16
19 See Wilson, op. cit., p. 35
20 See Marks, op. cit., p. 96
21 Ibid.
22 See Wilson, op. cit., p. 35
23 See Stanley, *Historical Monuments of Westminster Abbey*, pp. 383–4
24 Ibid.
25 See Marks, op. cit., p. 105

26 See Scott, *Gleanings from Westminster Abbey*, pp. 38–40
27 See Stow, op. cit., pp. 229–30
28 See Marks, op. cit., p. 105
29 Ibid.
30 See Shakespeare, *Henry VI Pt 2*, Act II, Scene 3
31 See Marks, op. cit., p. 124
32 Ibid.
33 Ibid.
34 See Harrison, *The Tower of London Prisoner Book*, p. 523
35 See Marks, op. cit., p. 120
36 Ibid., p. 117
37 Ibid.
38 Ibid., p. 133
39 Ibid., pp. 134–6

CHAPTER TWO

1 See Impey and Parnell, *The Tower of London*, p. 18
2 See Wilson, *The Tower*, p. 11
3 Ibid., p. 5
4 Ibid., pp. 27–8
5 Ibid., pp. 62–3
6 Ibid., p. 64
7 See Impey and Parnell, op. cit., p. 46
8 See Wilson, op. cit., pp. 68–9
9 Ibid., p. 72
10 Ibid., p. 73
11 Ibid.
12 See Harrison Ainsworth, *The Tower of London*, p. 173
13 See Wilson, op. cit., p. 84
14 See Marks, *Tyburn Tree*, p. 121
15 See http://digital.library.upenn.edu/women/yonge/deeds/daughter.html,
    quoting from Yonge, Charlotte M., *A Book of Golden Deeds*, Blackie &
    Son Ltd., London, 1864
16 See Wilson, op. cit., p. 96
17 Ibid.
18 Ibid., p. 101
19 See Harrison, *The Tower of London Prisoner Book*, p. 534
20 Ibid., p. 530
21 Ibid., p. 519

22 See Harrison Ainsworth, op. cit., p. 175
23 See Harrison, op. cit., p. 530
24 Ibid., p. 530
25 See Harrison Ainsworth, op. cit., p. 175
26 See Wilson, op. cit., p.109
27 Ibid., p. 110
28 Ibid., p. 110
29 Ibid., p. 110
30 See Harrison Ainsworth, op. cit., p. 323
31 Ibid., p. 511
32 Elizabeth I at the Tower of London during her coronation ceremonies, 1559, from *Records of St Giles' Cripplegate* by William Denton, G Bell & Son, London, 1883
33 See Harrison, op. cit., p. 260
34 See Trevelyan, *Sir Walter Raleigh*, p. 552
35 See Harrison Ainsworth, op. cit., p. 168
36 Ibid.
37 Ibid., p. 169
38 Ibid.
39 See http://briancatling.com/Site/Tower_2.html

CHAPTER THREE

1 See Spraggs, *Outlaws and Highwaymen*, p. 68
2 Ibid.
3 See Marks, *Tyburn Tree*, p. 137
4 See Salgado, *The Elizabethan Underworld*, p. 147
5 Ibid.
6 Ibid. p. 153
7 See Hitchcock and Shoemaker, *Tales from the Hanging Court*, p. xi
8 See Salgado, op. cit., pp. 6–7
9 See Linnane, *The Encyclopedia of London, Crime and Vice*, p. 6
10 Ibid. p. 192
11 See Salgado, op. cit., p. 33
12 Ibid. p. 11
13 Ibid. p. 15
14 Ibid. p. 11
15 See Picard, *Elizabeth's London*, p. 246
16 See Salgado, op. cit., p. 22
17 See Picard, op. cit., p. 247

18 Ibid.
19 See Salgado, op. cit., p. 19
20 Ibid., p. 17
21 Ibid.
22 Ibid., p. 11
23 See Jonson, *Bartholomew Fair*, Act II, Scene 6, lines 10–15
24 See Kinney, *Rogues, Vagabonds and Sturdy Beggars,* p. 37
25 See Jonson, op. cit., Act III, Scene 2, 35–37
26 See http://www.exclassics.com/foxe/foxe174.htm
27 See Brandon and Brooke, *London*, p. 67
28 Ibid., p. 70
29 See Marks, op. cit., pp. 21–2

CHAPTER FOUR

1 See Hooper, *History of Newgate and the Old Bailey*, p. 26
2 Ibid.
3 Ibid., pp. 74–5
4 See Rivlin, *Understanding the Law*, p. 224
5 Ibid.
6 Ibid.
7 See http://www.usask.ca/english/turne_backe/taylor_bio.html
8 Ibid.
9 Ibid.
10 See http://www.british-history.ac.uk/report.aspx?compid=45054, quoting from Thornbury, Walter, *Old and New London, Volume 1*, 1878
11 See Stow, *A Survey of London*, p. 351
12 See Salgado, *The Elizabethan Underworld*, p. 171
13 Ibid.
14 Ibid.
15 See Herber, *Legal London*, p. 106
16 See Burford, *A Short History of the Clink Prison*, p. 9
17 See Hooper, op. cit., p. 6
18 Ibid., p. 26
19 Ibid., p. 6
20 See Babington, *The English Bastille*, p. 23
21 Ibid., p. 25
22 See Marks, *Tyburn Tree*, p. 104
23 See http://www.british-history.ac.uk/report.aspx?compid=45045
24 See Halliday, *Newgate*, p. 7

25 See Babington, op. cit., p. 24

26 See Hooper, op. cit., p. 35

27 See Babington, op. cit., p. 23

28 Ibid.

29 See http://www.exclassics.com/foxe/foxe174.htm, quoting from Foxe, John, *Book of Martyrs*, 1563

30 See Grovier, *The Gaol*, pp. 66–7

CHAPTER FIVE

1 See Bulwer-Lytton, *Paul Clifford*, p. 136

2 See Jonson, *The Alchemist*, Act I, Scene I

3 See Spraggs, *Outlaws and Highwaymen*, pp. 147–50

4 See Spraggs, http://www.outlawsandhighwaymen.com/index.htm

5 See http://www.exclassics.com/newgate/ng2.htm

6 See Marks, *Tyburn Tree*, p. 194

7 See http://www.exclassics.com/newgate/ng2.htm

8 Ibid.

9 Ibid.

10 See Marks, op. cit., pp. 209–11

11 Ibid., pp. 211–3

12 Ibid., pp. 229–30

13 Ibid.

14 See Spraggs, op. cit., p. 1

15 See Faller, *Turned to Account*, p. 162

16 See Cruikshank, *The Secret History of Georgian London*, p. 335

17 See Spraggs, op. cit., p. 1

18 See Griffith, *The Newgate Calendar*, pp. 183–96

19 See Spraggs, http://www.outlawsandhighwaymen.com/index.htm

20 See Babington, *The English Bastille*, p. 119

21 See Marks, op. cit., pp. 258–9

22 See Bulwer-Lytton, op. cit., p. 147

CHAPTER SIX

1 See Babington, *The English Bastille*, p. 34

2 Ibid., p. 19

3 See Babington, *A House in Bow Street*, p. 15

4 See Foucault, *Discipline and Punish*, p. 61

5 See Defoe, *Moll Flanders*, pp. 273–4
6 See Babington, *The English Bastille*, p.113
7 Ibid., p.117
8 Ibid., p.115
9 See Griffith, *The Newgate Calendar*, p. 107
10 See Gatrell, *The Hanging Tree*, p. 59
11 See Marks, *Tyburn Tree*, pp. 221–3
12 Ibid., pp. 225–6
13 Ibid.
14 See Griffith, op. cit.
15 Ibid.
16 See *Mist's Weekly Journal*, 2 April 1726
17 Ibid.
18 See *London Journal*, 5 May 1726
19 Ibid.
20 See Marks, op. cit., p. 251
21 See http://www.exclassics.com/newgate/ng186.htm
22 See http://www.capitalpunishmentuk.org/malcolm.html
23 Ibid.
24 Ibid.
25 Ibid.
26 See Gatrell, op. cit., p. 62
27 See Griffith, op. cit.
28 See Marks, op. cit., p. 256
29 Ibid., p. 247
30 Ibid., pp. 260–2
31 Ibid., p. 263
32 Ibid.
33 Ibid.
34 Ibid., pp. 266–7
35 See Babington, *The English Bastille*, p. 147
36 See Marks, op. cit., p. 267

CHAPTER SEVEN

1 See Babington, *A House in Bow Street*, p. 17
2 See Thompson, *The Story of Scotland Yard*, p. 23
3 Ibid., p. 20
4 See Babington, op. cit., pp. 35–7
5 Ibid., p. 58

6 Ibid., p. 57
7 Ibid.
8 Ibid., p. 62
9 See Thompson, op. cit., p. 33
10 Ibid. p.30
11 See Halliday, *Newgate*, p. 138
12 See Thompson, op. cit., pp. 34–5
13 See Babington, op. cit., pp. 159–60
14 Ibid.
15 See Linnane, *Encyclopaedia of London Crime and Vice*, p. 110
16 See Babington, op. cit., p. 164
17 Ibid., p. 179
18 Ibid., pp. 210–11
19 See http://www.thamespolicemuseum.org.uk/h_
   ratcliffehighwaymurders_1.html
20 Ibid.
21 Ibid.
22 See James and Critchley, *The Maul and the Pear Tree*, p. 225
23 See Babington, op. cit., p. 210
24 See Thompson, op. cit., p. 46
25 Ibid.
26 Ibid., p. 51
27 See Gatrell, *The Hanging Tree*, p. 308
28 Ibid.
29 See *The Traveller*, May 1820
30 See Thompson, op. cit., p. 54
31 See 'From the archive, 18 August 1821: Two killed in Queen's
   funeral procession', *Guardian*, 18 August 2011

CHAPTER EIGHT

1 See Mayhew, *London Labour and the London Poor*, p. 63
2 See *Illustrated London News*, 18 September 1852
3 See Dickens, *Oliver Twist*, p. 69
4 Ibid. p. 77
5 See Chesney, *The Victorian Underworld*, p. 146
6 See Mayhew, *London's Underworld*, p. 291
7 Ibid., p. 293
8 Ibid., p. 196
9 Ibid.

10 Ibid.
11 Ibid., p. 181
12 Ibid., pp. 214–30
13 See Chesney, op. cit., p. 160
14 See Mayhew, op. cit., p. 230
15 See Thomas, *The Victorian Underworld*, pp. 255–6
16 Ibid., pp. 206–29
17 See Babington, *The English Bastille*, p. 191
18 See *Punch*, 31 January 1857
19 See Babington, op. cit., pp. 132–5
20 Ibid., p. 105
21 Ibid., p. 104
22 See http://utilitarianism.com/jeremy-bentham/index.html
23 See Babington, op. cit., p. 199
24 Ibid., p. 210
25 Ibid., p. 213
26 See Herber, *Legal London*, p. 118
27 See Babington, op. cit., p. 210
28 Ibid., p. 197
29 Ibid., p. 210
30 Ibid., p. 191
31 Ibid., p. 199
32 See Thomas, op. cit., p. 268
33 See Babington, op. cit., p. 192
34 Ibid., p. 214
35 Ibid., p. 218
36 Ibid.
37 See Dickens, op. cit., p.500
38 Ibid. p. 504

CHAPTER NINE

1 See Babington, *The English Bastille*, p.146
2 Ibid.
3 See Halliday, *Newgate*, p. 177
4 See Gatrell, *The Hanging Tree*, p. 54
5 See Babington, op. cit., p. 163
6 See http://www.exclassics.com/newgate/ng567.htm
7 See Gatrell, op. cit., p.359
8 Ibid., pp. 363–7

9 Ibid., p. 357

10 Ibid., p. 356

11 See http://www.exclassics.com/newgate/ng567.htm

12 See Gatrell, op. cit., p. 368

13 See Babington, op. cit., p. 163

14 See Gatrell, op. cit., p. 51

15 See http://www.exclassics.com/newgate/ng622.htm

16 See Gatrell, op. cit., p. 69

17 Ibid., p. 39

18 *Weekly Chronicle*, 7 May 1837

19 See Babington, op. cit., p.225

20 Ibid., p. 224

21 See http://www.met.police.uk/history/daniel_good.htm

22 See http://www.capitalpunishmentuk.org/mannings.html

23 See Gatrell, op. cit., p. 605

24 See Babington, op. cit., p. 226

25 See Gatrell, op. cit., p. 606

26 See Babington, op. cit., p. 226

27 See Berresford Ellis, *A History of the Irish Working Class*, p. 140

28 *Daily Telegraph* and *Daily News*, 27 May 1868

CHAPTER TEN

1 See http://www.victorianlondon.org/crime/harrietlane.htm

2 Ibid.

3 See Fido, *Murder Guide to London*, p. 29

4 See http://www.victorianlondon.org/crime/harrietlane.htm

5 See *Bell's Life in London and Sporting Chronicle*, 27 January 1883

6 See http://www.readbookonline.net/readOnLine/2527, quoting from Dickens, Charles, 'The Detective Police', London, 1838

7 See Thomson, *The Story of Scotland Yard*, p. ix

8 See http://www.hawthornedvrt.org/Women-and-Domestic-Violence.htm

9 See *The Times*, 9 April 1872

10 See Thomas, *The Victorian Underworld*, p. 66

11 See 'Skull found in Sir David Attenborough's garden that solves 1879 Barnes murder mystery', *Daily Mail*, 26 October 2010

12 See Fido, op. cit., p. 96

13 See Thomas, op. cit., p. 66

14 See http://www.met.police.uk/history/ripper.htm

15 Ibid.

16 Ibid.

17 See Pearsall, *The Worm in the Bud*, p. 310

18 See http://www.met.police.uk/history/ripper.htm

19 Ibid.

20 Ibid.

21 See Thomas, op. cit., p. 66

22 Ibid.

23 Ibid.

24 Ibid.

25 Ibid.

26 Ibid.

CHAPTER ELEVEN

1 See *Daily Mail,* 16 August 1902

2 See Babington, *The English Bastille*, p. 236

3 See Hooper, *History of Newgate and the Old Bailey*, p. 115

4 See   http://www.lawgazette.co.uk/news/the-great-defender-sir-edward-marshall-hall

5 Ibid.

6 See http://www.netcharles.com/orwell/essays/decline-of-the-english-murder.htm

7 See http://www.flickr.com/photos/brizzlebornandbred/4803874483/

8 See http://www.met.police.uk/history/dr_crippen.htm

9 See   http://www.oldbaileyonline.org/browse.jsp?id=t19101011-74&div=t19101011-74

10 Ibid.

11 See http://en.wikipedia.org/wiki/Hawley_Harvey_Crippen

12 See http://www.nickelinthemachine.com/tag/funeral/

13 See Fido, *Murder Guide to London*, p. 52

14 See http://www.capitalpunishmentuk.org/edith.html

15 See Wild and Curtis-Bennett, *Curtis*, p. 163

16 Ibid., p. 166

17 See Young, *Trial of Fredrick Bywaters and Edith Thompson*, p. 146

18 Ibid., p. 143

19 See http://www.capitalpunishmentuk.org/edith.html

20 See Wild and Curtis-Bennett, op. cit., p. 165

21 Ibid.

22 See http://www.nickelinthemachine.com/tag/egypt/

23 Ibid.
24 See Majoribanks, *For the Defence*, pp. 363–80
25 Ibid.
26 Ibid.
27 Ibid.
28 See http://www.nickelinthemachine.com/tag/egypt/
29 Ibid.
30 See Fido, op. cit., p. 75

CHAPTER TWELVE

1   See http://eastlondonhistory.com/isaac-bogard-and-arthur-harding/
2   See Campbell, *The Underworld*, p. 18
3   See http://eastlondonhistory.com/isaac-bogard-and-arthur-harding/
4   Ibid.
5   See Darbyshire and Hilliard, *The Flying Squad*, p. 25
6   Ibid.
7   See Campbell, op. cit., p. 29
8   Ibid.
9   See Campbell, op. cit., p. 19
10 See http://observer.guardian.co.uk/drugs/story/0,,686503,00.html
11 See http:/www.nickelinthemachine.com/2010/02/sample-post.
    html/limehouse/
12 Ibid.
13 See http://www.victorianlondon.org/entertainment/opiumsmok-
    ingdens.htm
14 See Campbell, op. cit., pp. 216–7
15 Ibid., p. 214
16 Ibid., p. 215
17 See Fabian, *London After Dark*, p.36
18 Ibid.
19 See http://eastlondonhistory.com/isaac-bogard-and-arthur-harding/
20 See Campbell, op. cit., p. 23
21 See *Daily Express*, 20 November 1922

CHAPTER THIRTEEN

1 See http://www.murderpedia.org/male.H/h/hulten-karl.htm
2 See Webb, *Crime Is My Business*, p.70
3 See Webb, op. cit., p. 73
4 Ibid., p. 73
5 Ibid., p. 71
6 See http://murderpedia.org/male.H/h/hulten-karl.htm
7 Anecdotal
8 See http://www.netcharles.com/orwell/essays/decline-of-the-english-murder.htm
9 See Webb, op. cit., p. 213
10 Ibid., p. 214
11 Ibid., p. 215
12 Ibid., p. 218
13 Ibid., pp. 221–2
14 See Hodge, *Famous Trials 5*, pp. 55–106
15 Ibid.
16 See Honeycombe, *Murders of the Black Museum*, p. 257
17 Ibid., p. 279
18 See Webb, op. cit., p. 222
19 Ibid., p. 79
20 Ibid., p. 80
21 Ibid., p. 84
22 Ibid., p. 85
23 Ibid., p. 87
24 See Honeycombe, op. cit., p. 279
25 See *Daily Express*, 29 April 1945
26 Paul Willetts, via email correspondence with the author
27 Ibid.

CHAPTER FOURTEEN

1 See http://www.trutv.com/library/crime/serial_killers/history/christie/place_7.html
2 Ibid.
3 Ibid.
4 Ibid.
5 See http://news.bbc.co.uk/onthisday/hi/dates/stories/june/25/newsid_3721000/3721267.stm

6 Ibid.

7 See Honeycombe, *Murders of the Black Museum*, p. 314

8 See http://www.bailii.org/ew/cases/EWHC/Admin/2004/2779.html, quoting 'Mary Westlake v Criminal Cases Review Commission', England and Wales High Court, 17 November 2004

9 Paul Willetts, via email correspondence with the author

10 See http://www.murderuk.com/one_off_bentley_craig.html

11 See Yallop, *To Encourage the Others*, p.115

12 Ibid.

13 See http://news.bbc.co.uk/onthisday/hi/dates/stories/january/28/newsid_3393000/3393807.stm

14 Ibid.

15 See http://news.bbc.co.uk/onthisday/hi/dates/stories/july/13/newsid_2745000/2745023.stm

16 See Webb, *Line-Up for Crime*, p. 213

17 See http://www.nickelinthemachine.com/2008/05

18 See Webb, op. cit., p. 213

19 Ibid., p. 216

20 Ibid., p. 217

21 Ibid.

22 Ibid., p. 218

23 Ibid., p. 224

24 Ibid.

25 Ibid.

26 Ibid.

27 Ibid.

28 See http://en.wikipedia.org/wiki/William_Connor

29 See Webb, op. cit., p. 224

30 See Hiney, *Raymond Chandler*, p. 224

31 See 'My sister Ruth', *Guardian*, 27 January 1997

32 See http://www.nickelinthemachine.com/2008/05

33 Ibid.

34 See http://copperknob.wordpress.com/category/albert-pierrepoint/

35 See Foot, *Who Killed Hanratty?*, p.26

36 Ibid., p. 31

37 Ibid., p. 33

38 Ibid., p. 41

39 Ibid., p. 51

40 Ibid., p. 54

41 Ibid., p. 55

42 Ibid., p. 54

43 Ibid., p. 142

44 See 'Hanratty's body is reburied after DNA testing', *Daily Telegraph*, 28 June 2001

45 See 'We will never know the truth about the A6 killer', *Independent*, 7 February 2009

46 See Pierrepoint, *Executioner: Pierrepoint*, p.169

47 See http://www.bbc.co.uk/news/uk-14402195

CHAPTER FIFTEEN

1 See 'When crime grabbed the limelight', *Guardian*, 30 July 2008

2 See Linnane, *The Encyclopaedia of London Crime and Vice*, p. 160

3 See *The Times*, 23 May 1952

4 See Linnane, op., cit. p. 261

5 See Watts, *The Men in My Life*, p. 195

6 See Webb, *Crime Is My Business*, p. 138

7 Ibid.

8 See Watts, op. cit., p. 230

9 See Campbell, *The Underworld*, p. 70

10 Ibid., p. 69

11 See http://www.nickelinthemachine.com/2009/02/no1-eaton-square-lord-boothby-and-ronnie-kray/

12 See http://www.thekrays.co.uk

13 See Campbell, op. cit., p. 130

14 Ibid., p. 134

15 Ibid., p. 104

16 See Pearson, *The Profession of Violence*, pp. 237–9

17 See Campbell, op. cit., pp. 79–81

18 Ibid.

19 See Pearson, op. cit., p. 265

20 See Campbell, op. cit., p. 262

21 Ibid.

22 See http://news.bbc.co.uk/1/hi/uk/714289.stm

23 See 'Dome robbery: how it happened', *Guardian*, 18 February 2002

24 See 'Who are the Yardies?', *BBC News*, 19 June 1999 http://news.bbc.co.uk/1/hi/uk/371604.stm

25 See Heale, *One Blood*, p. 75

26 See 'Man stabbed to death on Oxford Street', *Guardian*, 26 December 2011

27 See 'Ex-street thug becomes trainee barrister', *Evening Standard*, 8
    September 2011

CHAPTER SIXTEEN

1 See St Paul's protest: Occupy London Camp evicted 28 February
   2012 http://www.bbc.co.uk/news/uk-17187180
2 See http://www.bbc.co.uk/news/uk-england-london-14439970
3 See 'London riots: three-quarters charged over riots had previous
   criminal convictions', *Guardian*, 15 September 2011
4 See Madox Ford, *The Soul of London*, p. 27
5 Ibid.
6 See Marks, *Tyburn Tree*, p. 268

Illustration Credits

p. 42   Lady Jane Grey © Mary Evans Picture Library

p. 132   The Gordon Riots © Mary Evans Picture Library

p. 168   Exercise Yard at Pentonville © Mary Evans Picture Library

p. 169   Coldbath Fields © Mary Evans Picture Library

p. 202   Henry Wainwright © City of London

p. 221   Dr Crippen Trial © Illustrated London News Ltd/Mary Evans

p. 263   Murder in Soho © Getty Images

p. 267   10 Rillington Place © Getty Images

p. 274   Ruth Ellis © Corbis

Index

Abbeline, CI Frederick 209, 211, 213, 214
Acts of Parliament *see* laws
Agar, Robert 160–62
Agate, Stan 294
Ainsworth, William Harrison 37, 93–4
Akerman, Richard 133
Alexander, Andrew 77
Alexander, James 115, 116
Alexander of Pershore 15
Alexander, William 115, 116
Ali Fahmy Bey, Prince 230–33
Allen, Peter 286
Alphon, Peter 281, 282, 284, 285
Ann (servant of Lydia Duncomb) 115
ap Llewlyn, Gruffydd 27–8
Applebee, John 102, 106, 107
Arif, Dennis 299
Arif, Dogan 299
Arif, Mehmet 299
Arif gang 299
Askew, Anne 40–41
Aston, Sir David 268
Attenborough, Sir David 206
Austin, John 123
Avershaw, Lewis 3
Avory, Mr Justice 237

Babington, Anthony 43
Bailly, Charles 44–5
Baker, Kenny 299
Barney, Elvira 234
Barrett, Michael 196–7
Bartholomew Fair 59–61
Barton, Elizabeth 22
Bayes, Richard 93
Beggar's Opera, The (Gay and Rich) 90–91
Bentham, Jeremy 165–6
Bentham, Samuel 165
Bentley, Derek 269–72

Bentley, Iris 272
Beveridge, CS Peter 266
Biggs, Ronnie 294
Billings, Thomas 112, 113
Binny, John 167, 168, 171–2
Bishop, John 181–2
Black, Anthony 299
Black Dog of Newgate 77–9
Blake, Joseph ('Blueskin') 101, 102
Blakely, David 273–7, 278
Blantyre, Lady 190
Bloody Code 121
Bogard, Isaac 'Ikey' 236–7
Bogarde, Dirk 263
Boleyn, Anne 35–6
Bolingbroke, Roger 17–18
Bond, George 182–3
Bonner, Bishop 'Bloody' 62
Boothby, Lord 293
Borough Compter 68
Boswell, James 91
Bousfield, William 195–6
Bow Street Runners 131, 142
Brabazun, Sir Robert 13
Bread Street Compter 69
Brennan, Lord 268–9
Briant, Alexander 38
Bridewell Prison 68, 134
Bridgeman, William 229
Brink's-MAT robbery 299–300
Brown, Beresford 266
Brown, Hannah 184–5
Brownrigg, Elizabeth 120–21
Brummagen Boys 247–8
Brunt, John 141–4
Buckingham, Duke of 33, 35
Bull, William 52
Bulwer-Lytton, Edward 80
Burgess (train guard) 160, 161, 162

Burke, William 182
Burney, Fanny 126
burnings (executions) 17, 21–2, 41, 62, 111, 113–15, 176
Burton, Sidney 280
Butcher, Susan 188, 189
Butler, R. A. 284
Byfield, Richard 62
Bywaters, Frederick 226–9, 230

Calcraft, William 181, 194, 195–6
Campbell, Duncan 294
capital punishment, abolition 263–4, 279, 286
    see also miscarriages of justice
Carleton, Billie 241–3
Caroline, Queen 145–6
Casswell, J. D. 257
Castlereagh, Lord 142
Catling, Brian 45
Cato Street Conspiracy 141–5
Chandler, Raymond 277
Chang, Brilliant 244–5
Chapman, Annie 209–210
Chapman, George (Severin Klosovski) 213
Charlies 126–7
Chesterfield, Lord 122
Chesterton, Capt George 162–3
child criminals 150–54, 156–7, 159, 303–4
Christie, Ethel 266, 268
Christie, John 266–9
Church, John 205
Churchill, Winston 289
CID (Criminal Investigation Department) 190
Clarence, Duke of 215
Clavell, John 82
Clement, Henry 11
Clifford, Mary 120
Clink Prison 72–3
Cobham, Eleanor, Duchess of Gloucester 17–18
Coldbath Fields Prison 162–3, 169–70, 171
Cole, Len 255–6
Coles, Frances 214
Collins, Wilkie 198–9
Colquhoun, Patrick 135
Comer, Jack 'Spot' 288–9
Comer, Rita 289
Conan Doyle, Arthur 203–4

Conley, Maurie 273
Connor, William 277
constables of the watch 50–51
cony-catchers 57–9
Cooper, Alan 297
Cooper, Lady Diana 246
Cordrey, Roger 294
Cornell, George 296
Cortesi, Alexander Tomaso 248, 249
Cortesi, George 248, 249
Cortesi, Gus 248, 249
Cortesi, Harry 'Frenchie' 248–9
Cortesi, Paul 248, 249
Cortesi gang 248–9
Cotell, John 19–20
Cotton, Reverend 179
Courvoisier, François 186–7
Cox, Billy 303
Craig, Christopher 269–72
crank (prisoner task) 170
Cream, Dr Thomas 213–14
Crichton, Charles 207
Criminal Investigation Department (CID) 190
Crippen, Cora 220–25
Crippen, Dr Hawley Harvey 220–25
Critchley, T. A. 140
Cromwell, Thomas 35
Crook, G. T. 238–9
Cruickshank, Robert 179
Culpepper, George 36
Curtis (collier) 117
Curtis-Bennett, Derek 268
Curtis-Bennett, Sir Henry 227, 230
Curwen, Benett 63
Cussens, Desmond 274, 275, 277, 278

Dagoe, Hannah 119–20
Dalyvell, Robert 40
Dance, George 175
Dando, Jill 4
Darling, Mr Justice 249
Davidson, William 141–4
Davies, Edmund 295
Davies, John 209–210
Davis, William 86
Day, Alice 199–200
de Antiquis, Alec 262–3
de Podlicote, Richard 15–16
De Turberville, Sir Thomas 12–13

De Veil, Sir Thomas 126, 128
de Veulle, Reggie 242–3
death penalty *see* capital punishment
Defoe, Daniel 100
Dekker, Thomas 54, 71
Dereham, Francis 36
Dew, CI Walter 222–4
Diarrassouba, Seydou 303–4
Dickens, Charles 150, 172, 180, 186–7, 194–5, 203
Dixblanc, Marguerite 204–5
Dodd, Dr William 122–3
Donoghue, Albert 296, 297
Doralli, Louisa 248
Dowe, Robert 71
Downer, Tony 299
Draper, Hugh 44
drawing, hanging and quartering 6
Driberg, Tom 293
drugs 241–6
Druitt, Montague 212–13
Du Vall, Claude 83–6
Dudley, Earl of 42
Dudley, Lord 141
Duggan, Mark 306
Duncomb, Lydia 115
Dunne, PC Patrick 302
Durand-Deacon, Olive 259–60
Dyer, Amelia 215

Eady, Muriel 266
Eddowes, Catherine 210
Ede, Chuter 289–90
'Edgworth Bess' 101–2, 105
'Edward' (criminal) 156–8
Edward I, King 14
Edward II, King 16
Edward III, King 74
Edward IV, King 29–30
Edward VI, King 68
Edward VII, King 218
Edward, Prince (Edward V) 31–3
Edwards, Buster 294, 295
Edwards, George 141–3
Eglinton, Earl of 95–7
Elizabeth I, Queen 43
Ellis, Andy 278–9
Ellis, George 273, 278
Ellis, Georgina 273, 278, 279
Ellis, John 229, 230

Ellis, Ruth 272–9
Enani, Said 232, 233
Essex Gang 92–3
Evans, Beryl 267, 268
Evans, Geraldine 267, 268
Evans, Gwynne 286
Evans, Timothy 265–9
Ewart, William 195
Ewer, William 281, 282
executions
    see also Tyburn
    public, end of 186–7, 195–7
    survivors 106
executions, men
    Allen, Peter 286
    Austin, John 123
    Babington, Anthony 43
    Barrett, Michael 196–7
    Bentley, Derek 271–2
    Bishop, John 181–2
    Bolingbroke, Roger 18
    Bousfield, William 195–6
    Buckingham, Duke of 35
    Byfield, Richard 62
    Bywaters, Frederick 229
    Cato Street conspirators 143–5
    Christie, John 268
    Courvoisier, François 186–7
    Crippen, Dr Hawley Harvey 225
    Cromwell, Thomas 35
    Davis, William 86
    De Turberville, Sir Thomas 12–13
    Dodd, Dr William 122–3
    Du Vall, Claude 85–6
    Dudley, Earl of 42
    Evans, Gwynne 286
    Fitzosbert, William 6–10
    Forest, John 62
    Frith, John 62
    George, Duke of Clarence 30
    Geraghty, Christopher 263
    Good, Daniel 190
    Gordon rioters 134
    Greenacre, James 185–6
    Haggerty, Owen 177
    Haigh, John George 261
    Hanratty, James 284
    Harrison, Major-General 2
    Hastings, William 31
    Head, Thomas 181–2

executions, men – *continued*
  Heath, Neville 257–8
  Hewitt, Andrew 62
  Hind, Capt James 83
  Holloway, John 177
  Hulten, Karl 254
  Hutton, Luke 79
  Ignes, William 20
  Jenkins, Charles 263
  Jonston, Sir John 87
  Mackay, Alexander 197
  MacLaine, James 97
  Manning, Frederick 194
  Marsh, William 11–12
  Matthew, William 20
  More, Sir Thomas 35
  Mortimer, Roger 16
  Oldcastle, Sir John 28
  Perreau twins 122
  Phillips, Thomas 90
  Raleigh, Sir Walter 44
  Ratsey, Gamaliel 82
  religious dissenters 20–24
  Rouse, Richard 63
  Senex, John 11
  Sheppard, Jack 106–7
  Shirley, Laurence, Earl Ferrers 118–19
  Shoreditch murderers 74
  Skitch, William 176
  Spiggot, William 90
  Stafford, Capt Philip 83
  Turner, Col John 2
  Turpin, Dick 93
  Wainwright, Henry 202–3
  Wallace, William 13–14
  Warbeck, Perkin 34–5
  White, Charles 180–81
  Whitney, James 88
  Wild, Jonathan 110
executions, women 110
  Askew, Anne 41
  Barton, Elizabeth 22
  Boleyn, Anne 35–6
  Brownrigg, Elizabeth 120–21
  Dagoe, Hannah 119–20
  Ellis, Ruth 277–8
  Fenning, Eliza 177–80
  Gordon rioters 134
  Gourdemaine, Margery 18
  Grey, Lady Jane 41–3

  Harris, Phoebe 176
  Hayes, Catherine 113–15
  Howard, Katherine 36
  Hungerford, Agnes 20
  Jones, Mary 121
  Malcolm, Sarah 116
  Manning, Maria 193–5
  Murphy, Catherine 176
  Pearcey, Mary 208
  Pole, Margaret 36
  Thompson, Edith 229–30
  Webster, Kate 206

Fabian, Robert 245–6, 262
Fahmy, Prince Ali 230–33
Fahmy, Marguerite 230–34
Fairfax, DS Frederick 270
Feckenham, John 43
Feltham, Inspector 184
Fenning, Eliza 177–80
Fennor, William 69–71, 82
Fielding, Henry xi, 99, 129–31
Fielding, John 129–31, 133
Findlater, Seaton 274–5
Firmin, Stanley 245
Fisher, John, Bishop of Rochester 62, 63
Fitzosbert, William 6–10
Flambard, Bishop Ranulf 27
Fleet Prison 72, 134
Fleetwood, William 52
Flying Squad 238–9
Foot, Paul 285, 286
Forbes, Laverne 302
Ford, Ford Madox 307–8
Foreman, Freddie 'the Mean Machine' 292, 296
Forest, John 62
Foucault, Michel 165
Fox, Caroline 169–70
Foxe, John 28, 62, 77
Foxon, John 181
France, Carol 284
France, Charles 283–4
Fraser, 'Mad' Frankie 247, 289, 295
Fraser, Simon 14
Frater, Mark 249
Frith, John 62
Fry, Elizabeth xi, 171
Fuerst, Ruth 266

Gale, Sarah 184–5
gallows 5, 10–11, 175–7
  see also Tyburn
gambling 56–7, 247–9
gangs 235–7, 247–50, 287–304
Gardiner, Archbishop 40, 42
Gardner, Margery 255–8
Gardner, PC William 188
Gatehouse Prison 68
Gay, John 91
Gay, Mr (stockbroker) 183–4
George, Duke of Clarence 29, 30
George, Prince Regent (*later* George IV) 145
Geraghty, Christopher 262–4
Gerard, John 39
gibbets 2–3, 5–6
Girdwood, Mr (surgeon) 183
Gladstone, Sir Herbert 216
Goldstein, Lillian 239–40
Good, Daniel 188–90
Good, Jane 188–90
Good, Molly 189
Goodwin, Eric 246
Goody, Gordon 294
Gordon, Lord George 132, 134
Gordon Riots 131–4
Gourdemaine, Margery 17–18
Gowan, James 136
Grayson, Georgina (Betty Jones) 252–5
Great Train Robbery 293–5
Great Victorian Train Robbery 159–62
Greenacre, James 182–6
Greene, Anne 106
Greene, Graham 249
Gregory, William 92, 93
Gregsten, Janet 281, 282, 284–5
Gregsten, Michael 280
Grey, Lady Jane 41–3
Gundulf, Bishop of Rochester 26
Gunnell, Clive 275
gypsies 48–9

Haggerty, Owen 177
Haigh, John George 258–61
Hall, Edward 34–5
Hambrook, Detective Inspector 238
Hanfield, Benjamin 177
Hanratty, James 279–86
hard labour 169–70

Harding, Arthur 236–7, 247
Hardy, John 19
Hare, William 182
Harpham, Ralph 110
Harrington, Bridget 138
Harris, Joseph 99
Harris, Phoebe 176
Harrison, Major-General 2
Harrison, Mrs (companion of Lydia
  Duncomb) 115
Harrison, William 48
Hart, Cornelius 137, 140
Hastings, Patrick 234
Hastings, William 31
Havers, Sir Cecil 275, 277, 278
Hayes, Catherine 110–115
Hayes, John 111–13
Hayes, Superintendent 193
Head, Thomas 181–2
Heath, George 253
Heath, Neville 256–8
Henderson, Mr and Mrs (murder victims)
  260–61
Henry I, King 10, 27
Henry III, King 11, 73
Henry V, King 28
Henry VI, King 17, 29–30
Henry VII, King 33, 34
Henry VIII, King 22, 35–6, 39–40, 41,
  61–2, 68
Hentzner, Paul 60
Herbert, William, Earl of Pembroke 72
Hereward the Wake 81
Herrmann, Marie 218
Hewitt, Andrew 62
Higgins, DCI Bob 262
highwaymen 80–97, 130–31
Hill, Billy 287–9
Hill, Doctor 271
Hind, Capt James 83
Hobhouse, John 143
Hodge, Violet 252
Hogarth, William 90, 97, 116, 128
Hogg, Phoebe 207–8
Hogg, Phoebe (mother of Phoebe) 207–8
Hogg, Thomas 207–8
Holinshed, Raphael 73
Holland, Henry 38
Holloway, John 177
Hone, William 179

Horton, Charles 137
Houghton, Fr John 23–4
Howard, John 164, 172–3
Howard, Katherine 36
Howard, Philip, Earl of Arundel 44
Hugh of Lincoln 21
hulks (prisons) 166–7
Hulten, Karl (Ricky Rafeld) 252–5
Humphreys, Christmas 276, 279
Hungerford, Agnes 18–20
Hungerford, Sir Edward 19–20
Husband, Richard 69
Hutton, Luke 78–9

Ignes, William 19–20
Ings, James 141–4
Inns of Court murders 115–16
Irish Republicanism 196–7
Isabella, Queen 16

'Jack Ketch's Kitchen' 75–6
Jack the Ripper 208–215
James I, King 44
James, P. D. 140
James, Roy 294, 295
Jenkins, Charles 262–4
Jewell, Margaret 136
Jews 20–21
Johnson, John 117
Johnson, Dr Samuel 122, 123–4
Jones, Betty (Georgina Grayson) 252–5
Jones, Jane (*married name* Good) 188–90
Jones, Mary 121
Jonson, Ben 46–7, 61, 82
Jonston, Sir John 86–7
jury trials 66
Justices of the Peace 127

Kelly, Mary Jane 212
Kemp, Gary 298
Kemp, Martin 298
Kempton, Freda 243–5
Kendell, Capt Henry 223, 224
Kennedy, Ludovic 268
Kennett, Richard 133
Kent, James 210
Kimber, Billy 236, 247, 249
Kimberley, Henry 254
Klosovski, Severin (George Chapman) 213
Knolleys, Thomas 75

Knyvett, Sir Anthony 40–41
Kosminski, Aaron 212
Kray, Charlie 292, 298
Kray, Frances 296
Kray, Reggie 291–3, 296–8
Kray, Ronnie 291–3, 296–8

Lambourne, WPS Alexandra 259
Lambrianou, Chris 297
Lambrianou, Tony 297
Lamplugh, Suzy 4
landlord of the Cock, Cheapside 17
Lane, Constance 259
Lane, Harriet 199–202
Lane, Mr (father of Harriet) 201
Langdale, Roy 283
Lau Ping, Ada 242
Lau Ping You 242–3
Laurie, Peter 176
Law, CI Percy 266
law enforcement 125–47
    Bow Street Runners 131
    Colquhoun's proposals 135
    De Veil's court 128
    early 50–51, 126–7
    enhanced reputation 203–4
    Fieldings 129–31
    Flying Squad 238–9
    Metropolitan Police 146–7,
        188–90
    Scotland Yard 128, 203
Lawrence, Mr (robbery victim) 93
Lawrence, Fr Robert 22–3
laws 48, 65, 121
    Acts of Parliament 3, 48–9, 88, 90, 97,
        109, 131, 196, 241, 279, 286
Le Blanc, Abbe 91
le Lorimer, Edmund 76
Le Neve, Ethel 221–4, 225
le Skirmisour, Roger 74
Leeds gang 248
Leopold, Duke of Austria 7
Littlechild, DCI John 213
Liverpool, Lord 141–2, 146
Llewellyn, Dr Ralph 209
Lloyd Lane, Ethel 254
Loader, Mr (tailor) 96
Lollards 21–2
Ludgate Prison 75
Lusk, George 211

Macaulay, Thomas Babington 51
McDonald, CI James 200–201
Mackay, Alexander 197
MacLaine, James 94–7
McLennan, Hectorina 266
Macmanus (Bow Street Runner) 133
Macnaghten, Sir Melville 212
McSwann, William 260
McVitie, Jack 'the Hat' 296–7
Malcolm, Sarah 115–16
Maloney, Kathleen 266
Manning, Eddie 246
Manning, Frederick 191–4
Manning, James 76–7
Manning, Maria 190–95
Mansfield, Michael 285
Map, John 113
Marks, Alfred 10, 83, 308
Marr, Celia 136–7
Marr, Timothy 136–7
Marr, Timothy (son of Timothy) 136–7
Marsh, William 11–12
Marshall, Doreen 257
Marshall, John 178
Marshall, Thomas 40
Marshall Hall, Sir Edward 4, 218, 225, 232, 233, 234
Martinetti, Mrs (friend of Cora Crippen) 222
Marwood, William 206
Marx, Karl 196–7
Mary I, Queen 41–2, 62
Mason, Mr (robbery victim) 92
Massiah, Tony 304
Matheson, Doctor 271
Matthew, William 19–20
Maxwell Fyfe, David 271, 272
Mayhew, Henry 107, 148, 149, 150, 154, 156, 167, 168, 170, 171–2
Mayne, Richard 146–7
M. C. (Turpin victim) 91–2
Melford Stevenson, Aubrey 276
Meredith, Sir William 121
Messina, Alfredo 291
Messina, Attilio 290
Messina, Gino 290, 291
Messina gang 289–91
Metropolitan Police 146–7, 188–90
Meyrick, Kate 244
Miagh, Thomas 44

Miles, Mrs (widow of Sidney Miles) 271
Miles, PC Sidney 270
Millbank Prison 165–6, 167
Millennium Dome raid 300
Miller, Bruce 224
Milliner, Mary 108, 109
Mills, Jack 294–5
miscarriages of justice 16–17, 265–86
    see also capital punishment
    Bentley, Derek 269–72
    Ellis, Ruth 272–9
    Evans, Timothy 265–9
    Fenning, Eliza 177–80
    Hanratty, James 279–86
Mischon, Victor 277
Mitchell, Frank 'the Mad Axeman' 296
Mollere, Nicolas 74
Moore, Insp Henry 214
More, Sir Thomas 33, 35, 48
Mortimer, Roger 16
Morton, Bishop 31
Mounted Patrol 130–31
murderers, men
    Barrett, Michael 196–7
    Bishop, John 181–2
    Bousfield, William 195–6
    Burke, William 182
    Chapman, George (Severin Klosovski) 213
    Christie, John 266–9
    Courvoisier, François 186–7
    Craig, Christopher 269–72
    Cream, Dr Thomas 213–14
    Crippen, Dr Hawley Harvey 220–25
    Geraghty, Christopher 262–4
    Good, Daniel 188–90
    Greenacre, James 182–6
    Haggerty, Owen 177
    Haigh, John George 258–61
    Hanratty, James 279–86
    Hare, William 182
    Head, Thomas 181–2
    Heath, Neville 256–8
    Holloway, John 177
    Hulten, Karl (Ricky Rafeld) 252–5
    Ignes, William 19–20
    Jack the Ripper 208–215
    Jenkins, Charles 262–4
    Kray twins 291–3, 296–8
    Mackay, Alexander 197

murderers, men – *continued*
    Manning, Frederick 191–4
    Matthew, William 19–20
    Mortimer, Roger 16
    Richard III, King 30–33
    Rouse, Richard 63
    Sadler, Tom (acquitted) 214
    Shirley, Laurence, Earl Ferrers 117–19
    Shoreditch murderers 74
    Wainwright, Henry 199–203
    Williams, John 138–40
murderers, women
    Barney, Elvira (acquitted) 234
    Brownrigg, Elizabeth 120–21
    Dixblanc, Marguerite 204–5
    Dyer, Amelia 215
    Ellis, Ruth 272–9
    Fahmy, Marguerite (acquitted) 230–34
    Fenning, Eliza (attempted) 177–80
    Hayes, Catherine 110–115
    Herrmann, Marie (manslaughter) 218
    Hungerford, Agnes 18–20
    Malcolm, Sarah 115–16
    Manning, Maria 190–95
    Pearcey, Mary 207–8
    Thompson, Edith 225–30
    Webster, Kate 205–7
murders, unsolved 208–215
Murphy, Catherine 176

Nash, John 222
Nelson, Rita 266
Newgate Gaol 64, 73–9, 100–101, 132,
    133–4, 143, 163, 171–7, 216–18
Nicholls, Mary Ann 209
Norfolk, Duke of 40
Norton, Thomas 38
Noye, Kenneth 299–300
Nudds, William 281, 282

O'Connor, Patrick 191–3
Old Bailey 64–5, 218
Oldcastle, Sir John 28
Oldfield (hangman) 180
Oliver Twist (Dickens) 150–52, 172–3
ordeals (trials) 65
Orwell, George 219, 254–5
O'Sullivan, Tim 288

Page, James 183

Paris, Matthew 6, 9
parish constables 126–7
Parr, Catherine 40
Payne, Leslie 'Payne the Brain' 292, 296,
    297
Pearce, Insp Nicholas 189
Pearcey, Mary 207–8
Pearson, John 297
Peel, Sir Robert 146
penal reform 163–4, 171
Pentonville Prison 167–8
Pepys, Samuel 2
Perreau, Daniel 122
Perreau, Robert 122
Petersen, John 137, 140
Petty, Doctor 106
Phillips, Thomas 88–90
Pickering, Laurence 52
pickpockets 52–3, 57, 151–2, 154–6
Pierce, Edward 160–62
Pierrepoint, Albert 257–8, 261, 262, 263,
    265, 268, 271, 277–8, 286
Pizer, John 210
Plunkett, William 94–5
Pole, Margaret 36
police *see* law enforcement
Poulson, John 128
Poultry Compter 68–9, 71
prisons 64–79
    Bridewell 68, 134
    Clink 72–3
    Coldbath Fields 162–3, 169–70, 171
    Compters 68–72
    Fleet 72, 134
    Gatehouse 68
    hulks 166–7
    Ludgate 75
    Millbank 165–6, 167
    Newgate 64, 73–9, 100–101, 132, 133–4,
        143, 163, 171–7, 216–18
    Pentonville 167–8
    reform 163–4, 171
    Tower of London *see* Tower of London
public executions, end of 186–7, 195–7

Quekett, Mr (scientist) 15

Rachman, Peter 293
rack 38
Rafeld, Capt Ricky (Karl Hulten) 252–5

Raleigh, Carew 44
Raleigh, Sir Walter 43–4, 68
Ratcliffe Highway murders 135–41
Ratsey, Gamaliel 82
Read, CI 'Nipper' 292, 293, 297
religious dissenters 20–24, 62–3
Reynolds, Bruce 294
Rich, John 91
Rich, Richard 40–41
Richard, Duke of Gloucester see Richard
    III
Richard I, King 7
Richard III, King 31–3
    as Duke of Gloucester 30–31
Richard (of Shrewsbury), Prince 31–3
Richardson, Charlie 295–6
Richardson gang 295–6
Riel, Madame (murder victim) 204–5
riots 131–4, 141, 145–6, 306–7
Robin Hood 81
Robinson, Brian 299
Rogers, John 77
Rolt, Terence 262, 263
Roman Catholics 22–4
Rose, Thomas 189–90
Rouse, Richard 63
Rowan, Sir Charles 146–7
Rudd, Mrs (mistress of Robert Perreau) 122
Russell, William, Lord 186
Ruthven, George 142
Ryder, Robert 139

Sabini, Charles 'Darby' 248, 249–50
Sabini gang 248–9
Sach, Amelia 229
Sadler, Tom 214
St Paul's Cathedral 54–6, 306
Salander, Dr Tobias 60
Savile, Sir George 133
'Scavenger's Daughter' 38
Scotland Yard 128, 203
Scott, Captain 241
Scott, Sir Gilbert 15–16
Senex, John 11
Shackleton, Ernest 241
Shakespeare, William 30
Sharpe, Insp 'Nutty' 239, 240, 241, 245
Shaw, George Bernard 254
Shearman, Mr Justice 228
Sheppard, Jack 101–7

Shirley, Laurence, Earl Ferrers 117–19
Shoreditch, Sir John of 74
shot-drill 170
Sidmouth, Lord 143
silent system 171
Silverman, Sydney 286
Silvester, John 178
Simmons, Leon 277
Simnel, Lambert 34
Simpson, Keith 255
Skeffington, Leonard 38
'Skeffington's Gyves' 38
Skitch, William 176
Smirke, Robert 166
Smith (execution survivor) 106
Smith, Patrick 302
Smithers, Richard 142
Smithfield 59–63
Solomons, Alf 249
Solomons, Isaac 'Ikey' 151
Southey, Robert 3
Southwell, Canon Thomas 17–18
Sparks, John 'Ruby' 239–40
Spence, Thomas 141
Spicer, John 123
Spiggot, William 88–90
Spilsbury, Sir Bernard 223, 224, 228
Spink, James 'Spinky' 249
Spooner, Supt Reginald 255
Spratley, Inspector 209
Stafford, Capt Philip 82–3
Stanley, Dean 16
Stanley, Lord 31
Stephen, Scott 234
Stillwell, Kitty 138
Stokes, Albert 199–200
Storie, Valerie 280–84
Stow, John 9, 19, 69
Stride, 'Long Liz' 210
Surrey, Earl of 72
survivors of executions 106
'swell mob' (pickpockets) 154–6
Symes, CI Shelley 259
Symmonds, Yvonne 256

Taylor, John 67–9, 72, 73
Tester, William 160–62
Thackeray, William 186–7
Thames River Police 135
Thistlewood, Arthur 141–4

Thomas, Julia 205–6
Thompson, Alison 206
Thompson, Edith 225–30
Thompson, Percy 226–7
Thompson, Sir William 109
Thornhill, James 102
Thornton, Sgt Stephen 189
Throgmorton, Elizabeth 43–4
Tidd, Richard 141–4
torture 37–41, 88–90
Tower Green 35–6
Tower Hill 35
Tower of London 25–45
    construction 26
    escape attempts 27–8
    fate of the princes 31–3
    inscriptions 44–5
    torture 37–41
Tracey, Mary 115, 116
treadmills 169–70
trials, early 65–6
Tryppytt, Alyce 63
Tumblety, Dr Francis J. 213
Turner, Charlotte 178
Turner, Haldebart 178
Turner, Col John 2
Turner, Robert 177–9
Turpin, Dick 91–4
Tyburn
    see also executions; gallows
    condemned journey to 98–124
    early history 5–24
    last execution 123
Tyler, Wat 61
Tyrell, Sir James 33

unsolved murders 208–215

Vanstone, DS Charles 247
Vergil, Polydore 30, 33
Vermilloe, Robert 137, 138
Vigus, Henry 113

Wainwright, Henry 199–203
Wainwright, Thomas 201
Wakeley, Thomas 144–5
Wallace, William 13–14

Walpole, Sir Horace 95, 97, 101, 118–19, 134
Walter, Hubert 7–8, 9–10
Walters, Annie 229
Walworth, William 61
Warbeck, Perkin 34–5
Ward, Stephen 278
Warren, Sir Charles 212
Waterloo Bridge Mystery 208
Watson (under-sheriff) 104
Watts, Marthe 290, 291
Webb, Duncan 255, 258, 273, 275, 289, 290–91
Webster, Fr Augustine 22–3
Webster, Kate 205–7
Weller, Monica 278
Westcot (Bow Street Runner) 142
Wharton, Mary 86–7
Whitby, David 294–5
White, Charles 180–81
White, Harry 288
White, Jimmy 294
Whitechapel Murders 208–215
Whitney, James 87–8
Whittington, Sir Richard 75
Wild, Jonathan 91, 102, 107–110
William I, King 10
William III, King 87
William the Sacrist 15–16
Williams, Henry 159
Williams, John 138–40
Williamson, Elizabeth 138
Williamson, John 138
Willis, William 229
Woffinden, Bob 285
women see executions; murderers
Wood Street Compter 68, 69–71, 72
Wood, Thomas 112, 113
Woodville, Elizabeth 31
Wotton (criminal) 52–3
Wriothesley, Thomas 40–41
Wyatt, Sir Francis 73
Wycliffe, John 21

Yardies 302
Yiddishers 249
Yule, Gladys 275